TEXTBOOK OF MODERN PHARMACEUTICS

[According to the latest syllabus of M. Pharm of Pharmacy Council of India]

Dr. Sanghadeep Sukhadeo Gajbhiye

Associate Professor, Pharmaceutics

VIVA Institute of Pharmacy

(Mumbai University)

Shirgaon, Virar (E), India

Prof. Jayshree V. Patil

Associate Professor

Department of Pharmacy

G H Raisoni Institute of Life Sciences

Nagpur University

Hingna Wadi Link Road, Nagpur, India

Dr. Archana A. Bele

Associate Professor

Department of Quality Assurance

VIVA College of Pharmacy

(Mumbai University)

Shirgaon, Virar (E), India

Prof. Jayshree R. Aate

Assistant Professor

Department of Pharmacology

VIVA Institute of Pharmacy

(Mumbai University)

Shirgaon, Virar (E), India

Prof. Shikha Shukla

Assistant Professor

Department of Pharmacology

VIVA Institute of Pharmacy

(Mumbai University)

Palghar, Maharashtra, India

TEXT BOOK OF

MODERN PHARMACEUTICS

First Edition 2024

Published by:

NOTION PRESS

Publisher and distributor

Head office: Notion Press Media Pvt. Ltd.

7, Red Cross Road,

Egmore, Chennai, Tamil Nadu 60008

TEXT BOOK OF MODERN PHARMACEUTICS

NOTION PRESS

PREFACE

The authors feel great pleasure in presenting the first edition of the book **"Text Book of Modern Pharm Pharmaceutics"** for graduate and postgraduate students. The present book on **Text Book of Modern Pharm Pharmaceutics** has been written according to the syllabus of M. Pharm of Pharmacy Council of India and covers the full course of the subject.

THE SALIENT FEATURES OF THE BOOK ARE:-

- *Easy to understand style of writing which makes the book a self-study material.*
- *Each new concept has been introduced through day-today problem of interest to the students which makes the subject matter interesting.*
- *The language of the book, on the whole, is lucid and easy to understand.*
- *Wherever needed neatly labeled figures have been drawn.*

The authors hope that the students, teachers, and other readers will find the book interesting and to the point covering the course. We hope that the students will receive the book warmly.

I sincerely thank the Management of Advance Group of college and VIVA Institute of Pharmacy for their support during the writing of this book.

Every effort is made to keep the book error-free. The author will gratefully acknowledge the suggestions to improve the book to make it more useful.

Wishing our readers success in examination and life ahead. The authors feel that their efforts will be fully rewarded if the book serves the purpose for which it is written.

TEXT BOOK OF MODERN PHARMACEUTICS

CONTENTS

g. Linearity Concept of significance
h. Standard deviation
i. Chi square test
j. students T-test
k. ANOVA test

CHAPTER – 1

PREFORMATION CONCEPTS

INTRODUCTION:

Preformation is a historical concept in developmental biology that refers to the idea that the structures of an organism pre-existing in miniature form within the sperm or egg. Although it has largely been superseded by modern developmental biology, understanding this concept helps in appreciating the evolution of scientific thought regarding embryonic development.

Here's a detailed introduction to preformation concepts:

1. Definition and Historical Background:

Preformation is the theory that all the structures of an organism are pre-formed within the sperm or egg, and that development is merely a process of enlarging and unfolding these pre-existing structures. This idea was prominent from the 17th to the early 19th century.

a. **Early Proponents:**

   i. **Anton van Leeuwenhoek (1670s):** Observed spermatozoa and hypothesized that they contained miniature organisms.

   ii. **Caspar Friedrich Wolff (1759):** Proposed the idea of "preformation" as an extension of his work on embryonic development, although he was more of a proponent of epigenesis.

2. Types of Preformation:

1. **Spermist Theory:**

   a. **Definition:** The theory that the entire organism is pre-formed within the sperm cell.

   b. **Proponents:** Advocates included **Nicholas Hartsoeker**, who illustrated the concept of "animalcules" (tiny pre-formed organisms) within sperm.

2. **Ovist Theory:**

   a. **Definition:** The theory that the entire organism is pre-formed within the egg cell.

b. **Proponents: Maria Sibylla Merian** and other early biologists contributed to this idea by studying egg development and embryology.

3. Key Concepts and Contributions:

1. **Homunculus:**
   a. **Definition:** The idea of a fully-formed miniature human (homunculus) within the sperm.
   b. **Importance:** Represented a literal interpretation of preformation, illustrating the belief that all future generations were pre-formed.
2. **Embryology:**
   a. **Definition:** The study of embryos and their development.
   b. **Historical Impact:** Preformation was a significant theory before the acceptance of epigenesis and modern developmental biology.
3. **Epigenesis vs. Preformation:**
   a. **Epigenesis:** The theory that organisms develop through a series of gradual changes and differentiation from an initially undifferentiated state.
   b. **Comparison:** Preformation was challenged by epigenesis, which became widely accepted after the work of **Ernst Haeckel** and other scientists who observed development as a process of gradual differentiation.

4. Experiments and Observations:

1. **Microscopy:**
   a. **Contribution:** Early microscopes provided evidence for preformation by allowing scientists to observe sperm and eggs in detail, leading to the belief in pre-formed structures.
   b. **Limitation:** Microscopy was limited by the resolution and understanding of cellular structures at the time.
2. **Developmental Observations:**

a. **Contribution:** Observations of embryonic development in various organisms provided evidence for the gradual formation of structures, challenging preformation.
b. **Notable Figures: Carl Ernst von Baer** and **Rudolf Virchow** contributed to understanding the developmental process, leading to the decline of preformation theory.

5. Legacy and Modern Understanding:

1. **Historical Significance:**
   a. **Contribution:** Preformation was an important step in the evolution of developmental biology, highlighting early attempts to understand embryonic development.
   b. **Impact:** Provided a foundation for the development of modern theories of embryogenesis.
2. **Modern Developmental Biology:**
   a. **Current Understanding:** Modern biology supports **epigenesis**, where development involves gradual differentiation from a fertilized egg into a fully-formed organism.
   b. **Advances:** Techniques such as molecular biology, genetics, and advanced microscopy have replaced preformation with a more comprehensive understanding of developmental processes.
3. **Educational Value:**
   a. **Role in Teaching:** Preformation is often discussed in historical contexts to illustrate the progression of scientific understanding and the development of modern developmental biology.

Preformation, while now obsolete, represents an important chapter in the history of science, illustrating how early scientists grappled with the complexities of embryonic development. Its study provides valuable insights into the evolution of biological theories and the advancement of scientific methods.

DRUG EXCIPIENT INTERACTIONS

Drug-excipient interactions and their impact on drug stability are crucial in the pharmaceutical field, especially for ensuring the safety and efficacy of medications. Here's a detailed overview of drug-excipient interactions, including methods for studying these interactions, kinetics of stability, and stability testing:

1. Drug-Excipient Interactions:

Drug-Excipient Interactions refer to the interactions between a drug substance and other components (excipients) of a formulation. Excipients are inactive substances used to deliver the drug effectively and safely. These interactions can affect the stability, efficacy, and safety of the final pharmaceutical product.

Types of Interactions

1. **Chemical Interactions:**
    a. **Definition:** Chemical reactions between the drug and excipient, leading to degradation or altered drug properties.
    b. **Examples:** Hydrolysis, oxidation, reduction, or complex formation.
2. **Physical Interactions:**
    a. **Definition:** Non-chemical interactions that can affect the drug's physical properties.
    b. **Examples:** Changes in solubility, crystallinity, or hygroscopicity.
3. **Compatibility Issues:**
    a. **Definition:** Problems that arise from the incompatibility of drug and excipient, affecting drug performance or safety.
    b. **Examples:** Color changes, precipitate formation, or changes in drug release rates.

2. Methods for Studying Drug-Excipient Interactions:

1. **Spectroscopic Techniques:**

a. **Techniques:** Infrared Spectroscopy (IR), Nuclear Magnetic Resonance (NMR), Ultraviolet-Visible Spectroscopy (UV-Vis).
b. **Purpose:** Identify chemical changes or interactions by analyzing spectra and comparing with known standards.

2. **Chromatographic Techniques:**
   a. **Techniques:** High-Performance Liquid Chromatography (HPLC), Gas Chromatography (GC).
   b. **Purpose:** Separate and quantify components to detect degradation products or changes in drug composition.
3. **Microscopy:**
   a. **Techniques:** Scanning Electron Microscopy (SEM), Transmission Electron Microscopy (TEM).
   b. **Purpose:** Examine the physical morphology of drug-excipient mixtures to observe particle size or structure changes.
4. **Thermal Analysis:**
   a. **Techniques:** Differential Scanning Calorimetry (DSC), Thermogravimetric Analysis (TGA).
   b. **Purpose:** Study thermal behavior and stability of drug-excipient systems, including melting points and decomposition temperatures.
5. **Stability Studies:**
   a. **Techniques:** Accelerated Stability Testing, Long-Term Stability Testing.
   b. **Purpose:** Evaluate the impact of excipients on drug stability under various environmental conditions.

3. Kinetics of Stability

1. **Chemical Kinetics:**
   a. **Definition:** Study of the rates at which chemical reactions occur and the factors affecting these rates.
   b. **Importance:** Helps in understanding how quickly a drug might degrade in the presence of different excipients.

2. **Stability Kinetics:**
    a. **Definition:** Examines how the stability of a drug changes over time under various conditions (temperature, humidity, light).
    b. **Models:**
        i. **Zero-Order Kinetics:** Degradation rate is constant over time.
        ii. **First-Order Kinetics:** Degradation rate depends on the concentration of the drug.
        iii. **Second-Order Kinetics:** Degradation rate depends on the concentration of both the drug and another reactant.
3. **Arrhenius Equation:**
    a. **Definition:** A mathematical model that relates the rate of reaction to temperature.
    b. **Purpose:** Predict the effect of temperature on drug stability and calculate activation energy.
4. **Shelf-Life Prediction:**
    a. **Definition:** Estimate the period during which a drug remains effective and safe.
    b. **Purpose:** Utilize kinetic data to predict the drug's shelf life under various storage conditions.

4. Stability Testing in Preformation Concepts:

1. **Preformation Concepts in Stability Testing:**
    a. **Definition:** The theory that structures or characteristics of a drug are pre-formed before the testing phase.
    b. **Purpose:** Apply this concept to ensure that excipients do not alter the pre-formed stability characteristics of the drug.
2. **Testing Methods:**
    a. **Accelerated Stability Testing:**
        i. **Purpose:** Expose drug-excipient mixtures to higher temperatures and humidity to simulate long-term storage conditions.

ii. **Duration:** Typically involves testing over a period of 6 months to 1 year.

b. **Long-Term Stability Testing:**

   i. **Purpose:** Evaluate the stability of the drug-excipient system under normal storage conditions over extended periods.

   ii. **Duration:** Usually involves testing over a period of 2-5 years.

c. **Stress Testing:**

   i. **Purpose:** Assess the impact of extreme conditions (e.g., high temperatures, light exposure) on the drug-excipient system.

   ii. **Purpose:** Identify potential degradation pathways and optimize formulations.

3. **Regulatory Guidelines:**

   a. **Purpose:** Follow guidelines set by regulatory bodies (e.g., FDA, EMA) for stability testing and compatibility studies.

   b. **Importance:** Ensure that formulations meet safety and efficacy standards before market approval.

THEORIES OF DISPERSION AND PHARMACEUTICAL DISPERSION (EMULSION AND SUSPENSION, SMEDDS) PREPARATION

Theories of Dispersion and **Pharmaceutical Dispersion** involve the study and formulation of systems where substances are distributed within a medium, affecting the physical and chemical properties of the resulting formulations. These concepts are vital in the preparation and stabilization of various pharmaceutical formulations like emulsions, suspensions, and Self-Microemulsifying Drug Delivery Systems (SMEDDS). Here's a detailed exploration of these concepts:

1. Theories of Dispersion:

Dispersion refers to a system in which particles are distributed throughout a continuous phase. Theories of dispersion help in understanding how these particles interact with the medium and with each other.

1.1. Dispersion Theories

1. **Colloidal Theory:**
   a. **Definition:** Explains the behavior of colloidal particles (particles between 1 nm and 1 μm) dispersed in a medium.
   b. **Key Concepts:**
      i. **Brownian Motion:** Random movement of colloidal particles due to collisions with molecules of the dispersing medium.
      ii. **Tyndall Effect:** Scattering of light by colloidal particles, making the path of light visible.
      iii. **Electrical Double Layer:** Formation of a double layer of charge around colloidal particles, affecting stability.
2. **Thermodynamic Theory:**
   a. **Definition:** Describes the stability of dispersions based on thermodynamic principles.
   b. **Key Concepts:**
      i. **Gibbs Free Energy:** Determines the stability of the dispersion; a lower free energy indicates a more stable system.
      ii. **Surface Energy:** The energy associated with the surface of particles, influencing their interaction and dispersion stability.
3. **Kinetic Theory:**
   a. **Definition:** Focuses on the movement and interaction of particles within a dispersion.
   b. **Key Concepts:**
      i. **Sedimentation:** The process where particles settle out of the dispersion due to gravity.
      ii. **Flocculation:** The clustering of particles, which can lead to instability.

2. Pharmaceutical Dispersion:

Pharmaceutical dispersions include formulations where active ingredients are dispersed in a medium to enhance their delivery and stability. The major types are emulsions, suspensions, and Self-Microemulsifying Drug Delivery Systems (SMEDDS).

2.1. Emulsions

Definition: A type of dispersion where one liquid is dispersed in another immiscible liquid in the form of droplets. Emulsions are used to deliver drugs that are poorly soluble in water.

Preparation Methods:

1. **High-Shear Mixing:**
    a. **Process:** Using high-speed mixers or homogenizers to disperse droplets of one liquid into another.
    b. **Purpose:** Achieves fine droplet size and stable emulsion.
2. **Phase Inversion:**
    a. **Process:** Transition from one emulsion type to another (e.g., from water-in-oil to oil-in-water) during formulation.
    b. **Purpose:** Improves stability and enhances the delivery of active ingredients.
3. **Microfluidization:**
    a. **Process:** High-pressure fluid mixing to create smaller and more uniform droplets.
    b. **Purpose:** Produces stable emulsions with fine droplet sizes.

Stabilization:

a. **Emulsifiers:** Surfactants or stabilizers that reduce the surface tension between the two immiscible liquids, preventing coalescence.
b. **Viscosity Modifiers:** Thickeners to increase the viscosity and reduce droplet movement.

2.2. Suspensions

Definition: A type of dispersion where solid particles are suspended in a liquid medium. Suspensions are used for drugs that are insoluble or poorly soluble in the liquid.

Preparation Methods:

1. **Wet Grinding:**
    a. **Process:** Grinding solid particles in a liquid to achieve a desired particle size.
    b. **Purpose:** Ensures uniform dispersion and reduces particle size.
2. **High-Shear Mixing:**
    a. **Process:** Using high-speed mixers to disperse solid particles into the liquid.
    - **Purpose:** Enhances the uniformity of the suspension.

Stabilization:

a. **Suspending Agents:** Polymers or clays that increase viscosity to prevent sedimentation.
b. **Flocculating Agents:** Help in forming aggregates to reduce caking and improve re-dispersibility.

2.3. Self-Microemulsifying Drug Delivery Systems (SMEDDS)

Definition: Advanced systems that form microemulsions upon contact with gastrointestinal fluids, enhancing the solubility and bioavailability of poorly water-soluble drugs.

Preparation Methods:

1. **Phase Diagram-Based Method:**
    a. **Process:** Using phase diagrams to identify the optimal composition of oils, surfactants, and co-surfactants.
    b. **Purpose:** Ensures the formation of stable microemulsions.
2. **High-Shear Mixing:**
    a. **Process:** Mixing oils, surfactants, and co-surfactants at high speeds to create a pre-emulsion.

b. **Purpose:** Produces a homogeneous system that forms microemulsions upon dilution.

Stabilization:

a. **Surfactants and Co-Surfactants:** Essential for forming and stabilizing microemulsions.

b. **Optimized Composition:** Balancing the components to achieve stable and effective drug delivery.

3. Application of Preformation Concepts:

In the context of preformation concepts, the study of dispersions, emulsions, suspensions, and SMEDDS involves understanding how the initial formulation parameters (like concentration and particle size) influence the stability and performance of the final product. The theories and preparation methods are employed to ensure that the pharmaceutical products remain effective and safe throughout their shelf life and upon administration.

STABILITY LARGE AND SMALL VOLUME PARENTAL

Stability of Parenteral Formulations is crucial for ensuring the safety and efficacy of injectable medications. Parenteral formulations include both large and small volume parenterals, which must be carefully designed and tested to maintain stability throughout their shelf life and upon administration. Here's a detailed overview of the stability considerations for these formulations, with a focus on physiological and formulation aspects:

1. Large Volume Parenterals (LVPs):

Definition: Large Volume Parenterals are intravenous solutions administered in volumes greater than 100 mL. They are often used for fluid and electrolyte replacement, nutritional support, or drug delivery over an extended period.

Stability Considerations

1.1. **Physiological Considerations:**

a. **Osmolarity:** The osmotic concentration of the solution should be compatible with body fluids to avoid irritation or hemolysis. Solutions are typically isotonic with blood.
b. **pH:** The pH should be compatible with physiological pH (around 7.4) to prevent discomfort or tissue damage.
c. **Compatibility:** The formulation must be compatible with the infusion site, including the use of appropriate administration devices and techniques to prevent adverse reactions.

1.2. **Formulation Considerations:**

a. **Preservatives and Stabilizers:** These are used to prevent microbial growth and maintain chemical stability. However, their concentration must be optimized to avoid adverse effects.
b. **Container Material:** The choice of container (e.g., glass or plastic) can influence the stability of the formulation due to interactions between the container material and the drug.
c. **Storage Conditions:** LVPs must be stored under controlled conditions to prevent degradation. Factors like temperature, light, and humidity can affect stability.

1.3. **Testing and Stability Studies:**

a. **Accelerated Stability Testing:** To predict the shelf life of the product under stressed conditions (e.g., elevated temperatures).
b. **Long-Term Stability Testing:** To monitor the formulation's stability under recommended storage conditions over an extended period.

2. Small Volume Parenterals (SVPs):

Definition: Small Volume Parenterals are typically injectable solutions or suspensions administered in volumes less than 100 mL. They are often used for drugs that require precise dosing or have potent effects.

Stability Considerations

2.1. **Physiological Considerations:**

a. **Volume:** SVPs must be designed to be administered in small, controlled amounts to ensure accurate dosing.
b. **Injection Site:** Considerations include ensuring the formulation is compatible with subcutaneous, intramuscular, or intravenous administration, as appropriate.

2.2. **Formulation Considerations:**

a. **Concentration:** Higher concentrations of drugs in SVPs can lead to stability issues such as precipitation or aggregation.
b. **Buffering Agents:** Buffers are used to maintain the pH within a range that ensures drug stability and minimizes irritation at the injection site.
c. **Solvent and Vehicles:** The choice of solvents (e.g., water for injection, saline) and vehicles (e.g., oils) must ensure solubility and stability of the drug.

2.3. **Testing and Stability Studies:**

a. **Compatibility Testing:** To ensure that the drug remains stable when mixed with other medications or during administration.
b. **Long-Term Stability Testing:** To ensure the drug maintains its efficacy and safety throughout its intended shelf life.

3. Preformation Concepts in Stability

3.1. **Preformation Concepts:**

a. **Preformation in Formulation Design:** Understanding how the pre-existing state of a drug (e.g., its solid form, crystallinity) affects its stability and solubility in the final formulation.
b. **Pre-existing Conditions:** Factors such as the drug's inherent stability and its behavior in different formulations influence how it will perform in parenteral products.

3.2. **Key Considerations:**

a. **Drug Stability:** Addressing potential instability issues such as hydrolysis, oxidation, or crystallization that might arise from the formulation process.

b. **Formulation Adjustments:** Using preformation concepts to adjust the formulation to ensure compatibility and stability, such as altering pH or solvent systems.

3.3. **Testing Techniques:**

a. **Stability-Indicating Assays:** To monitor the chemical stability of the drug and detect any degradation products.

b. **Physical Stability Testing:** Includes assessing factors like particle size, appearance, and precipitate formation.

MANUFACTURING AND EVALUATION

Manufacturing and Evaluation of pharmaceutical formulations, including parenteral and non-parenteral products, are crucial stages in drug development. This process involves creating the drug product and ensuring its quality and effectiveness through rigorous evaluation. In the context of **preformation concepts**, understanding how these concepts apply to manufacturing and evaluation is essential for producing safe and effective pharmaceutical products.

1. Manufacturing:

Manufacturing involves the preparation of pharmaceutical products in a controlled environment to ensure consistency and quality. Here's how preformation concepts integrate into manufacturing:

1.1. Preformation Concepts in Manufacturing

1.1.1. **Drug Formulation:**

a. **Pre-Formed Structures:** Consideration of the drug's pre-existing state (e.g., crystalline form, polymorphs) to ensure proper dissolution and stability during manufacturing.

b. **Compatibility:** Ensuring that the pre-existing drug characteristics are compatible with excipients and other components in the formulation.

1.1.2. **Processing Techniques:**

a. **Granulation:** Using pre-formed granules or powders that maintain stability and enhance uniformity in the final product.

b. **Mixing and Blending:** Ensuring that pre-formed particles or drug substances are evenly distributed in the formulation to achieve consistent dosage.

1.1.3. **Quality Control During Manufacturing:**

a. **In-Process Testing:** Monitoring parameters like temperature, pH, and particle size during manufacturing to ensure that pre-formed components remain stable and effective.

b. **Equipment Calibration:** Ensuring that manufacturing equipment is calibrated to prevent deviations from the desired product specifications.

2. Evaluation:

Evaluation involves assessing the quality, efficacy, and safety of the manufactured pharmaceutical product. It includes both physical and chemical assessments to ensure that the product meets regulatory and quality standards.

2.1. Preformation Concepts in Evaluation

2.1.1. **Pre-Existing Conditions Assessment:**

a. **Initial Analysis:** Evaluating the pre-existing characteristics of the drug, such as its crystalline form or polymorphs, to understand how they affect stability and performance.

b. **Formulation Compatibility:** Testing how the pre-formed drug interacts with excipients and other formulation components.

2.1.2. **Physical Evaluation:**

a. **Appearance and Color:** Ensuring that the physical characteristics of the product (e.g., color, clarity) remain consistent with the pre-formed specifications.

b. **Particle Size and Distribution:** Analyzing the particle size of pre-formed powders or granules to ensure uniformity and proper dissolution.

2.1.3. **Chemical Evaluation:**

a. **Stability Testing:** Conducting accelerated and long-term stability studies to assess how the pre-formed drug remains stable under various conditions.

b. **Assay and Content Uniformity:** Testing the drug's concentration to ensure that it meets the specified limits and remains consistent throughout the product.

2.1.4. **Microbiological Evaluation:**

a. **Sterility Testing:** Ensuring that parenteral products are free from microbial contamination, especially if the drug is in a pre-formed state that could be sensitive to microbial growth.

b. **Preservative Efficacy Testing:** Evaluating the effectiveness of preservatives in preventing microbial growth and maintaining product safety.

2.1.5. **Performance Evaluation:**

a. **Dissolution Testing:** For solid dosage forms, assessing how quickly and completely the drug dissolves, considering the pre-formed state of the drug.

b. **Bioavailability Studies:** Evaluating how well the drug is absorbed and utilized in the body, taking into account the pre-formed characteristics that affect drug release.

3. Integration of Preformation Concepts:

3.1. **Design and Development:**

a. **Preformed State Utilization:** Incorporating the pre-existing characteristics of the drug (e.g., polymorphs, granules) to optimize formulation design.

b. **Formulation Stability:** Ensuring that the formulation maintains the pre-formed characteristics and remains stable over time.

3.2. **Regulatory Considerations:**

a. **Compliance with Guidelines:** Following regulatory guidelines that consider the pre-formed state of the drug and its impact on manufacturing and evaluation.

b. **Documentation and Reporting:** Providing detailed information on the pre-formed characteristics and their influence on the manufacturing and evaluation processes.

CLASSIFICATION:

Preformation concepts in pharmaceutical formulation refer to the theoretical and practical considerations of the state and behavior of a drug substance before and during the formulation process. These concepts are crucial for understanding how pre-existing conditions of a drug affect its stability, performance, and formulation. Here's a detailed classification of preformation concepts with examples:

1. Physical State of the Drug:

1.1. **Crystalline vs. Amorphous Forms:**

a. **Crystalline:** Drugs with a well-defined crystalline structure (e.g., **Sodium Chloride**).

b. **Amorphous:** Drugs lacking a defined crystalline structure (e.g., **Amorphous Metformin**).

c. **Example: Acetaminophen** can exist in different polymorphic forms. The physical state affects its solubility and stability.

1.2. **Polymorphism:**

a. **Definition:** The ability of a substance to exist in more than one crystalline form.

b. **Example: Ranitidine Hydrochloride** has multiple polymorphic forms, affecting its solubility and dissolution rate.

1.3. **Particle Size and Distribution:**

a. **Definition:** The size and distribution of particles in a formulation.

b. **Example: Pulmicort (budesonide)** for inhalation has a specific particle size to ensure effective delivery to the lungs.

2. Chemical Form:

2.1. **Salt vs. Free Base Forms:**

a. **Salt Form:** The drug is in its ionic form (e.g., **Lisinopril Dihydrate**).

b. **Free Base Form:** The drug is in its non-ionic form (e.g., **Ciprofloxacin** in free base form).

c. **Example: Ibuprofen** is often used as **Ibuprofen Sodium Salt** in oral formulations to improve solubility.

2.2. **Prodrugs:**

a. **Definition:** Inactive compounds that are metabolized into active drugs in the body.

b. **Example: Enalapril** is a prodrug that is converted to **Enalaprilat** upon administration.

3. Solubility and Dissolution:

3.1. **Solubility Characteristics:**

a. **Definition:** The extent to which a drug can dissolve in a solvent.

b. **Example: Diazepam** has poor solubility in water, which affects its formulation into oral and injectable forms.

3.2. **Dissolution Rate:**

a. **Definition:** The rate at which a drug dissolves in a solvent.

b. **Example: Extended-release formulations** of **Metformin** are designed to control the dissolution rate for prolonged action.

4. Stability Considerations:

4.1. **Chemical Stability:**

a. **Definition:** The drug's ability to retain its chemical integrity over time.

b. **Example: Penicillin** is known for its instability in aqueous solutions and requires careful formulation.

4.2. **Physical Stability:**

a. **Definition:** The drug's ability to maintain its physical properties, such as appearance and uniformity.

b. **Example: Insulin** formulations must be stable against aggregation and precipitation.

4.3. **Microbial Stability:**

a. **Definition:** The formulation's ability to resist microbial contamination.

b. **Example: Parenteral solutions** often include preservatives to maintain sterility.

5. Formulation Techniques:

5.1. **Granulation:**

a. **Definition:** Process of forming granules from powders to improve flow and compressibility.

b. **Example: Tablets** containing **Acetaminophen** are granulated to ensure uniform dosage.

5.2. **Coating:**

a. **Definition:** Applying a coating to tablets or granules to control release or protect the drug.

b. **Example: Enteric-coated Aspirin** prevents its release in the stomach and releases it in the intestines.

5.3. **Encapsulation:**

a. **Definition:** Enclosing the drug in a capsule to mask taste or control release.

b. **Example: Extended-release formulations** of **Oxycodone** are encapsulated for controlled drug release.

6. Formulation Considerations:

6.1. **Excipient Compatibility:**

a. **Definition:** Interaction between the drug and excipients used in the formulation.

b. **Example: Omeprazole** is formulated with specific excipients to prevent degradation in acidic environments.

6.2. **Manufacturing Processes:**

a. **Definition:** Methods used to produce the drug product, considering preformation states.

b. **Example: High-shear granulation** for **Oral Solid Dosage Forms** ensures uniform distribution of active ingredients.

7. Drug Delivery Systems:

7.1. **Controlled Release Systems:**

a. **Definition:** Systems designed to release the drug over an extended period.

b. **Example: Osmotic pump tablets** of **Hydrochlorothiazide** release the drug gradually.

7.2. **Self-Microemulsifying Drug Delivery Systems (SMEDDS):**

a. **Definition:** Systems that form microemulsions upon contact with gastrointestinal fluids.

b. **Example: SMEDDS formulations** of **Cyclosporine** enhance its bioavailability.

A. **Acetaminophen:**

Acetaminophen (also known as paracetamol) is a widely used analgesic and antipyretic agent. It is often used to relieve mild to moderate pain and reduce fever. Its pharmacological properties and formulation considerations are critical for effective drug delivery and stability.

Pharmacology of Acetaminophen

1. **Mechanism of Action:**

a. **Central Action:** Acetaminophen is primarily believed to exert its analgesic and antipyretic effects in the central nervous system (CNS). It is thought to inhibit the enzyme cyclooxygenase (COX) in the brain, leading to decreased production of prostaglandins, which are mediators of pain and fever.

b. **Peripheral Action:** While its peripheral COX inhibition is less significant compared to NSAIDs, some analgesic effects may be attributed to its action at the site of pain.

2. **Pharmacokinetics:**
   a. **Absorption:** Acetaminophen is well-absorbed from the gastrointestinal tract. Peak plasma concentrations are typically reached within 30 minutes to 2 hours after oral administration.
   b. **Distribution:** It is widely distributed throughout the body, including the CNS. It crosses the blood-brain barrier and is found in various tissues.
   c. **Metabolism:** Acetaminophen is primarily metabolized in the liver. It undergoes conjugation with sulfate and glucuronide. A small portion is metabolized via the cytochrome P450 enzyme system to a reactive metabolite.
   d. **Excretion:** The metabolites are excreted in the urine.
3. **Therapeutic Uses:**
   a. **Analgesic:** Used for the relief of mild to moderate pain, such as headaches, muscle aches, and toothaches.
   b. **Antipyretic:** Effective in reducing fever.
4. **Adverse Effects:**
   a. **Hepatotoxicity:** High doses or chronic use can lead to liver damage, especially in the presence of alcohol or other liver-affecting substances.
   b. **Allergic Reactions:** Rare but may include rashes and urticaria.
5. **Drug Interactions:**
   a. **Alcohol:** Increases the risk of hepatotoxicity.
   b. **Warfarin:** May enhance the anticoagulant effect of warfarin, increasing bleeding risk.

B. Ranitidine Hydrochloride:

Ranitidine Hydrochloride is an H2-receptor antagonist used primarily to treat conditions related to excessive stomach acid production, such as peptic ulcers and gastroesophageal reflux disease (GERD).

Pharmacology of Ranitidine Hydrochloride

1. **Mechanism of Action:**
   a. **H2 Receptor Antagonism:** Ranitidine selectively blocks H2 receptors in the stomach lining, reducing gastric acid secretion. This decreases the volume and acidity of gastric secretions, which helps in treating and preventing acid-related disorders.
2. **Pharmacokinetics:**
   a. **Absorption:** Ranitidine is rapidly absorbed from the gastrointestinal tract. Peak plasma concentrations are reached within 1 to 3 hours after oral administration.
   b. **Distribution:** It is distributed throughout the body and can cross the placenta. It binds to plasma proteins moderately.
   c. **Metabolism:** Ranitidine is primarily metabolized in the liver, but it is less extensively metabolized than some other H2 antagonists.
   d. **Excretion:** The drug and its metabolites are excreted mainly through the urine. A small portion is excreted in the feces.
3. **Therapeutic Uses:**
   a. **Peptic Ulcer Disease:** Used to treat and prevent peptic ulcers.
   b. **GERD:** Effective in treating symptoms of GERD and reducing acid reflux.
   c. **Zollinger-Ellison Syndrome:** Used to manage conditions involving excessive gastric acid secretion.
4. **Adverse Effects:**
   a. **Gastrointestinal:** Nausea, constipation, and diarrhea.
   b. **CNS:** Dizziness and headaches.

c. **Rare Effects:** Severe allergic reactions, including anaphylaxis, and blood dyscrasias.

5. **Drug Interactions:**

   a. **Antacids:** Can affect the absorption of ranitidine; it is generally advised to separate doses.

   b. **Warfarin:** Ranitidine can alter the effect of warfarin, requiring careful monitoring of INR.

Preformation Concepts

For Acetaminophen:

1. **Physical Form:**

   a. **Crystalline Form:** Acetaminophen exists in a crystalline form that affects its dissolution rate and stability. The crystalline form is generally stable but can be influenced by temperature and humidity.

2. **Solubility:**

   a. **Poor Water Solubility:** Acetaminophen has limited solubility in water, which can affect the formulation of oral solutions. Techniques such as solubilization and use of excipients to enhance solubility may be required.

3. **Stability:**

   a. **Chemical Stability:** Acetaminophen is stable in its solid form but can degrade in aqueous solutions, especially under acidic conditions or high temperatures.

4. **Formulation:**

   a. **Tablet Formulation:** In tablet formulations, acetaminophen is usually granulated to ensure uniform distribution and improve tablet characteristics.

For Ranitidine Hydrochloride:

1. **Physical Form:**

a. **Salt Form:** Ranitidine is used as the hydrochloride salt, which is more soluble in water compared to the free base form, facilitating its use in oral and injectable formulations.

2. **Solubility:**
   a. **Good Water Solubility:** The hydrochloride salt form of ranitidine is highly soluble in water, which aids in its formulation into various dosage forms, including tablets and injectables.

3. **Stability:**
   a. **Chemical Stability:** Ranitidine hydrochloride is relatively stable but can be sensitive to light and moisture. Proper storage conditions are essential to maintain its potency.

4. **Formulation:**
   a. **Tablet and Injectable Formulation:** In tablets, ranitidine is often combined with excipients to ensure uniformity and stability. Injectable forms are prepared under stringent conditions to avoid contamination and degradation.

C. Pulmicort (Budesonide):

Pulmicort is a brand name for **budesonide**, a corticosteroid used in the management of asthma and chronic obstructive pulmonary disease (COPD). It is an inhaled corticosteroid that helps reduce inflammation in the airways.

Pharmacology of Budesonide

1. **Mechanism of Action:**
   a. **Anti-Inflammatory:** Budesonide works by binding to glucocorticoid receptors in the cytoplasm of target cells. This complex then translocates to the nucleus, where it regulates the expression of anti-inflammatory genes and inhibits the expression of pro-inflammatory genes.
   b. **Reduction of Inflammatory Mediators:** The drug reduces the production of inflammatory mediators such as cytokines, prostaglandins, and leukotrienes, leading to decreased inflammation in the airways.

2. **Pharmacokinetics:**
   a. **Absorption:** When inhaled, budesonide is rapidly absorbed in the lungs. Systemic absorption is relatively low, which reduces the risk of systemic side effects.
   b. **Distribution:** The drug is distributed throughout the body after systemic absorption, but its primary site of action is the lungs.
   c. **Metabolism:** Budesonide is metabolized in the liver by the enzyme CYP3A4 into inactive metabolites.
   d. **Excretion:** The metabolites are excreted primarily through the feces, with a small amount excreted in the urine.
3. **Therapeutic Uses:**
   a. **Asthma:** Used as a maintenance therapy to reduce the frequency and severity of asthma attacks.
   b. **COPD:** Used to manage chronic inflammation and symptoms associated with COPD.
4. **Adverse Effects:**
   a. **Local:** Common adverse effects include oral candidiasis (thrush), hoarseness, and cough.
   b. **Systemic:** Although less common due to low systemic absorption, potential systemic effects include adrenal suppression and bone loss.
5. **Drug Interactions:**
   a. **CYP3A4 Inhibitors:** Concomitant use with strong CYP3A4 inhibitors (e.g., ketoconazole) can increase budesonide levels and the risk of systemic side effects.

D. Ibuprofen:

Ibuprofen is a nonsteroidal anti-inflammatory drug (NSAID) used for its analgesic, anti-inflammatory, and antipyretic properties. It is commonly used to treat pain, inflammation, and fever.

Pharmacology of Ibuprofen

1. **Mechanism of Action:**
    a. **COX Inhibition:** Ibuprofen exerts its effects by inhibiting cyclooxygenase (COX) enzymes, particularly COX-1 and COX-2. This inhibition reduces the synthesis of prostaglandins, which are responsible for pain, inflammation, and fever.
2. **Pharmacokinetics:**
    a. **Absorption:** Ibuprofen is well-absorbed from the gastrointestinal tract. Peak plasma concentrations are generally reached within 1 to 2 hours after oral administration.
    b. **Distribution:** It is widely distributed throughout the body and binds extensively to plasma proteins.
    c. **Metabolism:** Ibuprofen is metabolized in the liver primarily by the enzyme CYP2C19 into inactive metabolites.
    d. **Excretion:** The metabolites are excreted mainly through the urine.
3. **Therapeutic Uses:**
    a. **Analgesic:** Used to relieve mild to moderate pain, such as headaches, menstrual cramps, and muscle aches.
    b. **Anti-Inflammatory:** Used for conditions involving inflammation, such as arthritis.
    c. **Antipyretic:** Effective in reducing fever.
4. **Adverse Effects:**
    a. **Gastrointestinal:** Common adverse effects include nausea, dyspepsia, and gastrointestinal bleeding or ulcers.
    b. **Renal:** Can cause renal impairment, especially with long-term use or in individuals with pre-existing kidney conditions.
    c. **Cardiovascular:** Long-term use can increase the risk of cardiovascular events such as heart attack and stroke.
5. **Drug Interactions:**

a. **Anticoagulants:** Can increase the risk of bleeding when used with anticoagulants (e.g., warfarin).
b. **Antihypertensives:** May reduce the efficacy of antihypertensive medications.

Preformation Concepts

For Budesonide (Pulmicort):

1. **Physical Form:**
    a. **Powder for Inhalation:** Budesonide is often formulated as a dry powder for inhalation. Its physical form needs to be optimized to ensure proper dispersion and deposition in the lungs.
    b. **Suspension:** Budesonide can also be formulated as a suspension in metered-dose inhalers (MDIs) or nebulizer solutions.
2. **Solubility:**
    a. **Limited Solubility in Water:** Budesonide has limited solubility in water, which influences its formulation into inhalable forms. Using appropriate solvents and carriers helps achieve the desired delivery form.
3. **Stability:**
    a. **Chemical Stability:** Budesonide is relatively stable in dry powder form but may degrade in solution or under high humidity conditions.
    b. **Formulation Stability:** Stability in inhaler devices must be ensured to prevent clumping or aggregation of the drug.
4. **Formulation:**
    a. **Particle Size:** Particle size is crucial for effective lung deposition. Fine particles are preferred for inhalation to reach the lower airways.

For Ibuprofen:

1. **Physical Form:**

a. **Tablets and Capsules:** Ibuprofen is commonly formulated as tablets or capsules. The physical form affects dissolution and absorption rates.

b. **Suspensions:** For pediatric use or for patients who have difficulty swallowing tablets, ibuprofen is formulated as a liquid suspension.

2. **Solubility:**

a. **Moderate Solubility:** Ibuprofen has moderate solubility in water, which can be enhanced with formulation techniques such as the use of solubilizers or dissolution enhancers.

3. **Stability:**

a. **Chemical Stability:** Ibuprofen is stable in solid dosage forms but can degrade in high humidity or heat. Proper storage conditions are required to maintain its stability.

b. **Formulation Stability:** Stability of ibuprofen formulations, such as tablets and suspensions, must be monitored to prevent degradation and ensure efficacy.

4. **Formulation:**

a. **Extended-Release Forms:** For prolonged action, ibuprofen can be formulated into extended-release tablets to maintain therapeutic levels over a longer period.

E. **Enalapril:**

Enalapril is an oral angiotensin-converting enzyme (ACE) inhibitor used primarily in the treatment of hypertension and heart failure.

Pharmacology of Enalapril

1. **Mechanism of Action:**

a. **ACE Inhibition:** Enalapril works by inhibiting the enzyme angiotensin-converting enzyme (ACE), which is responsible for converting angiotensin I to angiotensin II. Angiotensin II is a potent vasoconstrictor that also stimulates aldosterone release, leading to sodium and water retention.

b. **Effects:** By inhibiting ACE, enalapril reduces the levels of angiotensin II, resulting in vasodilation, reduced blood pressure, and decreased workload on the heart.

2. **Pharmacokinetics:**
   a. **Absorption:** Enalapril is well-absorbed from the gastrointestinal tract. However, it undergoes significant first-pass metabolism.
   b. **Distribution:** Enalapril is distributed throughout the body and can cross the placenta. It binds moderately to plasma proteins.
   c. **Metabolism:** Enalapril is converted to its active form, enalaprilat, primarily in the liver. Enalaprilat is responsible for the drug's therapeutic effects.
   d. **Excretion:** Both enalapril and enalaprilat are excreted mainly through the kidneys.
3. **Therapeutic Uses:**
   a. **Hypertension:** Used to lower blood pressure in patients with hypertension.
   b. **Heart Failure:** Helps reduce symptoms and improve outcomes in patients with heart failure.
   c. **Chronic Kidney Disease:** Used to protect renal function in patients with diabetic nephropathy and other forms of chronic kidney disease.
4. **Adverse Effects:**
   a. **Common:** Cough, hyperkalemia, dizziness, and headache.
   b. **Serious:** Angioedema (swelling of the deeper layers of the skin), renal impairment, and hypotension.
5. **Drug Interactions:**
   a. **Diuretics:** Concurrent use with diuretics can increase the risk of hypotension.

b. **Potassium-Sparing Diuretics:** Can lead to hyperkalemia when used together.

F. Diazepam:

Diazepam is a benzodiazepine used for its anxiolytic, sedative, muscle relaxant, and anticonvulsant properties.

Pharmacology of Diazepam

1. **Mechanism of Action:**
   a. **GABA-A Receptor Modulation:** Diazepam works by enhancing the effect of the neurotransmitter gamma-aminobutyric acid (GABA) at the GABA-A receptor. This leads to increased inhibitory neurotransmission, resulting in sedative, anxiolytic, and muscle relaxant effects.
   b. **Effects:** The enhancement of GABAergic activity helps in reducing anxiety, promoting sedation, and controlling seizures.
2. **Pharmacokinetics:**
   a. **Absorption:** Diazepam is well-absorbed from the gastrointestinal tract, with peak plasma concentrations typically reached within 1 to 2 hours after oral administration.
   b. **Distribution:** It is widely distributed throughout the body, including the CNS, and is highly protein-bound.
   c. **Metabolism:** Diazepam is metabolized in the liver by the cytochrome P450 enzyme system into active metabolites, such as desmethyldiazepam.
   d. **Excretion:** The drug and its metabolites are excreted primarily in the urine.
3. **Therapeutic Uses:**
   a. **Anxiety Disorders:** Used for the short-term management of anxiety.
   b. **Sedation:** Provides sedation for procedures and in cases of severe agitation.
   c. **Muscle Spasms:** Used to relieve muscle spasticity.
   d. **Seizures:** Utilized as an adjunctive treatment for certain types of seizures.

4. **Adverse Effects:**
    a. **Common:** Drowsiness, dizziness, and impaired coordination.
    b. **Serious:** Dependence and withdrawal symptoms with prolonged use, respiratory depression, and overdose.
5. **Drug Interactions:**
    a. **CNS Depressants:** Concurrent use with other CNS depressants (e.g., alcohol) can enhance sedative effects and increase the risk of respiratory depression.
    b. **CYP3A4 Inhibitors:** Can increase diazepam levels and effects when used with CYP3A4 inhibitors.

Preformation Concepts

For Enalapril:

1. **Physical Form:**
    a. **Tablet Formulation:** Enalapril is typically formulated as tablets. The physical form must ensure proper dissolution and absorption.
2. **Solubility:**
    a. **Moderate Solubility:** Enalapril has moderate water solubility. Formulation techniques may include using excipients that enhance solubility and ensure consistent release.
3. **Stability:**
    a. **Chemical Stability:** Enalapril is stable in solid dosage forms but may degrade in solution or under high humidity. Proper storage conditions are essential.
4. **Formulation:**
    a. **Extended-Release Forms:** Enalapril can be formulated into extended-release tablets to provide sustained antihypertensive effects.

For Diazepam:

1. **Physical Form:**

a. **Oral Tablets, Injectable Solutions:** Diazepam is available in various forms, including oral tablets, injectable solutions, and rectal gel. Each form requires specific considerations for stability and bioavailability.

2. **Solubility:**
    a. **Lipophilic Nature:** Diazepam is lipophilic, which affects its formulation. For injectable forms, solubilizers may be used to ensure proper dissolution.
3. **Stability:**
    a. **Chemical Stability:** Diazepam is relatively stable in its solid form but can degrade in solution. Stability is a concern, particularly for injectable forms, which must be stored properly to prevent degradation.
4. **Formulation:**
    a. **Extended-Release Forms:** For certain therapeutic indications, extended-release formulations may be used to provide prolonged effects.
    b. **Injectable Formulation:** Requires appropriate solubilizers and preservatives to ensure stability and prevent microbial contamination.

G. Penicillin:

Penicillin is a widely used antibiotic derived from the Penicillium mold. It is primarily used to treat bacterial infections.

Pharmacology of Penicillin

1. **Mechanism of Action:**
    a. **Inhibition of Cell Wall Synthesis:** Penicillin works by inhibiting the synthesis of bacterial cell walls. It binds to penicillin-binding proteins (PBPs) located in the bacterial cell wall, preventing cross-linking of peptidoglycan layers. This leads to cell lysis and death of the bacteria.

b. **Bactericidal Effect:** Penicillin is generally bactericidal, meaning it kills bacteria rather than just inhibiting their growth.

2. **Pharmacokinetics:**
   a. **Absorption:** Penicillin is absorbed from the gastrointestinal tract when administered orally. However, absorption can be affected by food. For intravenous (IV) or intramuscular (IM) administration, it reaches systemic circulation quickly.
   b. **Distribution:** It is widely distributed throughout the body, including into most tissues and fluids. Penicillin can cross the placenta and is found in breast milk.
   c. **Metabolism:** Penicillin is minimally metabolized in the liver.
   d. **Excretion:** It is primarily excreted unchanged in the urine. Renal function significantly affects the elimination rate.
3. **Therapeutic Uses:**
   a. **Infections:** Used to treat a variety of infections, including streptococcal, staphylococcal, and pneumococcal infections.
   b. **Preoperative Prophylaxis:** Often used as prophylaxis in surgical procedures to prevent infection.
4. **Adverse Effects:**
   a. **Allergic Reactions:** Includes rash, hives, and anaphylaxis in severe cases.
   b. **Gastrointestinal:** Nausea, vomiting, and diarrhea.
   c. **Superinfection:** Prolonged use can lead to superinfection by resistant organisms.
5. **Drug Interactions:**
   a. **Probenecid:** Can inhibit the renal excretion of penicillin, leading to increased penicillin levels.

b. **Oral Contraceptives:** Penicillin can reduce the effectiveness of oral contraceptives, though this is less commonly observed with newer formulations.

H. Omeprazole:

Omeprazole is a proton pump inhibitor (PPI) used to reduce gastric acid production.

Pharmacology of Omeprazole

1. **Mechanism of Action:**
   a. **Proton Pump Inhibition:** Omeprazole inhibits the hydrogen-potassium ATPase enzyme system (proton pump) in the parietal cells of the stomach. This enzyme is responsible for the final step in gastric acid secretion.
   b. **Reduction in Acid Secretion:** By inhibiting the proton pump, omeprazole effectively reduces gastric acid secretion, leading to decreased acidity in the stomach and duodenum.
2. **Pharmacokinetics:**
   a. **Absorption:** Omeprazole is well-absorbed from the gastrointestinal tract, with peak plasma concentrations reached within 1 to 2 hours after oral administration.
   b. **Distribution:** It is widely distributed in the body and can cross the placenta. It binds extensively to plasma proteins.
   c. **Metabolism:** Omeprazole is extensively metabolized in the liver by cytochrome P450 enzymes, particularly CYP2C19 and CYP3A4.
   d. **Excretion:** The metabolites are excreted primarily in the urine, with a smaller amount in the feces.
3. **Therapeutic Uses:**
   a. **Gastroesophageal Reflux Disease (GERD):** Used to treat GERD by reducing stomach acid and alleviating symptoms.

b. **Peptic Ulcer Disease:** Helps in the healing of peptic ulcers and reducing acid-related damage.
c. **Helicobacter pylori Eradication:** Used in combination with antibiotics to eradicate H. pylori infection.

4. **Adverse Effects:**
   a. **Common:** Headache, nausea, and diarrhea.
   b. **Serious:** Risk of Clostridium difficile infection, bone fractures, and kidney disease with long-term use.
5. **Drug Interactions:**
   a. **Clopidogrel:** Omeprazole can reduce the effectiveness of clopidogrel, an antiplatelet agent.
   b. **Warfarin:** Can alter the effect of warfarin, requiring careful monitoring of INR.

Preformation Concepts

For Penicillin:

1. **Physical Form:**
   a. **Powder for Injection:** Penicillin is often formulated as a powder for reconstitution into a solution for IV or IM injection. This form must be carefully prepared to ensure proper dosage and efficacy.
   b. **Oral Tablets/Capsules:** Penicillin is also available in oral forms, which need to be stable and have appropriate dissolution characteristics.
2. **Solubility:**
   a. **Variable Solubility:** Penicillin's solubility varies depending on the specific type (e.g., penicillin G is less soluble than penicillin V). Formulation must account for solubility to ensure effective delivery.
3. **Stability:**

a. **Chemical Stability:** Penicillin is sensitive to moisture, heat, and light. Dry powder forms are generally more stable, while solutions require proper storage to prevent degradation.

4. **Formulation:**
   a. **Extended-Release Forms:** Extended-release formulations can be used for sustained action and reduced dosing frequency.

For Omeprazole:

1. **Physical Form:**
   a. **Enteric-Coated Tablets:** Omeprazole is typically formulated as enteric-coated tablets or capsules to protect the drug from stomach acid and ensure it is released in the intestine where it is activated.
   b. **Oral Suspension:** Available as an oral suspension for patients who have difficulty swallowing tablets.
2. **Solubility:**
   a. **Acid-Sensitive:** Omeprazole is acid-sensitive, which is why enteric coating is used to protect the drug from degradation in the stomach.
3. **Stability:**
   a. **Chemical Stability:** Omeprazole is sensitive to moisture and light. Proper packaging and storage conditions are required to maintain stability.
4. **Formulation:**
   a. **Delayed-Release Forms:** The enteric coating ensures that the drug is released in the alkaline environment of the intestine, where it can be absorbed effectively.

Multiple-Choice Questions (Objective)

1. Preformation theory suggests that:
   a) Organisms develop from undifferentiated cells.
   b) Organisms are pre-formed in miniature form within the sperm or egg.

c) Organisms develop through random processes.
d) Organisms develop only after fertilization.

2. Which scientist was an early proponent of the spermist theory?
    a) Maria Sibylla Merian
    b) Anton van Leeuwenhoek
    c) Caspar Friedrich Wolff
    d) Carl Ernst von Baer
3. The ovist theory states that:
    a) Organisms are pre-formed within the sperm.
    b) Organisms are pre-formed within the egg.
    c) Development is a process of epigenesis.
    d) Development occurs after birth.
4. The homunculus concept refers to:
    a) A miniature form of an organism within the sperm.
    b) The gradual development of an organism.
    c) The study of embryos and their development.
    d) The theory that organisms develop from undifferentiated cells.
5. Preformation was challenged by the theory of:
    a) Spontaneous generation
    b) Biogenesis
    c) Epigenesis
    d) Germ theory
6. Which scientist's work contributed to the decline of preformation theory?
    a) Nicholas Hartsoeker
    b) Maria Sibylla Merian
    c) Carl Ernst von Baer
    d) Anton van Leeuwenhoek
7. Drug-excipient interactions that involve non-chemical changes are classified as:

a) Chemical interactions
b) Physical interactions
c) Biological interactions
d) None of the above

8. What type of analysis uses Differential Scanning Calorimetry (DSC)?
   a) Chromatographic analysis
   b) Microscopy
   c) Spectroscopic analysis
   d) Thermal analysis
9. Which equation is used to predict the effect of temperature on drug stability?
   a) Nernst Equation
   b) Arrhenius Equation
   c) Henderson-Hasselbalch Equation
   d) Michaelis-Menten Equation
10. Self-Microemulsifying Drug Delivery Systems (SMEDDS) are designed to:
   a) Form microemulsions upon contact with gastrointestinal fluids
   b) Enhance drug solubility in water
   c) Decrease drug absorption
   d) Increase drug hydrophilicity
11. Large volume parenterals (LVPs) typically have a volume greater than:
   a) 10 mL
   b) 50 mL
   c) 100 mL
   d) 500 mL
12. One of the main physiological considerations for large volume parenterals (LVPs) is:
   a) Viscosity
   b) Osmolarity
   c) Color

d) Particle size

13. What type of drug formulation is commonly used for extended-release effects?
    a) Suspension
    b) Tablet
    c) Granules
    d) Gel

14. Which of the following is not an example of a physical state consideration in preformation?
    a) Crystalline form
    b) Polymorphism
    c) Chemical stability
    d) Particle size distribution

15. What is the primary mechanism of action for acetaminophen?
    a) COX inhibition
    b) Serotonin reuptake inhibition
    c) GABA receptor modulation
    d) Inhibition of cyclooxygenase in the brain

16. Which form of acetaminophen is more soluble in water?
    a) Crystalline form
    b) Amorphous form
    c) Polymorphic form
    d) Hydrated form

17. Ranitidine Hydrochloride is primarily used to treat:
    a) Hypertension
    b) Infections
    c) Gastroesophageal reflux disease (GERD)
    d) Diabetes

18. Pulmicort (budesonide) is primarily used for:

a) Pain relief
b) Reducing inflammation in the airways
c) Reducing blood pressure
d) Treating infections

19. Ibuprofen works by:

a) Enhancing GABAergic activity
b) Inhibiting cyclooxygenase (COX) enzymes
c) Blocking H2 receptors
d) Inhibiting proton pumps

20. Which drug is an ACE inhibitor used for hypertension and heart failure?

a) Diazepam
b) Enalapril
c) Omeprazole
d) Penicillin

Short Answer Type Questions (Subjective)

1. Define preformation and explain its historical significance in developmental biology.
2. Differentiate between the spermist and ovist theories of preformation.
3. What is the concept of a homunculus in preformation theory?
4. How did microscopy contribute to the preformation theory?
5. What is the role of epigenesis in modern developmental biology?
6. Describe the types of drug-excipient interactions.
7. Explain the use of spectroscopic techniques in studying drug-excipient interactions.
8. How does the Arrhenius equation relate to drug stability?
9. What are Self-Microemulsifying Drug Delivery Systems (SMEDDS)?
10. Explain the physiological considerations for large volume parenterals (LVPs).

11. What are the key steps in preparing suspensions in pharmaceutical formulations?
12. Discuss the importance of preformation concepts in drug stability testing.
13. Define polymorphism and its significance in pharmaceutical formulations.
14. Describe the mechanism of action of acetaminophen.
15. What are the therapeutic uses of ranitidine hydrochloride?
16. How does the physical form of budesonide affect its delivery in Pulmicort?
17. Discuss the pharmacokinetics of ibuprofen.
18. Explain the primary uses of enalapril in clinical practice.
19. What are the adverse effects of diazepam?
20. How is omeprazole formulated to protect it from stomach acid?

Long Answer Type Questions (Subjective)

1. Discuss the evolution of developmental biology from preformation to epigenesis, highlighting key experiments and observations that led to the shift.
2. Explain the impact of drug-excipient interactions on the stability and efficacy of pharmaceutical products, providing examples.
3. Describe the methods used to study drug-excipient interactions and their importance in formulation development.
4. Explain the principles of Self-Microemulsifying Drug Delivery Systems (SMEDDS) and their applications in enhancing drug solubility and bioavailability.
5. Discuss the stability considerations for large volume parenterals (LVPs) and small volume parenterals (SVPs), including testing methods and regulatory guidelines.
6. Describe the manufacturing processes for pharmaceutical formulations and the role of preformation concepts in ensuring product quality.

7. Explain the importance of stability testing in preformation concepts, detailing the different types of stability studies conducted.
8. Discuss the pharmacology, therapeutic uses, and formulation considerations for acetaminophen.
9. Explain the mechanism of action, pharmacokinetics, and clinical applications of ranitidine hydrochloride.
10. Describe the formulation and stability challenges of penicillin and omeprazole, highlighting how preformation concepts address these issues.

Answer Key for MCQ Questions

1. b) Organisms are pre-formed in miniature form within the sperm or egg
2. b) Anton van Leeuwenhoek
3. b) Organisms are pre-formed within the egg
4. a) A miniature form of an organism within the sperm
5. c) Epigenesis
6. c) Carl Ernst von Baer
7. b) Physical interactions
8. d) Thermal analysis
9. b) Arrhenius Equation
10. a) Form microemulsions upon contact with gastrointestinal fluids
11. c) 100 mL
12. b) Osmolarity
13. b) Tablet
14. c) Chemical stability
15. d) Inhibition of cyclooxygenase in the brain
16. b) Amorphous form
17. c) Gastroesophageal reflux disease (GERD)
18. b) Reducing inflammation in the airways
19. b) Inhibiting cyclooxygenase (COX) enzymes
20. b) Enalapril

CHAPTER – 2

OPTIMIZATION TECHNIQUES IN PHARMACEUTICAL FORMULATION

INTRODUCTION:

Optimization techniques in pharmaceutical formulation are essential for developing effective, safe, and high-quality medications. These techniques help in refining the formulation process to achieve the desired therapeutic effect while minimizing side effects and improving patient compliance. Here's an overview of the key optimization techniques used in pharmaceutical formulation:

Formulation Development and Design:

Formulation development and design are critical stages in pharmaceutical formulation optimization. They involve creating and refining a drug product to achieve the desired therapeutic effect, ensure patient safety, and meet regulatory requirements. Here's a detailed look at formulation development and design in the context of optimization techniques:

1. Preformulation Studies

Purpose:

a. **Characterize Drug Properties:** Assess the drug's physical and chemical properties, including solubility, stability, and compatibility with excipients.

Key Aspects:

a. **Solubility Studies:** Determine the drug's solubility in various solvents, which impacts its bioavailability.
b. **Stability Studies:** Evaluate how the drug's chemical and physical properties change over time under different conditions.

c. **Compatibility Studies:** Test interactions between the drug and excipients to ensure no adverse effects on stability or efficacy.

Techniques:

a. **Solubility Testing:** Using techniques like shake-flask, dialysis, or solubility enhancement methods.

b. **Stability Testing:** Conducting accelerated stability studies and real-time stability studies.

c. **Compatibility Testing:** Using methods like differential scanning calorimetry (DSC) or Fourier-transform infrared spectroscopy (FTIR).

2. Design of Experiments (DoE)

Purpose:

a. **Efficiently Explore Formulation Space:** Systematically evaluate the effects of multiple factors and their interactions.

Key Aspects:

a. **Experimental Design:** Plan and conduct experiments to understand the effects of variables on responses.

b. **Data Analysis:** Analyze data to determine the optimal conditions for formulation.

Techniques:

a. **Factorial Designs:** Test all possible combinations of factors (full factorial) or a subset of combinations (fractional factorial).

b. **Response Surface Methodology (RSM):** Create and analyze polynomial models to find optimal conditions.

Tools:

a. **Software:** Minitab, JMP, Design-Expert for planning and analyzing experiments.

3. Formulation Design and Optimization

Purpose:

a. **Develop and Refine Formulations:** Optimize formulation parameters to achieve desired product characteristics.

Key Aspects:

a. **Formulation Components:** Select and optimize excipients such as binders, fillers, disintegrants, lubricants, and preservatives.

b. **Formulation Types:** Tailor the formulation based on the drug's properties and intended route of administration (e.g., oral tablets, injectable solutions, topical creams).

Techniques:

a. **Mixing and Granulation:** Optimize the mixing process and granulation parameters to ensure uniformity and desired release properties.

b. **Compression and Tablet Coating:** Adjust compression forces and coating processes to achieve optimal tablet hardness, dissolution, and stability.

Examples:

a. **Tablet Formulation:** Adjusting binder concentration and granulation parameters to achieve desired tablet hardness and dissolution.

b. **Oral Liquid Formulation:** Optimizing suspending agents and sweeteners to ensure stability and patient acceptability.

4. Quality by Design (QbD)

Purpose:

a. **Ensure Product Quality Through Understanding:** Focus on designing the formulation and process to consistently meet quality attributes.

Key Aspects:

a. **Critical Quality Attributes (CQAs):** Define attributes that are critical to the product's quality, such as dissolution rate and drug content uniformity.

b. **Critical Process Parameters (CPPs):** Identify parameters that significantly impact CQAs, such as mixing speed and granulation time.

c. **Design Space:** Define the range of conditions under which the product remains within acceptable quality limits.

Techniques:

a. **Risk Assessment:** Use tools like Failure Mode and Effects Analysis (FMEA) to identify and mitigate risks.

b. **Design Space Definition:** Use experimental data to establish a range of conditions that ensure product quality.

Tools:

a. **Software:** Risk management tools and statistical analysis software.

5. Process Optimization

Purpose:

a. **Improve Manufacturing Efficiency:** Ensure the formulation process is efficient, reproducible, and scalable.

Key Aspects:

a. **Scale-Up:** Adapt the formulation and process from laboratory to commercial scale while maintaining quality.

b. **Process Monitoring and Control:** Implement techniques to monitor and control process variables to ensure consistent product quality.

Techniques:

a. **Process Analytical Technology (PAT):** Use real-time measurements to monitor and control the manufacturing process.

b. **Scale-Up Studies:** Conduct pilot-scale studies to address challenges in scaling up and ensure reproducibility.

Examples:

a. **Granulation Process:** Optimize granulation parameters such as binder concentration and granulation time to achieve consistent granule size and flow properties.

b. **Tablet Coating:** Adjust coating conditions to ensure uniformity and stability of the final tablet.

6. Regulatory Considerations

Purpose:

a. **Ensure Compliance with Standards:** Meet regulatory requirements for drug formulation and manufacturing.

Key Aspects:

a. **Regulatory Guidelines:** Follow guidelines provided by agencies like the FDA, EMA, or ICH for formulation development and process optimization.

b. **Documentation:** Maintain thorough documentation of formulation development, optimization studies, and process controls.

Techniques:

a. **Regulatory Submissions:** Prepare and submit documents required for regulatory approval, including formulation details, process descriptions, and quality control data.

Examples:

a. **Regulatory Filing:** Prepare a comprehensive dossier including preformulation studies, stability data, and clinical trial results for regulatory review.

Optimization of Drug Delivery Systems:

Optimization of drug delivery systems (DDS) is a critical component in pharmaceutical formulation that focuses on enhancing the efficacy, safety, and patient compliance of drug therapies. This process involves designing and refining systems to ensure that drugs are delivered in the most effective way, considering factors like release rate, targeted delivery, and bioavailability. Here's a detailed overview of optimization techniques for drug delivery systems:

1. Types of Drug Delivery Systems

a. **Oral Drug Delivery Systems:**

i. **Tablets and Capsules:** Solid dosage forms optimized for controlled release, taste masking, and stability.

ii. **Oral Suspensions and Solutions:** Liquid forms designed for easier swallowing and quicker drug absorption.

b. **Topical Drug Delivery Systems:**

i. **Creams and Ointments:** Semi-solid forms optimized for localized treatment and controlled release.

ii. **Transdermal Patches:** Devices that deliver drugs through the skin over extended periods.

c. **Injectable Drug Delivery Systems:**

i. **Solutions and Suspensions:** Formulations for intravenous, intramuscular, or subcutaneous administration.

ii. **Implants:** Devices that provide prolonged drug release at a specific site.

d. **Inhalation Drug Delivery Systems:**

i. **Metered-Dose Inhalers (MDIs):** Devices that deliver drugs directly to the lungs.

ii. **Dry Powder Inhalers (DPIs):** Systems that deliver powdered drugs to the respiratory tract.

e. **Targeted Drug Delivery Systems:**

i. **Nanoparticles and Liposomes:** Vehicles that deliver drugs specifically to targeted cells or tissues.

ii. **Biodegradable Polymers:** Systems that provide controlled release of drugs over time.

2. Optimization Techniques

1. Formulation Optimization

a. Release Rate Control:

i. **Purpose:** Adjust the release profile of the drug to achieve desired therapeutic effects while minimizing side effects.

ii. **Techniques:**

   1. **Matrix Systems:** Use of polymers to control the release of the drug through diffusion or erosion.
   2. **Reservoir Systems:** Design of multi-layer or core-shell structures to modulate drug release.

iii. **Example:** Developing a sustained-release tablet by optimizing the ratio of polymer to drug to achieve a 12-hour release profile.

b. Solubility and Stability Enhancement:

i. **Purpose:** Improve the solubility and stability of poorly soluble drugs.

ii. **Techniques:**

   1. **Solid Dispersions:** Formulating the drug in a solid state with a solubility-enhancing polymer.
   2. **Cyclodextrin Complexes:** Using cyclodextrins to enhance drug solubility and stability.

iii. **Example:** Formulating a poorly soluble drug using solid dispersion with PEG to enhance its solubility.

c. Taste Masking:

i. **Purpose:** Improve the palatability of oral dosage forms.

ii. **Techniques:**

   1. **Coating:** Applying taste-masking coatings to tablets or granules.
   2. **Flavoring Agents:** Adding flavoring agents to improve taste.

iii. **Example:** Masking the bitter taste of a pediatric medication using a sugar coating.

2. Design of Experiments (DoE)

a. Factorial Designs:

i. **Purpose:** Evaluate the effects of multiple factors on the drug delivery system.

ii. **Techniques:**

   1. **Full Factorial Designs:** Study all possible combinations of factors.

2. **Fractional Factorial Designs:** Study a subset of combinations to reduce the number of experiments.

iii. **Example:** Optimizing the formulation of an oral suspension by varying the concentrations of suspending agents and sweeteners.

b. Response Surface Methodology (RSM):

i. **Purpose:** Model and analyze the relationship between factors and responses to find optimal conditions.

ii. **Techniques:**

1. **Central Composite Designs (CCD):** Used to build a second-order polynomial model for optimization.
2. **Box-Behnken Designs:** Used for optimization without requiring a full factorial design.

iii. **Example:** Optimizing the release profile of a controlled-release formulation by adjusting the concentration of hydrophilic and hydrophobic polymers.

3. Process Optimization

a. Process Analytical Technology (PAT):

i. **Purpose:** Monitor and control the manufacturing process in real-time.

ii. **Techniques:**

1. **Inline Sensors:** Measure critical parameters such as particle size, drug content, and dissolution rate.
2. **Real-Time Monitoring:** Use spectroscopy or chromatography to ensure consistent quality.

iii. **Example:** Implementing inline NIR spectroscopy to monitor the granulation process and ensure uniform drug content.

b. Scale-Up Studies:

i. **Purpose:** Ensure that the formulation process is reproducible at larger scales.

ii. **Techniques:**

1. **Pilot Studies:** Conduct small-scale trials to evaluate the feasibility of scaling up.
2. **Process Simulation:** Use computational models to predict scale-up challenges.

iii. **Example:** Scaling up the production of a transdermal patch from laboratory to commercial scale while maintaining consistent drug release.

4. Targeted Delivery Optimization

a. Nanoparticle Formulation:

i. **Purpose:** Enhance drug targeting and reduce side effects.

ii. **Techniques:**

1. **Surface Modification:** Modify the surface of nanoparticles to enhance targeting to specific cells or tissues.
2. **Controlled Release:** Design nanoparticles to release drugs in response to specific stimuli.

iii. **Example:** Developing targeted liposomes for cancer therapy that deliver drugs specifically to tumor cells.

b. Biodegradable Polymers:

i. **Purpose:** Provide controlled and sustained drug release over time.

ii. **Techniques:**

1. **Polymer Selection:** Choose polymers that degrade at controlled rates to release the drug gradually.
2. **Formulation Design:** Create polymer matrices or microspheres for sustained release.

iii. **Example:** Designing a biodegradable implant that releases an anti-inflammatory drug over several months.

5. Regulatory Considerations

a. Compliance with Guidelines:

i. **Purpose:** Ensure the drug delivery system meets regulatory standards.

ii. **Techniques:**

1. **Documentation:** Provide detailed information on formulation, manufacturing processes, and quality control.
2. **Stability Studies:** Conduct required stability testing to demonstrate the product's shelf life.

iii. **Example:** Submitting a comprehensive dossier for an oral controlled-release product, including stability data and clinical trial results.

Quality by Design (QbD):

Quality by Design (QbD) is a systematic approach to pharmaceutical formulation and development that emphasizes designing and understanding quality into the product from the outset. QbD focuses on defining and understanding the Critical Quality Attributes (CQAs) and Critical Process Parameters (CPPs) to ensure that the final product consistently meets the desired quality standards. Here's a detailed exploration of QbD in the context of pharmaceutical formulation optimization:

1. Core Concepts of QbD

a. Quality Target Product Profile (QTPP):

i. **Definition:** The QTPP is a comprehensive description of the desired product characteristics, including efficacy, safety, and performance criteria.

ii. **Purpose:** Guides the formulation and development process to ensure that the final product meets the intended therapeutic goals.

b. Critical Quality Attributes (CQAs):

i. **Definition:** Physical, chemical, biological, or microbiological properties or characteristics that must be within an appropriate limit, range, or distribution to ensure the desired product quality.

ii. **Examples:** Dissolution rate, drug content uniformity, particle size distribution, and stability.

c. Critical Process Parameters (CPPs):

i. **Definition:** Process parameters that have a significant impact on the CQAs.

ii. **Examples:** Mixing speed, granulation time, drying temperature, and compression force.

2. Steps in Implementing QbD:

a. Define the QTPP:

i. **Objective:** Establish clear, measurable product specifications based on the therapeutic goals and patient needs.

ii. **Process:** Engage in discussions with stakeholders, including regulatory agencies and clinicians, to outline the key attributes that the product must meet.

b. Identify CQAs:

i. **Objective:** Determine which attributes are crucial for product quality.

ii. **Process:** Use risk assessment tools and analytical methods to identify and define CQAs that are critical for achieving the QTPP.

c. Determine CPPs:

i. **Objective:** Identify the process parameters that influence CQAs.

ii. **Process:** Conduct experiments and studies to understand how different parameters affect the CQAs.

d. Develop a Design Space:

i. **Definition:** The range of conditions within which the CQAs are consistently achieved.

ii. **Purpose:** To ensure that variations in the process do not adversely affect the product quality.

iii. **Process:** Use experimental designs (e.g., factorial designs, response surface methodology) to determine the design space based on CPPs and CQAs.

e. Implement Control Strategies:

i. **Objective:** Develop and implement strategies to monitor and control the process to ensure consistent product quality.

ii. **Process:** Establish real-time monitoring systems (e.g., PAT) and define controls for critical process parameters.

f. Continuous Improvement:

i. **Objective:** Continuously evaluate and improve the formulation and process based on new data and technological advancements.

ii. **Process:** Use feedback from manufacturing and post-market data to refine the design and control strategies.

3. Tools and Techniques for QbD:

a. Risk Assessment:

i. **Purpose:** Identify potential risks that could impact product quality and implement mitigation strategies.

ii. **Tools:** Failure Mode and Effects Analysis (FMEA), Fault Tree Analysis (FTA), and Hazard Analysis and Critical Control Points (HACCP).

b. Design of Experiments (DoE):

i. **Purpose:** Efficiently explore the effects of various factors on CQAs and determine the optimal formulation and process conditions.

ii. **Techniques:** Factorial designs, response surface methodology (RSM), and fractional factorial designs.

c. Process Analytical Technology (PAT):

i. **Purpose:** Monitor and control the manufacturing process in real-time to ensure consistent product quality.

ii. **Techniques:** Inline sensors, spectroscopy (e.g., NIR, Raman), and chromatography.

d. Statistical Analysis:

i. **Purpose:** Analyze data to identify relationships between process parameters and CQAs, and to define the design space.

ii. **Techniques:** Regression analysis, variance analysis, and multivariate data analysis.

4. Applications of QbD:

a. Formulation Development:

i. **Example:** Developing a sustained-release tablet by defining CQAs such as release rate and tablet hardness, and optimizing CPPs like polymer concentration and compression force.

b. Process Optimization:

i. **Example:** Optimizing a granulation process by identifying key parameters (e.g., granulation time, binder concentration) that affect granule size and uniformity.

c. Quality Control and Assurance:

i. **Example:** Implementing real-time monitoring using PAT to ensure that the granulation process remains within the defined design space and maintains consistent product quality.

d. Scale-Up and Technology Transfer:

i. **Example:** Scaling up a formulation from lab to commercial scale by applying QbD principles to ensure that the process remains within the design space and meets product specifications.

e. Regulatory Submissions:

i. **Example:** Preparing a regulatory submission that includes detailed information on the QTPP, CQAs, CPPs, design space, and control strategies to demonstrate a thorough understanding of the formulation and process.

5. Benefits of QbD

a. Improved Product Quality:

i. **Benefit:** Ensures that the product consistently meets quality standards by designing and controlling the process to achieve desired attributes.

b. Increased Efficiency:

i. **Benefit:** Reduces the need for extensive testing and rework by identifying and controlling critical parameters early in the development process.

c. Regulatory Compliance:

i. **Benefit:** Meets regulatory requirements by providing a clear understanding of the formulation and process, and demonstrating robust control strategies.

d. Enhanced Innovation:

i. **Benefit:** Encourages the use of advanced technologies and methodologies to improve formulation and process design.

Statistical Optimization:

Statistical optimization in pharmaceutical formulation involves applying statistical methods to design, analyze, and interpret experiments to optimize the formulation and manufacturing processes. The goal is to systematically determine the effects of different variables on the quality and performance of the pharmaceutical product, thereby enhancing product consistency, efficacy, and safety.

1. Key Concepts in Statistical Optimization

a. Experimental Design:

i. **Definition:** A systematic approach to designing experiments to efficiently investigate the effects of variables and their interactions on responses.

ii. **Purpose:** To gain maximum information from a minimal number of experiments.

b. Response Variables:

i. **Definition:** Outcomes measured in an experiment that are influenced by the factors being tested.

ii. **Examples:** Drug release rate, tablet hardness, dissolution time, and stability.

c. Factors and Levels:

i. **Definition:** Factors are the independent variables manipulated during experiments, and levels are the different values or settings of these factors.

ii. **Examples:** Concentration of excipients, processing temperature, and mixing speed.

2. Statistical Techniques in Optimization

a. Factorial Designs

i. **Concept:** Investigate the effect of multiple factors simultaneously and their interactions.

ii. **Types:**

   1. **Full Factorial Design:** Evaluates all possible combinations of factors and levels.
   2. **Fractional Factorial Design:** Uses a subset of combinations to reduce the number of experiments.

iii. **Application:**

   1. **Example:** Optimizing the formulation of a tablet by varying excipient concentration and compression force to determine their effects on tablet hardness and dissolution.

b. Response Surface Methodology (RSM)

i. **Concept:** Models the relationship between factors and responses using polynomial equations to find optimal conditions.

ii. **Types:**

   1. **Central Composite Design (CCD):** A type of RSM design that allows for the creation of a second-order polynomial model.
   2. **Box-Behnken Design:** A design used for building second-order models that does not require a full factorial design.

iii. **Application:**

1. **Example:** Optimizing the release profile of a controlled-release formulation by adjusting polymer concentration and tablet compression force.

c. Taguchi Methods

i. **Concept:** Focuses on improving quality and reducing variation using orthogonal arrays to evaluate the effect of different factors efficiently.

ii. **Purpose:** To identify the optimal conditions that minimize variation and maximize performance.

iii. **Application:**

1. **Example:** Optimizing the coating process of tablets to achieve uniform coating thickness and consistency.

d. Design of Experiments (DoE)

i. **Concept:** A structured approach to planning, conducting, analyzing, and interpreting controlled tests.

ii. **Purpose:** To understand the relationship between factors and responses and to determine the best conditions for desired outcomes.

iii. **Application:**

1. **Example:** Developing a formulation for an oral liquid by varying the concentration of suspending agents and sweeteners to achieve optimal viscosity and taste.

3. Steps in Statistical Optimization

a. Define Objectives and Variables:

i. **Objective:** Clearly define what needs to be optimized (e.g., drug release rate, tablet hardness).

ii. **Variables:** Identify factors that might influence the outcome and determine their levels.

b. Design the Experiment:

i. **Approach:** Choose an appropriate experimental design (e.g., factorial design, RSM).

ii. **Planning:** Plan the number of experiments and the settings for each factor.

c. Conduct Experiments:

i. **Execution:** Carry out the experiments according to the design plan.

ii. **Data Collection:** Gather data on the response variables from each experiment.

d. Analyze Data:

i. **Statistical Analysis:** Use statistical methods to analyze the data, such as regression analysis, ANOVA (Analysis of Variance), and optimization algorithms.

ii. **Model Building:** Develop mathematical models to describe the relationship between factors and responses.

e. Interpret Results:

i. **Optimization:** Identify the optimal conditions that achieve the desired response.

ii. **Validation:** Verify the results by conducting additional experiments to ensure robustness.

f. Implement and Monitor:

i. **Implementation:** Apply the optimized conditions in the formulation process.

ii. **Monitoring:** Continuously monitor the process to ensure that it remains within the optimal range and consistently meets quality standards.

4. Applications of Statistical Optimization

a. Formulation Development:

i. **Example:** Optimizing the formulation of a sustained-release tablet to achieve the desired drug release profile by adjusting the polymer concentration and other excipient properties.

b. Process Optimization:

i. **Example:** Refining the granulation process by varying factors such as binder concentration and granulation time to improve granule size and consistency.

c. Quality Control:

i. **Example:** Using statistical process control methods to monitor the manufacturing process and ensure consistent product quality.

d. Scale-Up Studies:

i. **Example:** Applying statistical optimization techniques during scale-up to ensure that the formulation process remains effective and efficient at larger production scales.

5. Benefits of Statistical Optimization

a. Improved Efficiency:

i. **Benefit:** Reduces the number of experiments needed and provides a systematic approach to finding optimal conditions.

b. Enhanced Product Quality:

i. **Benefit:** Helps in designing formulations and processes that consistently meet quality standards.

c. Cost Savings:

i. **Benefit:** Minimizes resources and time spent on trial-and-error experimentation by using data-driven approaches.

d. Better Understanding:

i. **Benefit:** Provides a deeper understanding of how different factors influence the formulation and process, leading to more informed decisions.

Computational Techniques:

Computational techniques in pharmaceutical formulation are employed to optimize drug products and processes using advanced mathematical, statistical, and computational methods. These techniques leverage computational models and simulations to predict, analyze, and refine formulations and processes, enhancing efficiency and effectiveness in drug development. Here's a detailed overview of computational techniques used in pharmaceutical formulation optimization:

1. Computational Techniques Overview

a. Modeling and Simulation:

i. **Definition:** The use of mathematical models and simulations to represent and analyze complex systems in pharmaceutical formulation.

ii. **Purpose:** To predict how changes in formulation or process parameters affect the performance and quality of the drug product.

b. Optimization Algorithms:

i. **Definition:** Computational methods used to find the optimal conditions or parameters that maximize or minimize a specific objective function.

ii. **Purpose:** To improve formulation and process parameters to achieve desired product attributes.

2. Key Computational Techniques:

a. **Mathematical Modeling**

i. **Pharmacokinetic (PK) and Pharmacodynamic (PD) Modeling:**

1. **Purpose:** To predict how a drug is absorbed, distributed, metabolized, and excreted (PK), and to understand the drug's effects and mechanisms of action (PD).
2. **Models:**
    a. **Compartmental Models:** Simplify the body into compartments to model drug distribution and elimination.
    b. **Non-Compartmental Models:** Provide a more flexible approach to analyze PK data without assuming specific compartmental structures.
3. **Application:** Designing dosing regimens and predicting drug interactions.

ii. **Release Kinetics Models:**

1. **Purpose:** To predict the drug release profile from dosage forms.
2. **Models:**
    a. **Zero-Order Release Model:** Assumes constant release rate over time.
    b. **First-Order Release Model:** Assumes release rate is proportional to the amount of drug remaining.
    c. **Higuchi Model:** Describes drug release from a matrix system.
3. **Application:** Optimizing formulations to achieve desired release rates.

iii. **Stability Modeling:**

1. **Purpose:** To predict the stability of a drug product over time under various conditions.
2. **Models:**
    a. **Arrhenius Model:** Relates the rate of degradation to temperature.
    b. **Shelf-Life Prediction Models:** Estimate the product's shelf life based on stability data.
3. **Application:** Formulating and packaging strategies to ensure product stability.

b. **Design of Experiments (DoE)**

i. **Factorial Designs:**

1. **Purpose:** To evaluate the effect of multiple factors and their interactions on the responses.
2. **Approach:**
    a. **Full Factorial Design:** Tests all possible combinations of factors and levels.
    b. **Fractional Factorial Design:** Tests a subset of combinations to reduce the number of experiments.

3. **Application:** Optimizing excipient concentrations and processing conditions to achieve desired formulation attributes.

ii. **Response Surface Methodology (RSM):**

1. **Purpose:** To model and analyze the relationship between factors and responses and to find the optimal conditions.
2. **Approach:**
    a. **Central Composite Design (CCD):** Builds a second-order polynomial model to explore the design space.
    b. **Box-Behnken Design:** Provides a more efficient way to estimate the response surface.
3. **Application:** Refining formulations to optimize drug release profiles and other attributes.

c. **Computational Fluid Dynamics (CFD)**

i. **Definition:**

1. **Purpose:** To model and analyze fluid flow and interactions within pharmaceutical processes.
2. **Approach:** Uses numerical methods and algorithms to solve fluid dynamics equations.
3. **Application:** Designing mixing processes, optimizing fluid flow in reactors, and predicting the performance of drug delivery devices.

d. **Machine Learning and Artificial Intelligence (AI)**

i. **Predictive Modeling:**

1. **Purpose:** To predict formulation outcomes and optimize processes based on historical data.
2. **Approach:** Uses algorithms such as regression, classification, and clustering to analyze complex datasets.
3. **Application:** Predicting drug solubility, stability, and release characteristics.

ii. **Optimization Algorithms:**

1. **Purpose:** To find optimal conditions for formulation and processing.
2. **Algorithms:**
   a. **Genetic Algorithms (GA):** Mimic natural selection processes to optimize complex problems.
   b. **Simulated Annealing (SA):** Uses a probabilistic technique to explore the solution space.
   c. **Particle Swarm Optimization (PSO):** Simulates the social behavior of birds or fish to find optimal solutions.
3. **Application:** Optimizing multi-dimensional problems such as formulation parameters and processing conditions.

e. **Monte Carlo Simulations**

i. **Definition:**

1. **Purpose:** To model the impact of uncertainty and variability in formulation and process parameters.
2. **Approach:** Uses random sampling and statistical modeling to estimate the probability of different outcomes.
3. **Application:** Assessing the impact of variability on product quality and performance.

3. Applications in Pharmaceutical Formulation

a. **Formulation Development**

i. **Example:** Using PK/PD modeling to design dosing regimens and optimize the release profile of a drug formulation.

b. **Process Optimization**

i. **Example:** Applying CFD to optimize mixing processes in tablet manufacturing, ensuring uniformity and efficiency.

c. **Quality Assurance**

i. **Example:** Implementing machine learning algorithms to analyze quality control data and predict potential quality issues.

d. **Scale-Up Studies**

i. **Example:** Using stability modeling to predict how a formulation will perform at larger production scales and adjusting the process accordingly.

e. **Regulatory Compliance**

i. **Example:** Using mathematical modeling to provide data and evidence to support regulatory submissions and ensure product quality and consistency.

4. Benefits of Computational Techniques

a. **Enhanced Efficiency**

i. **Benefit:** Reduces the need for extensive trial-and-error experimentation by providing data-driven insights.

b. **Improved Accuracy**

i. **Benefit:** Offers precise predictions and optimizations based on complex models and simulations.

c. **Cost Savings**

i. **Benefit:** Minimizes resources and time spent on formulation development and process optimization.

d. **Better Understanding**

i. **Benefit:** Provides deeper insights into the relationships between formulation parameters and product performance.

CONCEPT AND PARAMETERS OF OPTIMIZATION

Optimization in pharmaceutical formulation involves systematically adjusting variables to achieve the best possible outcome in terms of efficacy, safety, and quality of a drug product. The goal is to develop a formulation that meets predefined criteria such as stability, bioavailability, and patient acceptability while minimizing potential risks and costs.

Key Parameters of Optimization

1. **Drug Properties:**

a. **Solubility:** The ability of the drug to dissolve in a given solvent. Poor solubility can affect the drug's bioavailability and efficacy.
b. **Stability:** The drug's ability to maintain its chemical and physical properties over time under various conditions (temperature, humidity, light).
c. **Compatibility:** The drug's interaction with excipients and other formulation components.

2. **Excipients:**
    a. **Type and Quantity:** The choice and amount of excipients can influence the drug's release rate, stability, and overall performance.
    b. **Function:** Excipients may serve as binders, fillers, disintegrants, lubricants, or preservatives, affecting the formulation's properties.
3. **Formulation Variables:**
    a. **Formulation Type:** Tablets, capsules, suspensions, injections, etc. Each type has unique requirements and considerations.
    b. **Processing Parameters:** Temperature, pressure, mixing speed, and duration of the formulation process.
4. **Quality Attributes:**
    a. **Critical Quality Attributes (CQAs):** Specific properties that must be controlled to ensure the drug's quality, including dissolution rate, drug content uniformity, and release profile.
    b. **Physical Characteristics:** Appearance, texture, hardness, and other physical properties that can affect the formulation's usability.
5. **Drug Release Profile:**
    a. **Release Rate:** The speed at which the drug is released from the dosage form. Controlled release or extended-release formulations require precise optimization.
    b. **Release Mechanism:** The manner in which the drug is released, such as diffusion, erosion, or osmosis.

6. **Pharmacokinetics:**
    a. **Bioavailability:** The proportion of the drug that reaches systemic circulation and is available for therapeutic effect.
    b. **Absorption, Distribution, Metabolism, and Excretion (ADME):** Understanding these factors helps in optimizing the formulation to ensure effective drug delivery.
7. **Patient Factors:**
    a. **Age, Gender, and Health Status:** These factors can affect how the drug is metabolized and how effective it is.
    b. **Compliance and Acceptability:** Formulation must be designed to be easy to use and acceptable to patients to ensure adherence.
8. **Regulatory Requirements:**
    a. **Compliance with Standards:** Adherence to guidelines and regulations set by agencies such as the FDA, EMA, or ICH.
    b. **Documentation:** Accurate recording and reporting of formulation development and optimization processes.

Techniques for Optimization

1. **Design of Experiments (DoE):**
    a. A systematic approach to designing experiments to efficiently study the effects of multiple variables on the desired outcome.
2. **Response Surface Methodology (RSM):**
    a. A statistical technique used to model and analyze the relationship between formulation variables and responses. It helps in finding the optimal combination of factors.
3. **Risk Assessment:**
    a. Identifying and evaluating potential risks that could affect the quality and performance of the formulation.
4. **Statistical Analysis:**

a. Using statistical tools to analyze data from experiments and optimize formulation parameters based on the results.

5. **Computational Modeling:**
   a. Employing molecular modeling and simulation techniques to predict and optimize drug-excipient interactions and formulation behavior.
6. **Scale-Up Studies:**
   a. Ensuring that the formulation process is reproducible at larger scales and meets quality requirements.

OPTIMIZATION TECHNIQUES IN PHARMACEUTICAL FORMULATION AND PROCESSING

Optimization techniques in pharmaceutical formulation and processing are essential to enhance the efficacy, safety, and quality of drug products. These techniques aim to refine both the formulation and the manufacturing process to meet the desired specifications and performance criteria. Here's a detailed overview of these techniques:

1. Formulation Optimization Techniques

Design of Experiments (DoE)

a. **Concept:** A systematic approach to designing and analyzing experiments to evaluate the effects of multiple variables simultaneously.
b. **Application:** Helps in identifying the optimal combination of formulation factors (e.g., excipient types and concentrations) to achieve desired drug release, stability, and bioavailability.
c. **Tools:** Software tools such as Minitab, JMP, and Stat-Ease.

Response Surface Methodology (RSM)

a. **Concept:** A collection of statistical techniques used for modeling and analyzing problems where several variables influence the response.

b. **Application:** Used to determine the relationships between formulation variables and responses such as dissolution rate, drug content uniformity, and stability. Helps in finding the optimal formulation conditions.
c. **Tools:** RSM software and statistical packages.

Quality by Design (QbD)

a. **Concept:** A systematic approach to pharmaceutical development that emphasizes understanding and controlling formulation variables and process parameters to ensure product quality.
b. **Application:** Involves defining Critical Quality Attributes (CQAs), Critical Process Parameters (CPPs), and Design Space. It ensures the formulation meets predefined quality criteria throughout its lifecycle.
c. **Tools:** Risk management tools like Failure Mode and Effects Analysis (FMEA) and Ishikawa diagrams.

Computational Modeling and Simulation

a. **Concept:** Utilizing computer-based models to predict and optimize drug-excipient interactions, drug release profiles, and formulation stability.
b. **Application:** Helps in understanding complex interactions and predicting outcomes without extensive experimental trials.
c. **Tools:** Molecular modeling software, pharmacokinetic modeling tools, and simulation platforms.

Stability Studies

a. **Concept:** Testing the formulation under various environmental conditions to assess its stability and shelf life.
b. **Application:** Includes accelerated stability testing (exposing the product to elevated conditions) and real-time stability testing (under recommended storage conditions) to ensure the product remains effective and safe.
c. **Tools:** Stability chambers and analytical techniques for monitoring chemical, physical, and microbiological stability.

2. Processing Optimization Techniques

Process Analytical Technology (PAT)

a. **Concept:** A framework for designing, analyzing, and controlling manufacturing processes through timely measurements of critical quality and performance attributes.
b. **Application:** Ensures that the manufacturing process remains within specified limits and consistently produces products meeting the desired quality attributes.
c. **Tools:** Inline and online sensors, spectroscopy, and chromatographic techniques.

Scale-Up and Technology Transfer

a. **Concept:** The process of adapting and scaling the formulation from laboratory scale to commercial production scale while maintaining quality and efficacy.
b. **Application:** Involves optimizing process parameters, equipment design, and production techniques to ensure consistency and reproducibility at larger scales.
c. **Tools:** Pilot plants, scale-up models, and process simulation software.

Six Sigma and Lean Manufacturing

a. **Concept:** Six Sigma focuses on reducing process variability and defects, while Lean Manufacturing aims at eliminating waste and improving process efficiency.
b. **Application:** Techniques such as DMAIC (Define, Measure, Analyze, Improve, Control) and value stream mapping are used to enhance process efficiency and product quality.
c. **Tools:** Statistical analysis tools, process mapping, and improvement methodologies.

Critical Process Parameter (CPP) Optimization

a. **Concept:** Identifying and controlling the parameters that significantly affect the product quality during the manufacturing process.
b. **Application:** Ensures that variations in process parameters do not lead to deviations in the product quality. This includes parameters like mixing speed, temperature, and pressure.
c. **Tools:** Process monitoring and control systems, statistical analysis.

Quality Control and Assurance

a. **Concept:** Ensuring that the final product meets the required specifications through rigorous testing and quality control measures.
b. **Application:** Involves routine testing of physical, chemical, and microbiological attributes of the drug product. Quality assurance processes ensure compliance with regulatory standards and good manufacturing practices (GMP).
c. **Tools:** Analytical testing methods, quality assurance frameworks, and regulatory guidelines.

STATISTICAL DESIGN, RESPONSE SURFACE METHOD, CONTOUR DESIGNS, FACTORIAL DESIGNS AND APPLICATION IN FORMULATION

In pharmaceutical formulation, statistical designs are crucial for optimizing processes and formulations. These designs help identify and understand the relationships between various factors (such as excipient types and concentrations) and their effects on the final product's quality attributes. Here's a detailed look at statistical designs, including Response Surface Methodology (RSM), Contour Designs, and Factorial Designs, and their applications in formulation:

1. Statistical Design in Pharmaceutical Formulation

Statistical designs involve structured approaches to conducting experiments and analyzing data to determine the effects of multiple factors on a response. These designs help in understanding interactions between variables and optimizing formulations efficiently.

2. Response Surface Methodology (RSM)

Concept:

a. **Purpose:** RSM is used to model and analyze the relationships between several independent variables (factors) and dependent variables (responses). It helps in optimizing the response by understanding the interactions between factors and their impact on the response.
b. **Models:** Typically involves polynomial models that approximate the relationship between factors and responses. The most common model is the second-order polynomial equation.

Application:

a. **Experimental Design:** Involves selecting a set of experiments that cover a range of factor levels. Common designs include central composite designs (CCD) and Box-Behnken designs.
b. **Optimization:** Helps in finding the optimal conditions for formulation variables to achieve desired product attributes, such as drug release rate or stability.
c. **Analysis:** Utilizes statistical software to analyze data, create response surfaces, and identify the optimal combination of factors.

Tools:

a. **Software:** Minitab, JMP, and Design-Expert are popular tools for conducting RSM analysis.

3. Contour Designs

Concept:

a. **Purpose:** Contour designs, or contour plots, are graphical representations used to visualize the relationship between two independent variables and a dependent variable. They are particularly useful in RSM to understand the shape of the response surface.

b. **Visualization:** Contour plots display lines of constant response, helping to identify regions where the response is optimal.

Application:

a. **Optimization:** Helps in identifying the regions of optimal response and understanding the interactions between two factors.

b. **Analysis:** Provides visual insights into how changes in factor levels affect the response, making it easier to find the best formulation conditions.

Tools:

a. **Software:** Contour plots are generated using RSM tools within statistical software like Minitab or JMP.

4. Factorial Designs

Concept:

a. **Purpose:** Factorial designs are used to study the effects of multiple factors simultaneously and their interactions. They involve conducting experiments where all possible combinations of factors are tested.

b. **Types:** Full factorial designs (where all possible combinations are tested) and fractional factorial designs (where only a subset of combinations is tested).

Application:

a. **Screening:** Useful for identifying which factors have significant effects on the response and determining the best levels for those factors.

b. **Optimization:** Helps in understanding the interactions between factors and their combined effect on the formulation.

c. **Efficiency:** Fractional factorial designs are used to reduce the number of experiments while still obtaining valuable information about factor effects and interactions.

Tools:

a. **Software:** Minitab, JMP, and Design-Expert provide tools for designing and analyzing factorial experiments.

5. Applications in Pharmaceutical Formulation

1. Drug Release Optimization:

a. **RSM and Contour Designs:** Used to optimize the release profile of a drug by adjusting factors like excipient type and concentration, tablet compression force, and coating conditions.

2. Stability Studies:

a. **Factorial Designs:** Employed to evaluate the effects of storage conditions, such as temperature and humidity, on the stability of drug products. Helps in identifying optimal packaging and storage conditions.

3. Formulation Development:

a. **Screening:** Factorial designs are used to screen various excipients and their levels to determine their impact on drug solubility, dissolution, and bioavailability.

b. **Optimization:** RSM helps in refining the formulation to achieve desired product characteristics, such as tablet hardness, disintegration time, and uniformity of drug content.

4. Process Optimization:

a. **RSM and Factorial Designs:** Applied to optimize manufacturing processes, such as mixing, granulation, and drying, to ensure consistent product quality and efficiency.

5. Patient Compliance:

a. **Contingent Designs:** Used to develop formulations with improved patient acceptability, such as taste-masked tablets or easy-to-swallow capsules.

CLASSIFICATION:

Optimization techniques in pharmaceutical formulation can be classified based on their approach and purpose. Here's a classification with examples for each category:

1. Experimental Design Techniques

a. Factorial Designs

i. **Concept:** Evaluates the effects of multiple factors and their interactions by testing all possible combinations.

ii. **Types:**

1. **Full Factorial Design:** Tests all possible combinations of factors at different levels (e.g., a 2^3 factorial design tests all combinations of three factors each at two levels).
2. **Fractional Factorial Design:** Tests a subset of all possible combinations to reduce the number of experiments (e.g., a 2^3-1 fractional factorial design).

iii. **Example:** Optimizing tablet formulation by studying the effects of excipient types (e.g., lactose, cellulose) and their concentrations on tablet hardness and dissolution rate.

b. Response Surface Methodology (RSM)

i. **Concept:** Models and analyzes the relationships between multiple factors and responses using polynomial equations to find optimal conditions.

ii. **Types:**

1. **Central Composite Design (CCD):** A type of RSM design used for building a second-order (quadratic) model.
2. **Box-Behnken Design:** A design used to build second-order models without needing a full factorial design.

iii. **Example:** Optimizing the release rate of a drug from an extended-release tablet by adjusting the polymer concentration and tablet compression force.

c. Design of Experiments (DoE)

i. **Concept:** A systematic approach to designing experiments to efficiently evaluate the effects of variables on outcomes.

ii. **Types:** Includes factorial designs, RSM, and Taguchi methods.

iii. **Example:** Developing a formulation for a liquid suspension by varying the concentration of suspending agents and the mixing speed to achieve optimal viscosity and stability.

2. Computational and Modeling Techniques

a. Molecular Modeling

i. **Concept:** Uses computational methods to predict drug-excipient interactions and the behavior of drug molecules in different formulations.

ii. **Example:** Modeling the interaction between a drug and various polymer matrices to predict release rates in controlled-release formulations.

b. Pharmacokinetic Modeling

i. **Concept:** Models the absorption, distribution, metabolism, and excretion (ADME) of drugs to optimize dosing regimens and formulation parameters.

ii. **Example:** Using pharmacokinetic models to optimize the formulation of a drug to ensure consistent blood levels over time.

3. Statistical Analysis Techniques

a. Statistical Process Control (SPC)

i. **Concept:** Monitors and controls the formulation process to ensure that it operates at its full potential.

ii. **Example:** Using control charts to monitor the consistency of tablet weight and hardness during manufacturing.

b. Risk Assessment Techniques

i. **Concept:** Identifies and evaluates risks associated with formulation variables and process parameters.

ii. **Example:** Conducting Failure Mode and Effects Analysis (FMEA) to assess potential risks in the formulation process and implement controls to mitigate those risks.

4. Quality by Design (QbD)

a. Design Space

i. **Concept:** Defines the range of conditions under which the product quality is ensured. It is determined based on experimental data and risk assessments.

ii. **Example:** Establishing a design space for the formulation of an oral solid dosage form to ensure consistent drug release and stability under various manufacturing conditions.

b. Critical Quality Attributes (CQAs) and Critical Process Parameters (CPPs)

i. **Concept:** Identifies attributes that are critical to the product's quality and parameters that are critical to the process.

ii. **Example:** Identifying tablet disintegration time as a CQA and compression force as a CPP in tablet formulation.

5. Practical Optimization Techniques

a. Taguchi Methods

i. **Concept:** Focuses on improving quality and reducing variation using orthogonal arrays and signal-to-noise ratios.

ii. **Example:** Optimizing the process of tablet coating to achieve uniform coating thickness and reduce defects.

b. Process Analytical Technology (PAT)

i. **Concept:** Uses real-time measurements to monitor and control the formulation process, ensuring consistent product quality.

ii. **Example:** Implementing inline NIR spectroscopy to monitor the composition of granules during the granulation process.

Summary of Examples:

1. **Factorial Designs:** Optimizing tablet hardness by varying excipient types and concentrations.
2. **Response Surface Methodology (RSM):** Fine-tuning drug release rates by adjusting polymer concentration and compression force.

3. **Molecular Modeling:** Predicting drug-polymer interactions for controlled-release formulations.
4. **Statistical Process Control (SPC):** Monitoring tablet weight and hardness consistency.
5. **Design Space:** Establishing conditions for consistent drug release in oral solid dosage forms.
6. **Taguchi Methods:** Reducing variation in tablet coating processes.

Multiple Choice Questions (MCQs)

1. What is the main goal of optimization techniques in pharmaceutical formulation?
   A) To reduce the cost of production
   B) To enhance the efficacy, safety, and quality of drug products
   C) To increase the shelf life of the drug
   D) To improve the taste of the medication
2. Which technique involves using statistical methods to model and analyze the relationship between multiple factors and responses?
   A) Taguchi Methods
   B) Process Analytical Technology (PAT)
   C) Response Surface Methodology (RSM)
   D) Factorial Design
3. What does Quality by Design (QbD) primarily focus on?
   A) Reducing production costs
   B) Understanding and controlling formulation variables and process parameters
   C) Improving the taste and appearance of medications
   D) Enhancing the speed of drug development
4. Which of the following is a key parameter of optimization in pharmaceutical formulation?

A) Color of the drug

B) Solubility

C) Marketing strategy

D) Packaging design

5. What is the purpose of using factorial designs in pharmaceutical formulation?

A) To identify potential drug interactions

B) To evaluate the effects of multiple factors and their interactions

C) To improve the taste of the medication

D) To reduce the number of clinical trials needed

6. Which computational technique is used to predict drug-excipient interactions?

A) Process Analytical Technology (PAT)

B) Molecular Modeling

C) Six Sigma

D) Taguchi Methods

7. What does Process Analytical Technology (PAT) aim to achieve in pharmaceutical manufacturing?

A) Faster production times

B) Real-time monitoring and control of the formulation process

C) Better marketing strategies

D) Improved packaging designs

8. In the context of QbD, what are Critical Quality Attributes (CQAs)?

A) Attributes that affect the cost of production

B) Attributes that must be controlled to ensure the drug's quality

C) Attributes related to the marketing strategy

D) Attributes affecting the drug's appearance

9. Which method focuses on improving quality and reducing variation using orthogonal arrays and signal-to-noise ratios?

A) Response Surface Methodology (RSM)

B) Six Sigma

C) Taguchi Methods

D) Factorial Design

10. What is the purpose of conducting stability studies in pharmaceutical formulation?

A) To improve the taste of the drug

B) To assess the drug's stability and shelf life

C) To reduce the production cost

D) To enhance the appearance of the drug

11. Which tool is commonly used for statistical analysis in the optimization of pharmaceutical formulations?

A) Photoshop

B) Minitab

C) AutoCAD

D) Microsoft Word

12. What is the main focus of Lean Manufacturing in pharmaceutical production?

A) Increasing product price

B) Eliminating waste and improving process efficiency

C) Enhancing drug flavor

D) Improving the packaging design

13. Which regulatory body is responsible for ensuring the safety, efficacy, and quality of drugs in the U.S.?

A) EMA

B) WHO

C) FDA

D) ICH

14. What does the acronym ADME stand for in pharmacokinetics?

A) Absorption, Distribution, Metabolism, Excretion

B) Administration, Distribution, Metabolism, Elimination

C) Absorption, Digestion, Metabolism, Excretion

D) Administration, Digestion, Metabolism, Elimination

15. What is the primary goal of using computational fluid dynamics (CFD) in pharmaceutical formulation?

A) To predict drug-excipient interactions

B) To model and analyze fluid flow within pharmaceutical processes

C) To enhance drug flavor

D) To improve the color of the drug

16. Which method is used to reduce variability and defects in pharmaceutical processes?

A) Lean Manufacturing

B) Six Sigma

C) Taguchi Methods

D) Factorial Design

17. What is the main benefit of applying the Design of Experiments (DoE) in pharmaceutical formulation?

A) Reducing the cost of packaging

B) Efficiently evaluating the effects of multiple variables on outcomes

C) Enhancing the drug's color

D) Improving marketing strategies

18. Which technique involves real-time measurements to monitor and control the manufacturing process?

A) Response Surface Methodology (RSM)

B) Design of Experiments (DoE)

C) Process Analytical Technology (PAT)

D) Taguchi Methods

19. What is the purpose of using Six Sigma in pharmaceutical manufacturing?

A) To enhance the drug's flavor

B) To reduce process variability and defects

C) To improve marketing strategies

D) To increase the drug's color

20. Which statistical design helps in creating a second-order polynomial model to explore the design space?

A) Factorial Design

B) Central Composite Design (CCD)

C) Taguchi Methods

D) Six Sigma

Short Answer Type Questions

1. Explain the main goal of optimization techniques in pharmaceutical formulation.
2. What is Response Surface Methodology (RSM) and how is it used in pharmaceutical formulation?
3. Describe the concept of Quality by Design (QbD) in pharmaceutical formulation.
4. List and briefly explain the key parameters of optimization in pharmaceutical formulation.
5. What is the purpose of using factorial designs in pharmaceutical formulation?
6. Explain the role of Process Analytical Technology (PAT) in pharmaceutical manufacturing.
7. Define Critical Quality Attributes (CQAs) and Critical Process Parameters (CPPs) in the context of QbD.
8. What are the Taguchi Methods and how are they applied in pharmaceutical formulation optimization?
9. Why are stability studies important in pharmaceutical formulation?

10. What is molecular modeling and how does it assist in pharmaceutical formulation?
11. Describe the importance of Design of Experiments (DoE) in optimizing pharmaceutical formulations.
12. How does Lean Manufacturing improve pharmaceutical production processes?
13. Explain the regulatory framework for pharmaceutical formulations in the U.S.
14. What does ADME stand for, and why is it important in pharmacokinetics?
15. Describe the purpose of computational fluid dynamics (CFD) in pharmaceutical processes.
16. How does Six Sigma contribute to pharmaceutical process optimization?
17. What are the benefits of using Design of Experiments (DoE) in pharmaceutical formulation?
18. How does Process Analytical Technology (PAT) ensure consistent product quality?
19. What are the main goals of applying Six Sigma in pharmaceutical manufacturing?
20. Explain the Central Composite Design (CCD) and its application in pharmaceutical formulation optimization.

Long Answer Type Questions

1. Discuss the role and importance of optimization techniques in pharmaceutical formulation. Provide examples to illustrate your points.
2. Explain the concept of Quality by Design (QbD) and its application in pharmaceutical formulation development.
3. Describe the key parameters of optimization in pharmaceutical formulation and how they influence the final product.

4. Explain the different types of experimental designs used in pharmaceutical formulation optimization, focusing on their applications and benefits.
5. Discuss the importance of stability studies in pharmaceutical formulation and the different types of stability testing.
6. Explain the use of Process Analytical Technology (PAT) in pharmaceutical manufacturing and its impact on product quality.
7. Describe the application of computational and modeling techniques in pharmaceutical formulation optimization.
8. Discuss the regulatory considerations in pharmaceutical formulation optimization and how they impact the development process.
9. Explain the concept of Six Sigma and Lean Manufacturing in the context of pharmaceutical process optimization. Provide examples.
10. Describe the role of patient-centric considerations in pharmaceutical formulation optimization and provide examples of how these considerations are implemented.

Answer Key for MCQs

1. B) To enhance the efficacy, safety, and quality of drug products
2. C) Response Surface Methodology (RSM)
3. B) Understanding and controlling formulation variables and process parameters
4. B) Solubility
5. B) To evaluate the effects of multiple factors and their interactions
6. B) Molecular Modeling
7. B) Real-time monitoring and control of the formulation process
8. B) Attributes that must be controlled to ensure the drug's quality
9. C) Taguchi Methods
10. B) To assess the drug's stability and shelf life
11. B) Minitab

12.B) Eliminating waste and improving process efficiency

13.C) FDA

14.A) Absorption, Distribution, Metabolism, Excretion

15.B) To model and analyze fluid flow within pharmaceutical processes

16.B) Six Sigma

17.B) Efficiently evaluating the effects of multiple variables on outcomes

18.C) Process Analytical Technology (PAT)

19.B) To reduce process variability and defects

20.B) Central Composite Design (CCD)

CHAPTER – 3

VALIDATION

INTRODUCTION:

Validation is a crucial process in many fields, including pharmacology, to ensure that methods, processes, and systems meet their intended purpose and produce reliable results. Here's a detailed introduction to the concept of validation:

Validation?

Validation is the process of evaluating and confirming that a system, method, or process meets specified criteria and performs as expected under defined conditions. It is designed to ensure that results are accurate, consistent, and reliable.

Types of Validation

a. Method Validation

This involves assessing the reliability and accuracy of analytical methods used in research and development. Key aspects include:

i. **Specificity**: Ability to measure the analyte without interference from other substances.

ii. **Accuracy**: The closeness of measurements to the true value.

iii. **Precision**: The consistency of repeated measurements under the same conditions.

iv. **Linearity**: The method's ability to produce results directly proportional to the concentration of analyte.

v. **Range**: The span between the minimum and maximum concentrations over which the method is accurate.

vi. **Limit of Detection (LOD) and Limit of Quantification (LOQ)**: The lowest concentration of the analyte that can be reliably detected or quantified.

b. Process Validation

This is the confirmation that a manufacturing process consistently produces a product that meets its predetermined specifications and quality attributes. Key components include:

i. **Process Design**: Initial design and understanding of the process.

ii. **Process Qualification**: Verification that the process works as intended in real-world conditions.

iii. **Continued Process Verification**: Ongoing monitoring and validation during production.

c. Software Validation

Involves ensuring that software systems used in data collection, analysis, or other critical functions perform accurately and reliably. It includes:

i. **Requirements Analysis**: Ensuring the software meets specified user needs.

ii. **System Testing**: Verifying that the software functions correctly in all scenarios.

iii. **Validation Documentation**: Recording all validation activities and results for regulatory compliance.

Importance of Validation

a. **Compliance**: Meets regulatory requirements and standards.

b. **Quality Assurance**: Ensures that products and processes are consistent and reliable.

c. **Risk Management**: Identifies and mitigates potential issues before they affect outcomes.

d. **Efficiency**: Improves the effectiveness and efficiency of processes and systems.

Validation Process

a. **Define Objectives**: Clearly state what you intend to validate and the criteria for success.

b. **Develop Validation Plan**: Outline the procedures, responsibilities, and resources needed.
c. **Execute Validation**: Perform the tests and evaluations as per the plan.
d. **Document Results**: Record all findings, procedures, and outcomes.
e. **Review and Report**: Analyze results, identify any issues, and prepare a validation report.
f. **Implement Changes**: Make necessary adjustments based on validation outcomes.

Challenges in Validation

a. **Complexity**: Some systems or processes may be complex and difficult to validate thoroughly.
b. **Cost**: Validation can be expensive and time-consuming.
c. **Regulatory Changes**: Keeping up with evolving regulations and standards.

INTRODUCTION TO PHARMACEUTICAL VALIDATION

Pharmaceutical Validation is a critical component of ensuring that pharmaceutical products are produced consistently and meet the required quality standards. It encompasses various validation activities to confirm that processes, equipment, systems, and methods used in drug manufacturing and testing are capable of producing products that are safe, effective, and of high quality.

1. What is Pharmaceutical Validation?

Pharmaceutical validation is the process of demonstrating, through documented evidence, that a pharmaceutical process, method, or system consistently performs as intended. It is aimed at ensuring the quality, safety, and efficacy of pharmaceutical products by verifying that they meet predefined specifications and standards.

2. Types of Pharmaceutical Validation

a. Process Validation

Process Validation involves confirming that manufacturing processes consistently produce pharmaceutical products that meet their predefined specifications and quality attributes. It typically includes:

i. **Process Design**: Establishing the design of the process based on scientific understanding and intended use.
ii. **Process Qualification**: Confirming that the process design performs as expected under real-world conditions.
iii. **Continued Process Verification**: Ongoing monitoring and verification of the process during routine production to ensure continued performance.

b. Analytical Method Validation

Analytical Method Validation is the process of proving that an analytical method used for testing pharmaceutical products performs reliably and accurately. Key aspects include:

i. **Specificity**: Ensuring that the method can distinguish the analyte from other substances.
ii. **Accuracy**: Determining how close the test results are to the true value.
iii. **Precision**: Measuring the reproducibility of the method under the same conditions.
iv. **Linearity**: Confirming that the method provides results that are directly proportional to the concentration of the analyte.
v. **Range**: Defining the interval over which the method can produce accurate results.
vi. **LOD and LOQ**: Establishing the lowest levels that can be reliably detected or quantified.

c. Equipment Validation

Equipment Validation ensures that equipment used in the manufacturing and testing of pharmaceutical products operates correctly and consistently. This includes:

i. **Installation Qualification (IQ)**: Verifying that equipment is installed correctly and in accordance with specifications.
ii. **Operational Qualification (OQ)**: Testing equipment to ensure it operates according to its intended purpose.
iii. **Performance Qualification (PQ)**: Confirming that equipment performs consistently in actual production conditions.

d. Computer System Validation

Computer System Validation (CSV) is focused on ensuring that computer systems used for data collection, analysis, and control meet regulatory requirements and function accurately. This includes:

i. **Requirements Specification**: Defining user requirements and system functionality.
ii. **System Testing**: Performing rigorous testing to verify system performance.
iii. **Documentation**: Maintaining detailed records of validation activities and results.

3. Importance of Pharmaceutical Validation

a. **Regulatory Compliance**: Ensures adherence to regulatory requirements set by agencies such as the FDA, EMA, and others.
b. **Product Quality**: Guarantees that products are produced consistently and meet quality standards.
c. **Patient Safety**: Minimizes risks associated with pharmaceutical products and protects patient health.
d. **Risk Management**: Identifies and addresses potential issues early to avoid costly problems and recalls.

4. Validation Process

a. **Planning**: Develop a comprehensive validation plan that outlines the scope, objectives, and procedures.

b. **Execution**: Perform validation activities according to the plan, including testing and documentation.
c. **Documentation**: Record all validation results, procedures, and findings to provide evidence of compliance.
d. **Review**: Analyze results to ensure that all criteria are met and address any deviations or issues.
e. **Report**: Prepare and submit validation reports summarizing the validation process and outcomes.
f. **Ongoing Monitoring**: Continuously monitor and review processes to ensure ongoing compliance and performance.

5. Challenges in Pharmaceutical Validation

a. **Complexity**: The complexity of pharmaceutical processes and systems can make validation challenging.
b. **Regulatory Changes**: Keeping up with evolving regulations and standards requires continuous updates and adjustments.
c. **Cost and Time**: Validation can be resource-intensive, involving significant time and financial investment.

SCOPE & MERITS OF VALIDATION

The scope of validation in the pharmaceutical industry encompasses a wide range of activities and processes to ensure that drugs are manufactured and tested according to predefined quality standards. Here's a detailed breakdown:

1. Process Validation

a. **Scope**: Validates the entire manufacturing process to ensure that it consistently produces products meeting specifications. This includes:
   i. **Manufacturing Processes**: From raw material handling to final product packaging.
   ii. **Cleaning Processes**: Ensures that cleaning procedures effectively remove residues and contaminants.

iii. **Sterilization Processes**: Validates methods used to sterilize equipment and products.

2. Analytical Method Validation

a. **Scope**: Validates analytical methods used for testing the quality and safety of pharmaceutical products. This includes:

i. **Chromatographic Methods**: Like HPLC (High-Performance Liquid Chromatography) for separation and analysis.

ii. **Spectroscopic Methods**: Like UV-Vis or IR (Infrared) spectroscopy for substance identification.

iii. **Microbiological Methods**: For detecting microbial contamination.

3. Equipment Validation

a. **Scope**: Validates equipment used in the manufacturing and testing processes to ensure proper operation. This includes:

i. **Installation Qualification (IQ)**: Verifies that the equipment is installed correctly.

ii. **Operational Qualification (OQ)**: Tests the equipment to ensure it operates according to specifications.

iii. **Performance Qualification (PQ)**: Ensures equipment performs consistently under actual production conditions.

4. Computer System Validation (CSV)

a. **Scope**: Validates computerized systems used for data management, control, and reporting. This includes:

i. **System Validation**: Ensures that software and hardware systems perform as intended.

ii. **Data Integrity**: Ensures accuracy and reliability of data generated and stored by the system.

iii. **Regulatory Compliance**: Ensures systems comply with regulatory standards like 21 CFR Part 11 (US FDA).

5. Cleaning Validation

a. **Scope**: Ensures that cleaning processes are effective in removing residues from equipment and surfaces. This includes:

  i. **Residue Limits**: Verifying that cleaning procedures meet predefined residue limits.

  ii. **Cleaning Procedures**: Validating methods and frequencies of cleaning.

6. Packaging Validation

a. **Scope**: Ensures that packaging materials and processes maintain product integrity. This includes:

  i. **Packaging Materials**: Validating that materials do not interact with the product.

  ii. **Packaging Processes**: Ensuring that packaging processes maintain sterility and protect the product.

Merits of Validation

1. Regulatory Compliance

a. **Ensures adherence to regulatory standards**: Validation ensures that processes and methods comply with regulations set by authorities like the FDA, EMA, and other agencies.

b. **Facilitates regulatory approvals**: Well-documented validation activities support the approval process for new drugs and changes to manufacturing processes.

2. Product Quality

a. **Consistency**: Ensures that products are manufactured consistently, meeting quality specifications every time.

b. **Safety**: Minimizes risks related to product contamination, dosage errors, or ineffective treatment.

c. **Efficacy**: Confirms that products perform as intended, providing the expected therapeutic benefit.

3. Risk Management

a. **Identifies potential issues**: Validation helps detect and address potential problems before they affect product quality or patient safety.

b. **Reduces the likelihood of recalls**: By ensuring that processes and products meet quality standards, validation decreases the chances of costly recalls and associated reputational damage.

4. Operational Efficiency

a. **Improves Process Reliability**: Validated processes are more reliable and predictable, leading to more efficient operations.

b. **Reduces Waste**: Helps minimize product waste by ensuring processes are optimized and effective.

5. Cost Savings

a. **Prevents Expensive Errors**: Reduces the risk of costly errors and recalls by ensuring processes and systems work correctly from the start.

b. **Optimizes Resource Use**: Efficient processes and validated methods can lead to better resource utilization and cost savings.

6. Customer Confidence

a. **Enhances Trust**: Demonstrating that products are validated and of high quality enhances consumer and healthcare professional trust in the pharmaceutical company.

b. **Improves Market Reputation**: A reputation for producing reliable and safe products can positively impact a company's market position.

VALIDATION AND CALIBRATION OF MASTER PLAN

1. What is a Validation Master Plan?

A Validation Master Plan (VMP) is a comprehensive document that outlines the strategy and framework for validation activities within a pharmaceutical organization. It provides a structured approach for validating systems, processes, and equipment to ensure they meet required quality standards and regulatory requirements.

Scope and Contents of a Validation Master Plan

a. **Objective**: Defines the purpose of validation activities and the goals to be achieved.
b. **Scope**: Describes the processes, systems, and equipment covered by the validation efforts.
c. **Responsibilities**: Identifies roles and responsibilities for validation activities within the organization.
d. **Validation Strategy**: Outlines the approach and methods for conducting validation, including:
    i. **Process Validation**: Manufacturing processes, cleaning procedures, etc.
    ii. **Analytical Method Validation**: Testing methods and procedures.
    iii. **Equipment Validation**: Installation, operational, and performance qualifications.
    iv. **Computer System Validation**: Software and hardware systems.
e. **Validation Schedule**: Provides timelines for completing validation activities and milestones.
f. **Documentation Requirements**: Specifies the documentation needed for validation activities, including protocols, reports, and records.
g. **Change Control**: Details procedures for managing changes to validated systems or processes and ensuring that changes do not affect validated status.
h. **Training**: Describes the training requirements for personnel involved in validation activities.
i. **Compliance and Regulatory Requirements**: Ensures alignment with regulatory guidelines and standards.

Importance of a Validation Master Plan

a. **Consistency**: Provides a standardized approach to validation across the organization.
b. **Efficiency**: Streamlines validation processes and helps manage resources effectively.
c. **Regulatory Compliance**: Ensures that validation activities meet regulatory requirements and standards.
d. **Risk Management**: Helps identify and mitigate potential risks associated with validation activities and processes.

2. Calibration

What is Calibration?

Calibration is the process of adjusting and verifying the accuracy of measurement instruments and equipment to ensure they produce correct and reliable results. Calibration ensures that instruments provide accurate readings and are functioning within specified tolerances.

Scope and Components of Calibration

a. **Calibration Procedure**: Detailed steps for calibrating instruments, including the methods, standards, and equipment used.
b. **Frequency**: Specifies how often calibration should be performed based on factors like instrument usage, manufacturer recommendations, and regulatory requirements.
c. **Calibration Standards**: Reference standards or calibration weights that are used to ensure accuracy.
d. **Documentation**: Records of calibration activities, including calibration certificates, results, and any adjustments made.
e. **Verification**: Confirmation that calibrated instruments maintain accuracy over time through periodic checks.

Importance of Calibration

a. **Accuracy and Reliability**: Ensures that measurement instruments produce precise and accurate results, which is crucial for quality control and regulatory compliance.
b. **Consistency**: Maintains consistency in measurements across different instruments and time periods.
c. **Regulatory Compliance**: Meets regulatory requirements for equipment and instrument accuracy, supporting quality assurance processes.
d. **Quality Control**: Helps prevent errors in manufacturing and testing processes by ensuring that instruments are functioning correctly.

3. Integration of Validation and Calibration in the Master Plan

Validation in the Master Plan

a. **Incorporates Validation Requirements**: The VMP integrates validation requirements for processes, systems, and equipment, ensuring a comprehensive validation approach.
b. **Defines Validation Activities**: Specifies the scope and methods for validation activities, including process validation, equipment validation, and analytical method validation.

Calibration in the Master Plan

a. **Calibration Procedures**: Includes calibration procedures and requirements for instruments and equipment used in validation and manufacturing.
b. **Monitoring and Maintenance**: Details how calibration will be monitored and maintained to ensure ongoing accuracy and reliability.
c. **Documentation**: Ensures that calibration records are maintained as part of the overall validation documentation.

ICH & WHO GUIDELINES FOR CALIBRATION AND VALIDATION OF EQUIPMENTS

ICH (International Council for Harmonisation) and WHO (World Health Organization) Guidelines provide comprehensive standards and practices for the calibration and validation of equipment in the pharmaceutical industry. These guidelines are crucial for ensuring that equipment operates correctly and consistently, meeting quality and regulatory requirements. Here's a detailed overview of these guidelines:

1. ICH Guidelines for Calibration and Validation:

The ICH guidelines are international standards designed to harmonize pharmaceutical regulations across different regions. Key guidelines related to calibration and validation include:

a. ICH Q7: Good Manufacturing Practice (GMP) for Active Pharmaceutical Ingredients

1. **Calibration and Qualification**: ICH Q7 emphasizes the importance of calibrating and qualifying equipment used in the manufacturing of active pharmaceutical ingredients (APIs). It includes:
    i. **Equipment Qualification**: Ensuring that equipment is installed, operated, and maintained properly.
    ii. **Calibration**: Regular calibration of equipment to ensure accuracy and reliability.
    iii. **Documentation**: Maintaining records of equipment qualification and calibration.

b. ICH Q8: Pharmaceutical Development

1. **Design and Development**: ICH Q8 includes guidelines on the development and validation of pharmaceutical processes, which covers:
    i. **Process Validation**: Ensuring that manufacturing processes are validated to produce consistent and high-quality products.
    ii. **Equipment Calibration**: Calibration practices are critical to ensure that equipment used in the development and production phases operates within specified parameters.

c. ICH Q9: Quality Risk Management

1. **Risk-Based Approach**: ICH Q9 recommends a risk-based approach to validation and calibration. This involves:
   i. **Risk Assessment**: Evaluating the potential risks associated with equipment and processes.
   ii. **Prioritization**: Prioritizing validation and calibration activities based on risk assessments.

d. ICH Q10: Pharmaceutical Quality System

1. **Quality Management**: ICH Q10 outlines a quality management system that includes:
   i. **Validation Practices**: Ensuring that validation activities are part of the quality management system, including equipment calibration.
   ii. **Continual Improvement**: Regular review and improvement of validation and calibration processes.

2. WHO Guidelines for Calibration and Validation:

The WHO guidelines provide standards for the calibration and validation of equipment, focusing on ensuring product quality and safety. Key guidelines include:

a. WHO Technical Report Series, No. 823: Good Manufacturing Practices for Pharmaceutical Products

1. **Equipment Qualification**: The WHO guidelines emphasize the need for thorough equipment qualification, which includes:
   i. **Installation Qualification (IQ)**: Ensuring that equipment is installed according to specifications.
   ii. **Operational Qualification (OQ)**: Verifying that equipment operates as intended.
   iii. **Performance Qualification (PQ)**: Confirming that equipment performs reliably in actual production conditions.
2. **Calibration**: Regular calibration of equipment is required to maintain accuracy and reliability.

b. WHO Technical Report Series, No. 908: Good Manufacturing Practices for Biological Products

1. **Validation Requirements**: Includes specific validation requirements for equipment used in the production of biological products, such as:
    i. **Qualification and Calibration**: Ensuring that equipment used in the production of biological products is qualified and calibrated according to stringent standards.

c. WHO Technical Report Series, No. 970: Guidelines on Validation of Analytical Procedures

1. **Analytical Method Validation**: Provides guidelines for the validation of analytical methods, including:
    i. **Calibration of Analytical Instruments**: Ensuring that instruments used in analytical procedures are calibrated and maintained to provide accurate and reliable results.

d. WHO Guidelines on Good Manufacturing Practices for Pharmaceuticals

1. **Validation and Calibration**: WHO guidelines stress the importance of:
    i. **Documented Procedures**: Having documented procedures for validation and calibration.
    ii. **Regular Reviews**: Conducting regular reviews and updates of validation and calibration practices.

3. Key Elements in Calibration and Validation According to ICH and WHO

a. Calibration

i. **Regular Calibration**: Both ICH and WHO guidelines emphasize the need for regular calibration of equipment to ensure accuracy.
ii. **Documentation**: Comprehensive records of calibration activities, including certificates and results, are required.
iii. **Standards and Procedures**: Calibration must be performed using recognized standards and procedures.

b. Validation

i. **Validation Planning**: Develop and document validation plans outlining objectives, scope, and procedures.

ii. **Qualification**: Ensure that equipment and processes are qualified through IQ, OQ, and PQ.

iii. **Risk Management**: Apply risk-based approaches to prioritize validation and calibration activities.

iv. **Documentation and Reporting**: Maintain detailed records of validation activities, results, and any deviations or corrective actions.

VALIDATION OF SPECIFIC DOSAGE FORM

Validation of Specific Dosage Forms is a specialized aspect of pharmaceutical validation that ensures that different types of dosage forms meet the required quality, safety, and efficacy standards. Each dosage form—whether it's a tablet, capsule, injection, or topical preparation—has unique characteristics and requires specific validation approaches. Here's a detailed look at the validation processes for various dosage forms:

1. Tablets:

a. Process Validation

i. **Granulation**: Validate the granulation process to ensure uniformity in particle size and distribution. This includes evaluating the mixing and compaction processes.

ii. **Compression**: Validate the tablet compression process to ensure that tablets are formed with consistent hardness, weight, and thickness.

iii. **Coating**: If applicable, validate the coating process to ensure uniform application and adherence of the coating material.

b. Analytical Method Validation

i. **Assay**: Validate methods for determining the drug content in tablets to ensure accuracy and precision.

ii. **Disintegration and Dissolution**: Validate methods for measuring tablet disintegration and dissolution rates to ensure that tablets release the drug at the appropriate rate.

c. Equipment Validation

i. **Tablet Press**: Validate the calibration and performance of tablet presses to ensure consistent tablet production.

ii. **Granulator**: Validate granulators used in the production of tablet granules.

2. Capsules:

a. Process Validation

i. **Filling**: Validate the capsule filling process to ensure consistent drug content and proper filling of capsules.

ii. **Sealing**: Validate the sealing process to ensure capsules are properly closed and free from defects.

b. Analytical Method Validation

i. **Assay**: Validate methods for determining the drug content in capsules.

ii. **Content Uniformity**: Validate methods for assessing the uniformity of drug content within capsules.

c. Equipment Validation

i. **Capsule Filling Machines**: Validate the performance and calibration of machines used for filling capsules.

ii. **Capsule Sealing Equipment**: Validate equipment used for sealing capsules to ensure proper closure and integrity.

3. Injectables:

a. Process Validation

i. **Sterilization**: Validate the sterilization process to ensure that injectables are free from microbial contamination.

ii. **Filling**: Validate the aseptic filling process to ensure that injectables are filled under sterile conditions.

iii. **Packaging**: Validate packaging processes to ensure that injectables are properly sealed and protected from contamination.

b. Analytical Method Validation

i. **Sterility Testing**: Validate methods for testing the sterility of injectables.

ii. **Assay**: Validate methods for determining the concentration of the drug in injectable solutions.

iii. **Particulate Matter**: Validate methods for detecting particulate matter in injectables.

c. Equipment Validation

i. **Sterilizers**: Validate the calibration and performance of autoclaves or other sterilization equipment.

ii. **Filling Equipment**: Validate equipment used for the aseptic filling of injectable products.

4. Topical Preparations:

a. Process Validation

i. **Mixing**: Validate the mixing process to ensure uniformity of the topical formulation.

ii. **Filling**: Validate the filling process for creams, ointments, and gels to ensure consistent product quantity and quality.

b. Analytical Method Validation

i. **Assay**: Validate methods for determining the drug content in topical preparations.

ii. **Uniformity**: Validate methods for assessing the uniformity of drug distribution within topical formulations.

c. Equipment Validation

i. **Mixers**: Validate equipment used for mixing topical formulations to ensure consistent product quality.

ii. **Filling Machines**: Validate machines used for filling and packaging topical products.

5. Oral Solutions and Suspensions:

a. Process Validation

i. **Mixing**: Validate the mixing process to ensure that the drug is uniformly dissolved or suspended in the solution.

ii. **Filtration**: Validate filtration processes to remove particulates and ensure solution clarity.

b. Analytical Method Validation

i. **Assay**: Validate methods for determining the drug concentration in oral solutions and suspensions.

ii. **Stability**: Validate methods for assessing the stability of solutions and suspensions over time.

c. Equipment Validation

i. **Mixers and Homogenizers**: Validate equipment used for mixing and homogenizing solutions and suspensions.

ii. **Filling Equipment**: Validate equipment used for filling liquid dosage forms.

6. General Considerations

i. **Regulatory Compliance**: Ensure that all validation activities align with regulatory requirements, such as those from the FDA, EMA, or other relevant agencies.

ii. **Documentation**: Maintain comprehensive documentation for all validation activities, including validation plans, protocols, reports, and records of any deviations or corrective actions.

iii. **Risk Management**: Apply risk-based approaches to prioritize validation activities based on the potential impact on product quality and patient safety.

TYPES OF VALIDATION

In the pharmaceutical industry, **validation** is a critical process that ensures equipment, processes, and systems operate consistently and meet quality standards. Validation can be categorized into various types based on the aspect being validated. Here's a detailed overview of the different types of validation:

1. Process Validation

Process Validation ensures that manufacturing processes consistently produce products that meet predefined quality specifications. It involves the following stages:

a. **Process Design**: Developing and designing the manufacturing process based on scientific knowledge and intended use.
b. **Process Qualification**:
    i. **Installation Qualification (IQ)**: Verifying that equipment and systems are installed according to design specifications.
    ii. **Operational Qualification (OQ)**: Confirming that equipment and systems operate within specified parameters.
    iii. **Performance Qualification (PQ)**: Ensuring that the process performs reliably under actual production conditions.
c. **Continued Process Verification**: Ongoing monitoring of the process to ensure it remains in a state of control during routine production.

2. Analytical Method Validation

Analytical Method Validation involves demonstrating that an analytical method used to test pharmaceutical products is suitable for its intended purpose. Key parameters include:

a. **Specificity**: Ability of the method to measure the analyte without interference from other substances.
b. **Accuracy**: Closeness of the test results to the true value.
c. **Precision**: Reproducibility of the method under the same conditions.
d. **Linearity**: The method's ability to provide results that are directly proportional to the concentration of the analyte.

e. **Range**: The interval over which the method provides accurate and reliable results.

f. **Limit of Detection (LOD) and Limit of Quantitation (LOQ)**: The lowest concentration that can be reliably detected or quantified.

3. Equipment Validation

Equipment Validation ensures that equipment used in manufacturing and testing functions correctly and consistently. It includes:

a. **Installation Qualification (IQ)**: Confirming that the equipment is installed correctly and in accordance with specifications.

b. **Operational Qualification (OQ)**: Testing the equipment to ensure it operates according to its design.

c. **Performance Qualification (PQ)**: Verifying that the equipment performs effectively in its intended operating environment.

4. Computer System Validation (CSV)

Computer System Validation ensures that computerized systems used for data management, control, and reporting are reliable and meet regulatory requirements. It involves:

a. **Requirements Specification**: Defining user requirements and system functionality.

b. **System Testing**: Performing rigorous testing to ensure the system operates as intended.

c. **Data Integrity**: Ensuring accuracy, completeness, and consistency of data handled by the system.

d. **Documentation**: Maintaining detailed records of validation activities, including validation plans, protocols, and reports.

5. Cleaning Validation

Cleaning Validation ensures that cleaning procedures are effective in removing residues from equipment and production areas. It involves:

a. **Cleaning Procedures**: Validating methods and procedures used for cleaning equipment and surfaces.
b. **Residue Limits**: Determining acceptable residue limits for cleaning agents and product residues.
c. **Verification**: Regular testing to confirm that cleaning processes are effective and residues are below acceptable levels.

6. Sterilization Validation

Sterilization Validation ensures that sterilization processes are effective in eliminating microbial contamination. It includes:

a. **Sterilization Methods**: Validating methods such as autoclaving, dry heat, or filtration to ensure they achieve the required sterility.
b. **Process Monitoring**: Regular monitoring and testing to confirm that sterilization processes are consistently effective.

7. Validation of Specific Dosage Forms

Validation of Specific Dosage Forms involves ensuring that different types of dosage forms meet quality standards. It includes:

a. **Tablets and Capsules**: Validating processes such as granulation, compression, filling, and coating.
b. **Injectables**: Validating processes such as sterilization, filling, and packaging.
c. **Topical Preparations**: Validating mixing, filling, and packaging processes for creams, ointments, and gels.
d. **Oral Solutions and Suspensions**: Validating mixing, filtration, and filling processes for liquid dosage forms.

8. Validation of Packaging Systems

Packaging System Validation ensures that packaging processes and materials maintain the integrity and quality of the product. It includes:

a. **Packaging Materials**: Validating that materials used for packaging do not interact with the product.

b. **Packaging Processes**: Ensuring that packaging processes effectively protect the product from contamination and degradation.

9. Validation of Laboratory Procedures

Laboratory Procedure Validation ensures that laboratory procedures and methods used for testing pharmaceutical products are accurate and reliable. It includes:

a. **Method Validation**: Ensuring that laboratory methods for testing drug quality and safety are validated.

b. **Instrument Calibration**: Validating that laboratory instruments are calibrated and maintained correctly.

10. Validation of IT Systems

IT Systems Validation ensures that IT systems used for managing and storing data are reliable and compliant with regulatory requirements. It includes:

a. **System Development Life Cycle (SDLC)**: Ensuring that all phases of the system development, including design, implementation, and maintenance, are validated.

b. **Data Security**: Validating measures to protect data from unauthorized access and loss.

GOVERNMENT REGULATION

Government regulation in validation ensures that pharmaceutical processes, systems, and products meet safety, efficacy, and quality standards. These regulations vary by country but generally align on core principles. Here's a detailed overview of government regulations related to validation:

1. United States (FDA):

a. 21 CFR Part 210 and 211: Current Good Manufacturing Practice (cGMP)

i. **Process Validation (21 CFR 211.100)**: Requires that manufacturing processes be validated to ensure they consistently produce products meeting quality standards.

ii. **Equipment Validation (21 CFR 211.63)**: Mandates that equipment used in production is validated, including installation, operation, and performance qualifications.

iii. **Analytical Method Validation (21 CFR 211.194)**: Requires that methods used for testing are validated to ensure accuracy and reliability.

iv. **Documentation (21 CFR 211.180)**: Requires detailed documentation of validation activities, including protocols, reports, and records of deviations and corrective actions.

b. 21 CFR Part 820: Quality System Regulation (QSR)

i. **Design Validation (21 CFR 820.30(g))**: Requires that design validation be conducted to ensure that the product meets user needs and intended uses.

ii. **Process Validation (21 CFR 820.75)**: Mandates validation of manufacturing processes to ensure consistent production of devices that meet specifications.

c. FDA Guidance Documents

i. **Guidance for Industry: Process Validation**: Provides detailed recommendations for process validation, including stages (process design, process qualification, and continued process verification).

ii. **Guidance for Industry: Analytical Procedures and Methods Validation**: Offers guidance on validating analytical methods used in drug testing.

2. European Union (EMA):

a. EU Good Manufacturing Practice (GMP) Guidelines

i. **Process Validation**: Requires validation of critical processes, including manufacturing and packaging, to ensure consistent product quality.

ii. **Equipment Qualification**: Mandates that equipment used in production be qualified through installation, operational, and performance qualifications.

iii. **Analytical Method Validation**: Requires that methods used for testing pharmaceutical products are validated for accuracy, precision, and reliability.

b. EU Guideline on Good Manufacturing Practice for Medicinal Products for Human and Veterinary Use

i. **Validation Requirements**: Emphasizes the need for validation of manufacturing processes, including documentation and ongoing verification.

ii. **Cleaning Validation**: Provides guidelines for validating cleaning processes to ensure equipment is free of residues.

c. European Medicines Agency (EMA) Guidelines

i. **Guideline on Process Validation**: Offers detailed recommendations for validating manufacturing processes to ensure product quality.

ii. **Guideline on Analytical Method Validation**: Provides guidance on the validation of analytical methods used in drug testing.

3. International Council for Harmonisation (ICH):

a. ICH Q7: Good Manufacturing Practice for Active Pharmaceutical Ingredients

i. **Process Validation**: Provides guidance on the validation of manufacturing processes for active pharmaceutical ingredients, including installation, operational, and performance qualifications.

ii. **Documentation**: Emphasizes the need for comprehensive documentation of validation activities.

b. ICH Q8: Pharmaceutical Development

i. **Process and Analytical Method Validation**: Outlines requirements for validating processes and analytical methods to ensure consistent product quality and efficacy.

c. ICH Q9: Quality Risk Management

i. **Risk-Based Approach**: Encourages a risk-based approach to validation and quality management, focusing on critical aspects that impact product quality.

d. ICH Q10: Pharmaceutical Quality System

i. **Integration of Validation into Quality Systems**: Encourages integration of validation activities into the overall pharmaceutical quality system, emphasizing continuous improvement.

4. World Health Organization (WHO):

a. WHO Good Manufacturing Practice (GMP) Guidelines

i. **Process Validation**: Requires validation of manufacturing processes to ensure that products consistently meet quality specifications.

ii. **Equipment Qualification**: Mandates qualification of equipment used in manufacturing, including installation and performance testing.

iii. **Analytical Method Validation**: Requires that analytical methods used for testing are validated to ensure accuracy and reliability.

b. WHO Technical Report Series

i. **Technical Report Series No. 823**: Provides guidelines on GMP for pharmaceutical products, including process and equipment validation.

ii. **Technical Report Series No. 908**: Offers guidelines on GMP for biological products, including specific validation requirements.

5. Other Regional and National Guidelines:

a. Health Canada

i. **Guidelines for Process Validation**: Provides requirements for validating manufacturing processes to ensure product quality and safety.

ii. **Equipment Qualification and Validation**: Requires that equipment used in pharmaceutical manufacturing is properly qualified and validated.

b. Australian Therapeutic Goods Administration (TGA)

i. **GMP Guidelines**: Includes requirements for process and equipment validation to ensure product quality and compliance with regulatory standards.

c. Japan's Pharmaceuticals and Medical Devices Agency (PMDA)

i. **GMP Standards**: Provides guidelines for validating manufacturing processes and equipment to ensure consistent product quality.

MANUFACTURING PROCESS MODEL

A **Manufacturing Process Model** in the context of validation is a structured representation of the processes involved in the production of pharmaceutical products. This model serves as a blueprint for understanding, evaluating, and validating each stage of the manufacturing process to ensure consistent product quality and regulatory compliance. Here's a detailed overview:

1. Introduction to Manufacturing Process Model:

A Manufacturing Process Model outlines the sequence of operations, equipment, and controls used to produce a pharmaceutical product. It helps in identifying critical process parameters and quality attributes that need to be controlled and validated.

2. Components of a Manufacturing Process Model:

a. Process Flow Diagram (PFD)

i. **Purpose**: Provides a high-level overview of the manufacturing process, showing the sequence of operations and interactions between different stages.

ii. **Components**: Includes inputs, outputs, process steps, equipment, and control points.

b. Process Description

i. **Purpose**: Details each step in the manufacturing process, including the purpose of the step, materials used, and expected outcomes.

ii. **Components**: Describes raw materials, intermediate steps, equipment used, and conditions required (e.g., temperature, pressure).

c. Critical Process Parameters (CPPs)

i. **Purpose**: Identifies key parameters that influence the quality of the final product.

ii. **Components**: Includes parameters such as temperature, mixing speed, pressure, and time.

d. Quality Attributes

i. **Purpose**: Defines the characteristics of the product that must be measured and controlled to ensure quality.

ii. **Components**: Includes attributes such as potency, purity, dissolution rate, and appearance.

e. Control Strategy

i. **Purpose**: Outlines how the CPPs and quality attributes are monitored and controlled during the manufacturing process.

ii. **Components**: Includes process controls, monitoring methods, and response actions for deviations.

f. Validation Protocols

i. **Purpose**: Provides a structured plan for validating the manufacturing process, including methods and criteria for validation.

ii. **Components**: Includes Installation Qualification (IQ), Operational Qualification (OQ), and Performance Qualification (PQ) protocols.

3. Process Validation Stages:

a. Process Design

i. **Objective**: Develop and document the process design based on scientific principles and intended use.

ii. **Activities**:

1. Define process flow and key parameters.
2. Develop process maps and flow diagrams.

3. Establish process requirements and specifications.

b. Process Qualification

i. **Installation Qualification (IQ)**: Verify that equipment and systems are installed according to design specifications.

   1. **Activities**: Check equipment installation, utility connections, and environmental conditions.

ii. **Operational Qualification (OQ)**: Confirm that equipment and systems operate as intended under normal operating conditions.

   1. **Activities**: Test equipment performance, calibrate instruments, and validate control systems.

iii. **Performance Qualification (PQ)**: Ensure that the process performs consistently under actual production conditions.

   1. **Activities**: Conduct trials using production-scale equipment and materials to confirm process performance and product quality.

c. Continued Process Verification

i. **Objective**: Ensure that the manufacturing process remains in a state of control throughout routine production.

ii. **Activities**:

   1. Monitor and review process data.
   2. Implement ongoing validation activities and periodic re-evaluation.
   3. Address any process deviations or changes.

4. Risk Management:

a. Risk Assessment

i. **Objective**: Identify and evaluate potential risks associated with the manufacturing process.

ii. **Activities**:

   1. Perform risk assessments to determine the impact of process variations on product quality.

2. Use tools like Failure Modes and Effects Analysis (FMEA) or Fault Tree Analysis (FTA).

b. Risk Mitigation

i. **Objective**: Develop strategies to mitigate identified risks and ensure process robustness.

ii. **Activities**:

1. Implement control measures for critical process parameters.
2. Develop contingency plans for potential process deviations.

5. Documentation and Reporting:

a. Documentation

i. **Objective**: Maintain comprehensive records of the manufacturing process, validation activities, and quality control.

ii. **Activities**:

1. Document process design, qualification results, and process control data.
2. Maintain records of validation protocols, reports, and deviations.

b. Reporting

i. **Objective**: Provide detailed reports on validation activities, including process performance and compliance with specifications.

ii. **Activities**:

1. Prepare validation summary reports.
2. Review and approve validation documentation.

6. Case Study: Validation of a Tablet Manufacturing Process:

a. Process Flow Diagram

i. **Overview**: Shows steps such as granulation, compression, and coating.

ii. **Details**: Includes equipment used (e.g., granulators, tablet presses), and process connections.

b. Process Description

i. **Granulation**: Describes mixing of active ingredients with excipients, granulation conditions, and equipment used.
ii. **Compression**: Details the compression of granules into tablets, including tablet press settings and quality checks.
iii. **Coating**: Outlines the coating process, including coating materials and application methods.

c. Critical Process Parameters

i. **Granulation**: Moisture content, granulation time.
ii. **Compression**: Tablet hardness, weight variation.
iii. **Coating**: Coating thickness, uniformity.

d. Quality Attributes

i. **Potency**: Drug content in tablets.
ii. **Dissolution Rate**: Rate at which the tablet releases the drug.
iii. **Appearance**: Tablet color, shape, and surface texture.

e. Control Strategy

i. **Monitoring**: Regular measurement of CPPs and quality attributes.
ii. **Controls**: Procedures for adjusting process parameters and addressing deviations.

f. Validation Protocols

i. **IQ**: Verify installation of granulators and tablet presses.
ii. **OQ**: Test equipment performance under standard conditions.
iii. **PQ**: Conduct production runs to confirm consistent tablet quality.

URS, DQ, IQ, OQ & P.Q. OF FACILITIES

URS, DQ, IQ, OQ, and PQ are key elements in the validation of facilities, equipment, and systems in the pharmaceutical industry. Each term represents a specific stage or document in the validation process, ensuring that facilities and equipment are qualified to produce pharmaceutical products that meet required quality standards. Here's a detailed overview of each:

1. User Requirements Specification (URS)

Definition: The URS is a document that defines the needs and requirements for a facility, equipment, or system from the user's perspective. It serves as the foundation for the design and validation process.

Purpose:

a. To ensure that the facility, equipment, or system will meet the specific needs of the user and comply with regulatory requirements.
b. To provide a clear and detailed description of what the system or equipment must achieve.

Contents:

a. **Functional Requirements**: Describes what the equipment or system should do, including performance criteria, capacity, and capabilities.
b. **Design Requirements**: Details the design specifications, including materials, dimensions, and layout.
c. **Compliance Requirements**: Includes relevant regulations and standards that the facility or equipment must meet (e.g., GMP, ISO).
d. **Operational Requirements**: Outlines how the system or equipment will be used in practice, including operating conditions and user interactions.

Example: For a new tablet press, the URS might specify requirements such as production capacity (e.g., 500,000 tablets per day), tablet dimensions, and compliance with GMP guidelines.

2. Design Qualification (DQ):

Definition: DQ is the process of confirming that the design of a facility, equipment, or system meets the requirements specified in the URS.

Purpose:

a. To ensure that the design is capable of meeting the user requirements and regulatory standards before the construction or installation begins.
b. To identify and address any design-related issues early in the process.

Contents:

a. **Design Specifications**: Detailed drawings and specifications of the facility or equipment.
b. **Compliance**: Verification that the design meets all relevant regulations and standards.
c. **Risk Assessment**: Evaluation of potential risks associated with the design and implementation.

Example: For a new cleanroom, the DQ would review architectural and engineering plans to ensure that the design meets requirements for air cleanliness, temperature control, and space layout.

3. Installation Qualification (IQ)

Definition: IQ verifies that equipment or systems are installed according to design specifications and that they function as intended within the intended environment.

Purpose:

a. To ensure that equipment or systems are installed correctly and meet the design requirements specified in the DQ.
b. To confirm that installation procedures are followed and that all components are in place.

Contents:

a. **Installation Checks**: Verification of equipment placement, utility connections, and environmental conditions.
b. **Documentation**: Records of installation procedures, including calibration and setup.
c. **Equipment Verification**: Confirm that all equipment components are installed correctly and operational.

Example: For a new HVAC system, the IQ would involve checking that the system is installed according to the manufacturer's specifications, including proper ductwork, controls, and connections.

4. Operational Qualification (OQ):

Definition: OQ confirms that equipment or systems operate as intended under normal operating conditions and meet the specified operational criteria.

Purpose:

a. To ensure that the equipment or system performs as expected when operated within its specified range.
b. To validate that operational procedures and controls are effective.

Contents:

a. **Operational Testing**: Verification that the equipment operates correctly and consistently within specified parameters (e.g., temperature, pressure).
b. **Performance Data**: Collection of data to demonstrate that the equipment meets operational specifications.
c. **Documentation**: Records of test results and any deviations observed during testing.

Example: For a new tablet coating machine, the OQ would involve testing the machine's performance, including coating thickness, consistency, and temperature control, to ensure it meets operational specifications.

5. Performance Qualification (PQ):

Definition: PQ verifies that the equipment or system performs effectively and consistently under actual production conditions and meets the required quality standards.

Purpose:

a. To confirm that the equipment or system operates reliably and produces products that meet quality specifications during routine production.
b. To ensure that the equipment or system performs as intended over an extended period.

Contents:

a. **Performance Testing**: Conducting production runs to validate that the equipment or system produces products within specified quality attributes.

b. **Quality Control**: Monitoring and documenting product quality during production to ensure it meets standards.

c. **Long-Term Stability**: Assessing the equipment's performance over time to confirm consistent operation.

Example: For a new filling line, the PQ would involve running several production batches to ensure that the line consistently fills bottles to the correct volume and maintains product quality.

Summary

a. **User Requirements Specification (URS)**: Defines what the facility or equipment needs to achieve from the user's perspective.

b. **Design Qualification (DQ)**: Ensures the design meets the URS and regulatory requirements before installation.

c. **Installation Qualification (IQ)**: Verifies that the equipment or system is installed correctly and in accordance with design specifications.

d. **Operational Qualification (OQ)**: Confirms that the equipment or system operates as intended under normal operating conditions.

e. **Performance Qualification (PQ)**: Validates that the equipment or system performs reliably and produces quality products during actual production.

Multiple-Choice Questions (Objective)

1. What is the primary purpose of validation in pharmaceutical processes?
    a) To increase production speed
    b) To ensure methods, processes, and systems meet their intended purpose
    c) To reduce costs
    d) To automate production
2. Which type of validation involves assessing the reliability and accuracy of analytical methods?

a) Process validation
b) Method validation
c) Equipment validation
d) Software validation

3. What is the main goal of process validation?
   a) To ensure software performs correctly
   b) To confirm manufacturing processes consistently produce quality products
   c) To test analytical methods
   d) To validate cleaning procedures
4. Which of the following is NOT a key aspect of method validation?
   a) Specificity
   b) Accuracy
   c) Calibration
   d) Precision
5. What does the Limit of Detection (LOD) refer to in method validation?
   a) The highest concentration that can be reliably quantified
   b) The lowest concentration of an analyte that can be reliably detected
   c) The precision of repeated measurements
   d) The linearity of the method
6. What is the main focus of equipment validation?
   a) Ensuring manufacturing processes meet specifications
   b) Confirming software functions accurately
   c) Ensuring equipment operates correctly and consistently
   d) Validating cleaning processes
7. What does IQ stand for in the context of equipment validation?
   a) Installation Qualification
   b) Integration Qualification
   c) Initial Qualification

d) Instrument Qualification

8. What is the purpose of Operational Qualification (OQ)?
    a) To verify equipment installation
    b) To test equipment under specified operational conditions
    c) To confirm that the process design performs as expected
    d) To validate the cleaning process
9. What is a key component of continued process verification?
    a) Initial design
    b) Ongoing monitoring and validation during production
    c) Installation checks
    d) Requirements analysis
10. What is the purpose of a Validation Master Plan (VMP)?
    a) To automate the manufacturing process
    b) To outline the strategy and framework for validation activities
    c) To manage financial resources
    d) To train personnel
11. Which guideline emphasizes a risk-based approach to validation?
    a) ICH Q7
    b) ICH Q8
    c) ICH Q9
    d) ICH Q10
12. According to WHO guidelines, what is a key requirement for equipment qualification?
    a) System testing
    b) Installation checks
    c) Performance Qualification (PQ)
    d) Documentation of all activities
13. Which validation stage involves verifying that a process performs reliably under actual production conditions?

a) Installation Qualification (IQ)
b) Operational Qualification (OQ)
c) Performance Qualification (PQ)
d) Design Qualification (DQ)

14. What does the Validation Master Plan (VMP) typically include?
a) Manufacturing schedule
b) Detailed design drawings
c) Validation objectives, procedures, and timelines
d) Cost estimates

15. What is the primary focus of cleaning validation?
a) Ensuring equipment functions correctly
b) Removing residues from equipment and surfaces
c) Validating software systems
d) Confirming analytical methods

16. Which type of validation ensures that computer systems used for data management meet regulatory requirements?
a) Equipment validation
b) Process validation
c) Analytical method validation
d) Computer System Validation (CSV)

17. What is the purpose of sterility testing in injectables validation?
a) To measure drug concentration
b) To confirm the absence of microbial contamination
c) To ensure proper packaging
d) To test the dissolution rate

18. What does the Design Qualification (DQ) process confirm?
a) That equipment is installed correctly
b) That the design meets user requirements and regulatory standards
c) That the system operates under specified conditions

d) That cleaning processes are effective

19. In the context of a tablet manufacturing process, what is typically validated during the compression stage?
    a) Mixing speed
    b) Tablet hardness and weight
    c) Coating thickness
    d) Dissolution rate

20. Which document provides a high-level overview of the manufacturing process and shows the sequence of operations?
    a) Process Description
    b) Process Flow Diagram (PFD)
    c) Control Strategy
    d) Validation Protocol

Short Answer Type Questions (Subjective)

1. Define validation and explain its importance in the pharmaceutical industry.
2. What are the key aspects of method validation?
3. Describe the steps involved in process validation.
4. What is the difference between Installation Qualification (IQ) and Operational Qualification (OQ)?
5. Explain the purpose of a Validation Master Plan (VMP).
6. What is continued process verification and why is it important?
7. How does risk management play a role in validation?
8. What are the key components of a Process Flow Diagram (PFD)?
9. Describe the purpose of equipment validation.
10. What is the role of the International Council for Harmonisation (ICH) guidelines in validation?
11. Explain the significance of the Limit of Detection (LOD) and Limit of Quantitation (LOQ) in method validation.

12. What are the stages of performance qualification (PQ)?
13. How is cleaning validation conducted?
14. What are the key elements of computer system validation (CSV)?
15. Why is calibration important in the validation process?
16. Describe the process of analytical method validation.
17. What is the significance of regulatory compliance in validation?
18. Explain the concept of critical process parameters (CPPs).
19. What are the key requirements of WHO guidelines for equipment qualification?
20. How does the validation of specific dosage forms differ for tablets and injectables?

Long Answer Type Questions (Subjective)

1. Discuss the different types of validation and their significance in ensuring pharmaceutical product quality.
2. Explain the process and importance of equipment validation, including Installation Qualification (IQ), Operational Qualification (OQ), and Performance Qualification (PQ).
3. Describe the stages involved in process validation and their importance in manufacturing.
4. Discuss the role and components of a Validation Master Plan (VMP) in pharmaceutical validation.
5. Explain the concept and importance of analytical method validation, including key parameters such as specificity, accuracy, and precision.
6. Discuss the regulatory guidelines provided by ICH and WHO for calibration and validation of equipment.
7. Explain the process of cleaning validation and its significance in maintaining product quality and safety.

8. Describe the validation process for specific dosage forms, using tablets and injectables as examples.
9. Discuss the challenges and solutions in implementing a comprehensive validation program in the pharmaceutical industry.
10. Explain the role of risk management in validation, including how risk assessments are conducted and mitigated.

Answer Key for MCQ Questions

1. b) To ensure methods, processes, and systems meet their intended purpose
2. b) Method validation
3. b) To confirm manufacturing processes consistently produce quality products
4. c) Calibration
5. b) The lowest concentration of an analyte that can be reliably detected
6. c) Ensuring equipment operates correctly and consistently
7. a) Installation Qualification: "Installation Qualification (IQ)
8. b) To test equipment under specified operational conditions
9. b) Ongoing monitoring and validation during production
10. b) To outline the strategy and framework for validation activities
11. c) ICH Q9
12. c) Performance Qualification (PQ)
13. c) Performance Qualification (PQ)
14. c) Validation objectives, procedures, and timelines
15. b) Removing residues from equipment and surfaces
16. d) Computer System Validation (CSV
17. b) To confirm the absence of microbial contamination
18. b) That the design meets user requirements and regulatory standards
19. b) Tablet hardness and weight
20. b) Process Flow Diagram (PFD)

CHAPTER – 4

GOOD MANUFACTURING PRACTICE

INTRODUCTION:

Good Manufacturing Practice (GMP) refers to a set of regulations and guidelines established to ensure that products, particularly in the pharmaceutical, food, and medical device industries, are consistently produced and controlled according to quality standards. GMP covers all aspects of production, from the raw materials, facilities, and equipment to the training and hygiene of staff. Adherence to GMP is essential for preventing contamination, mix-ups, and errors, thereby ensuring that products are safe for consumers and meet their intended use.

The principles of GMP require manufacturers to establish strong quality management systems, maintain clean and hygienic production areas, implement robust procedures, and ensure thorough documentation. Regular inspections and audits are conducted to verify compliance, and any deviations must be promptly addressed.

GMP is a critical component of product safety and efficacy, and it is legally mandated in many countries. Compliance with GMP not only protects consumers but also enhances the credibility and reliability of manufacturers in the global market.

OBJECTIVES OF CURRENT GOOD MANUFACTURING PRACTICES

Current Good Manufacturing Practices (cGMP) are regulatory standards designed to ensure that pharmaceutical products are consistently produced and controlled according to quality standards. The objectives of cGMP are crucial for maintaining the safety, efficacy, and quality of drugs and other products. Here are the detailed objectives of cGMP:

1. Ensure Product Quality and Safety

a. **Consistent Quality:** cGMP ensures that products are manufactured consistently according to predefined quality standards. This consistency is achieved through well-documented processes, controlled environments, and regular quality checks.
b. **Safety Assurance:** By adhering to cGMP, manufacturers minimize the risk of contamination, mix-ups, and errors, thereby safeguarding the health and safety of consumers.

2. Compliance with Regulatory Requirements

a. **Regulatory Adherence:** cGMP establishes a framework for meeting the legal and regulatory requirements set by authorities like the FDA (Food and Drug Administration), EMA (European Medicines Agency), and other global regulatory bodies.
b. **Documentation and Record-Keeping:** Detailed documentation and records are maintained to demonstrate compliance and facilitate inspections and audits by regulatory agencies.

3. Risk Management and Mitigation

a. **Identification and Control:** cGMP guidelines require the identification of potential risks and the implementation of controls to manage those risks effectively. This includes controlling the manufacturing environment, equipment, and processes.
b. **Preventive Measures:** cGMP emphasizes preventive measures to avoid defects and ensure that corrective actions are taken promptly when issues arise.

4. Standardization of Manufacturing Processes

a. **Process Consistency:** Establishing standardized procedures for manufacturing processes helps ensure that products are produced consistently and meet quality specifications.

b. **Validation and Qualification:** cGMP requires the validation of manufacturing processes and the qualification of equipment to ensure they perform as intended.

5. **Training and Competence of Personnel**
   a. **Training Requirements:** cGMP mandates that personnel involved in manufacturing, quality control, and other relevant areas receive appropriate training and demonstrate competence in their roles.
   b. **Continuous Improvement:** Regular training and skill enhancement are encouraged to keep personnel updated with the latest practices and regulations.
6. **Effective Quality Control and Assurance**
   a. **Quality Control (QC):** cGMP includes rigorous QC measures to test and verify the quality of raw materials, in-process materials, and finished products.
   b. **Quality Assurance (QA):** QA activities ensure that the manufacturing processes and systems are in place to produce high-quality products consistently.
7. **Proper Documentation and Record Keeping**
   a. **Documentation Standards:** cGMP requires comprehensive documentation of all manufacturing processes, procedures, and quality control activities. This ensures traceability and accountability.
   b. **Record Retention:** Records must be maintained for specified periods to support product traceability and regulatory compliance.
8. **Facility and Equipment Maintenance**
   a. **Facility Conditions:** cGMP mandates that manufacturing facilities be designed, maintained, and cleaned to prevent contamination and cross-contamination.

b. **Equipment Maintenance:** Regular maintenance, calibration, and validation of equipment are required to ensure accurate and reliable operation.

9. Inspection and Audits

a. **Internal Audits:** Regular internal audits are conducted to assess compliance with cGMP standards and identify areas for improvement.

b. **Regulatory Inspections:** cGMP prepares manufacturers for external inspections by regulatory authorities to verify adherence to standards and regulations.

10. Consumer Confidence

a. **Trust Building:** By adhering to cGMP, manufacturers build consumer trust by ensuring that products are safe, effective, and of high quality. This trust is essential for maintaining a good reputation in the market.

POLICIES OF CURRENT GOOD MANUFACTURING PRACTICES

Current Good Manufacturing Practices (cGMP) policies are detailed guidelines and regulations that govern the manufacturing process to ensure product quality and safety. These policies are designed to ensure that pharmaceutical products and other regulated goods are consistently produced and controlled according to high standards. Here's a detailed overview of cGMP policies:

1. Quality Management System (QMS)

a. **Quality Policy:** Establishes the overall quality objectives and commitment to producing products that meet regulatory requirements and customer expectations.

b. **Quality Manual:** A comprehensive document outlining the QMS, including organizational structure, responsibilities, and procedures.

c. **Document Control:** Policies for creating, reviewing, updating, and maintaining documentation to ensure accuracy and integrity.

2. Personnel and Training

a. **Qualifications:** Ensures that personnel involved in manufacturing, quality control, and other critical functions have the necessary qualifications and experience.
b. **Training Programs:** Ongoing training for employees to keep them informed of new procedures, regulations, and technologies.
c. **Competency Assessment:** Regular evaluations to ensure that personnel are competent in their roles and responsibilities.

3. Facility and Equipment

a. **Facility Design and Maintenance:** Policies for the design, construction, and maintenance of manufacturing facilities to prevent contamination and ensure product safety.
b. **Equipment Qualification:** Requirements for the qualification, calibration, and maintenance of equipment used in manufacturing processes.
c. **Environmental Controls:** Measures to control environmental conditions, such as temperature, humidity, and cleanliness, to prevent contamination.

4. Raw Materials and Components

a. **Supplier Qualification:** Policies for evaluating and selecting suppliers to ensure the quality and reliability of raw materials and components.
b. **Material Testing:** Procedures for testing raw materials and components to verify their quality before use in manufacturing.
c. **Storage and Handling:** Guidelines for the proper storage and handling of raw materials to maintain their quality and prevent contamination.

5. Manufacturing Processes

a. **Standard Operating Procedures (SOPs):** Detailed procedures for each manufacturing step to ensure consistency and compliance with quality standards.

b. **Process Validation:** Validation of manufacturing processes to demonstrate that they consistently produce products that meet quality specifications.

c. **In-Process Controls:** Monitoring and controlling manufacturing processes to ensure they remain within specified limits.

6. Quality Control and Assurance

a. **Quality Control (QC):** Procedures for testing and inspecting raw materials, in-process materials, and finished products to ensure they meet quality standards.

b. **Quality Assurance (QA):** Policies for ensuring that manufacturing processes are in place and functioning to produce high-quality products consistently.

c. **Change Control:** Procedures for managing changes to processes, equipment, or materials to ensure they do not negatively impact product quality.

7. Documentation and Record-Keeping

a. **Record Maintenance:** Policies for maintaining accurate and complete records of all manufacturing activities, including batch records, test results, and equipment logs.

b. **Data Integrity:** Ensuring the accuracy, reliability, and security of data related to manufacturing processes and product quality.

c. **Audit Trails:** Maintaining detailed audit trails to track changes and activities related to manufacturing and quality control.

8. Complaint Handling and Product Recall

a. **Complaint Management:** Procedures for receiving, investigating, and addressing complaints related to product quality and safety.

b. **Product Recall:** Policies and procedures for recalling products from the market in case of quality or safety issues, including notification of regulatory authorities and affected parties.

9. Regulatory Compliance

a. **Regulatory Requirements:** Adherence to local and international regulations and guidelines set by regulatory agencies such as the FDA, EMA, and others.

b. **Inspection Readiness:** Ensuring that the facility, processes, and documentation are always in a state of readiness for regulatory inspections.

10. Risk Management

a. **Risk Assessment:** Identifying, assessing, and mitigating risks related to manufacturing processes, product quality, and safety.

b. **Preventive and Corrective Actions (CAPA):** Implementing actions to prevent the recurrence of issues and address any identified deficiencies.

11. Customer and Market Focus

a. **Customer Requirements:** Ensuring that products meet customer specifications and expectations.

b. **Market Surveillance:** Monitoring the market for feedback and potential issues related to product performance and safety.

12. Continuous Improvement

a. **Quality Improvement:** Ongoing efforts to improve manufacturing processes, product quality, and overall operational efficiency.

b. **Benchmarking:** Comparing practices with industry standards and best practices to identify areas for improvement.

LAYOUT OF BUILDINGS

The layout of buildings in a cGMP (current Good Manufacturing Practice) facility is crucial for ensuring the quality and safety of pharmaceutical products. The design and arrangement of facilities must minimize the risk of contamination, cross-contamination, and errors. Here's a detailed overview of the key aspects of building layout in cGMP facilities:

1. Facility Zones and Segregation

a. **Production Areas:** Areas where active manufacturing takes place. These should be designed to prevent contamination and ensure proper flow of materials and personnel.
b. **Clean Areas:** High cleanliness standards are required, often categorized by cleanroom classifications (e.g., ISO Class 5 to 8). These areas should have controlled temperature, humidity, and air quality.
c. **Support Areas:** Includes spaces for equipment storage, maintenance, and utility services. These areas should be designed to support the main production areas without risking contamination.

2. Flow of Materials and Personnel

a. **Unidirectional Flow:** The layout should ensure a logical flow of materials from receipt through to finished product, minimizing the risk of cross-contamination. Typically, raw materials enter through a dedicated area and flow through the production process to the packaging area.
b. **Personnel Flow:** Separate routes for personnel to prevent cross-contamination between different areas. This includes distinct entry and exit points for different zones to prevent cross-contact.

3. Cleanroom Design

a. **Air Filtration:** Cleanrooms must have high-efficiency particulate air (HEPA) filters or ultra-low penetration air (ULPA) filters to maintain the required air cleanliness levels.
b. **Controlled Environment:** Temperature, humidity, and pressure should be controlled and monitored to ensure they remain within specified limits.
c. **Surface Materials:** Walls, floors, and ceilings should be made of smooth, non-porous materials that are easy to clean and maintain.

4. Containment and Safety

a. **Containment Areas:** For handling hazardous materials or products, specialized containment facilities are required to protect personnel and the environment. These areas might include biological safety cabinets or isolators.

b. **Safety Zones:** Areas dedicated to safety equipment such as eye wash stations, showers, and fire extinguishers. These should be easily accessible and clearly marked.

5. Utilities and Ancillary Areas

a. **Utilities:** Facilities must have dedicated areas for utilities such as water, steam, and air supply systems, as well as waste management. These areas should be designed to avoid contamination and facilitate maintenance.

b. **Maintenance and Storage:** Areas for the storage of spare parts, tools, and maintenance equipment should be well-organized and separate from production areas to prevent cross-contamination.

6. Quality Control and Laboratories

a. **QC Laboratories:** These areas should be located to avoid contamination from production areas and have controlled environments for testing and analysis.

b. **Testing and Analysis:** Laboratories must have dedicated spaces for different types of tests (e.g., microbiological, chemical) and be equipped with the necessary instruments and safety features.

7. Office and Administrative Areas

a. **Administrative Offices:** Located separately from production and quality control areas to avoid disruption. These include offices for management, human resources, and other administrative functions.

b. **Meeting Rooms:** Spaces for meetings, training, and planning that are separate from production areas to avoid cross-contamination and ensure a focused environment.

8. Receiving and Shipping Areas

a. **Receiving Areas:** Designated areas for receiving raw materials and components, equipped with facilities for inspection and quarantine before they enter the production areas.
b. **Shipping Areas:** Separate areas for packing and shipping finished products. These areas should be designed to avoid contamination of the finished product.

9. Emergency and Contingency Areas

a. **Emergency Exits:** Clearly marked and accessible exits to ensure safe evacuation in case of an emergency.
b. **Contingency Facilities:** Areas designated for handling unexpected situations, such as spills or equipment failures, to minimize impact on the production process.

10. Visitor and Administrative Access

a. **Visitor Access:** Controlled access for visitors to prevent unauthorized entry into sensitive areas. Visitors should follow specific protocols to avoid contamination.
b. **Administrative Access:** Separate administrative areas for management and support staff that does not interfere with production activities.

11. Design Considerations for Future Expansion

a. **Scalability:** The layout should allow for future expansion or modification without disrupting existing operations.
b. **Flexibility:** Modular design elements can help accommodate changes in production needs or regulatory requirements.

12. Compliance with Regulations

a. **Regulatory Guidelines:** The layout must comply with guidelines from regulatory bodies such as the FDA, EMA, or other relevant authorities, which outline requirements for facility design and operation.

SERVICES

In a cGMP (current Good Manufacturing Practice) facility, various services are essential to maintain the quality, safety, and efficiency of the manufacturing process. These services support the primary manufacturing activities and ensure that the facility operates in compliance with regulatory requirements. Here's a detailed overview of the key services in a cGMP facility:

1. Utility Services

a. **Water Supply:**

i. **Purified Water:** Used for production processes and cleaning. Must meet strict quality standards (e.g., USP Purified Water, WFI - Water for Injection).

ii. **Water Treatment:** Includes filtration, reverse osmosis, and distillation to ensure the water meets quality requirements.

b. **Steam Supply:**

i. **Clean Steam:** Used in sterilization processes and must be free from contaminants. It is produced using dedicated steam generators and treated to ensure purity.

c. **Compressed Air:**

i. **Pharmaceutical Grade Air:** Used in processes where contamination could impact product quality. It must be filtered and monitored to meet specific quality standards.

d. **Heating, Ventilation, and Air Conditioning (HVAC):**

i. **Temperature and Humidity Control:** Maintains the required environmental conditions in production and storage areas.

ii. **Air Filtration:** Uses HEPA or ULPA filters to ensure clean and controlled air quality.

2. Cleaning and Sanitation Services

a. **Cleaning Procedures:**

i. **Cleaning Validation:** Ensures that cleaning processes effectively remove residues and contaminants from equipment and surfaces.

ii. **Cleaning Agents:** Selection and use of appropriate detergents and sanitizers that do not leave residues or affect product quality.

b. **Sanitation:**

i. **Routine Cleaning:** Regular cleaning schedules for floors, walls, equipment, and other surfaces to prevent contamination.

ii. **Sanitization:** Use of sanitizers and disinfectants to control microbial contamination.

3. Maintenance Services

a. **Preventive Maintenance:**

i. **Scheduled Maintenance:** Regular inspection and servicing of equipment and facilities to prevent breakdowns and ensure consistent performance.

ii. **Documentation:** Maintenance records must be kept to demonstrate adherence to maintenance schedules.

b. **Corrective Maintenance:**

i. **Repairs and Troubleshooting:** Addressing and fixing any equipment malfunctions or failures promptly to minimize impact on production.

ii. **Root Cause Analysis:** Identifying and addressing the underlying causes of equipment issues to prevent recurrence.

4. Quality Control and Assurance Services

a. **Laboratory Services:**

i. **Analytical Testing:** Testing of raw materials, in-process materials, and finished products to ensure they meet quality specifications.

ii. **Microbiological Testing:** Detection and quantification of microbial contamination.

b. **Quality Assurance:**

i. **Documentation Review:** Ensuring that all manufacturing activities are documented and comply with cGMP standards.

ii. **Audit Services:** Internal and external audits to verify compliance with cGMP regulations and identify areas for improvement.

5. Safety and Environmental Services

a. **Safety Management:**

i. **Personal Protective Equipment (PPE):** Provision and enforcement of the use of PPE to protect personnel from exposure to hazardous materials.

ii. **Emergency Response:** Plans and equipment for responding to emergencies such as spills, fires, or chemical exposures.

b. **Environmental Control:**

i. **Waste Management:** Procedures for handling and disposing of waste materials, including hazardous waste, in compliance with environmental regulations.

ii. **Environmental Monitoring:** Regular monitoring of the facility's environment to ensure it meets specified cleanliness and safety standards.

6. Information Technology Services

a. **Data Management:**

i. **Electronic Batch Records (EBR):** Digital records of manufacturing processes, reducing errors and improving traceability.

ii. **Data Integrity:** Ensuring that data related to manufacturing and quality control is accurate, complete, and secure.

b. **System Maintenance:**

i. **Software Updates:** Regular updates and maintenance of software systems used for manufacturing and quality control.

ii. **Cybersecurity:** Protecting systems from unauthorized access and data breaches.

7. Logistics and Supply Chain Services

a. **Material Handling:**

   i. **Storage:** Proper storage of raw materials, in-process materials, and finished products to prevent contamination and ensure quality.

   ii. **Inventory Management:** Monitoring and managing inventory levels to ensure the availability of materials while avoiding overstocking.

b. **Shipping and Receiving:**

   i. **Inspection and Documentation:** Inspecting incoming and outgoing materials and products and maintaining appropriate documentation for traceability.

8. Training and Development Services

a. **Employee Training:**

   i. **Induction Training:** Introduction to cGMP principles, procedures, and safety practices for new employees.

   ii. **Ongoing Training:** Regular training updates to keep employees informed about changes in regulations, technologies, and best practices.

b. **Competency Assessment:**

   i. **Skills Evaluation:** Assessing employees' competencies to ensure they can perform their roles effectively and adhere to cGMP standards.

9. Regulatory and Compliance Services

a. **Regulatory Affairs:**

   i. **Compliance Monitoring:** Ensuring that all operations and processes comply with local and international regulations.

   ii. **Documentation and Reporting:** Preparing and submitting required reports and documentation to regulatory authorities.

b. **Inspection Readiness:**

i. **Preparation:** Ensuring that the facility is always prepared for inspections by regulatory agencies by maintaining compliance and up-to-date documentation.

EQUIPMENT'S AND THEIR MAINTENANCE

In a cGMP (current Good Manufacturing Practice) facility, the proper management and maintenance of equipment are crucial to ensuring the production of high-quality and safe pharmaceutical products. Equipment must be qualified, maintained, and calibrated to operate reliably and within specified parameters. Here's a detailed overview of equipment and their maintenance in a cGMP environment:

1. Equipment Qualification

a. **Installation Qualification (IQ):**

i. **Purpose:** Ensures that equipment is installed correctly according to the manufacturer's specifications.

ii. **Activities:** Verification of equipment installation, including utilities and environmental controls. Documented evidence of correct installation is required.

b. **Operational Qualification (OQ):**

i. **Purpose:** Confirms that the equipment operates correctly and consistently within its specified operating ranges.

ii. **Activities:** Testing the equipment's functionality under normal operating conditions to ensure it performs as expected.

c. **Performance Qualification (PQ):**

i. **Purpose:** Ensures that the equipment performs consistently and reliably during actual production runs.

ii. **Activities:** Testing equipment with production materials to verify that it consistently produces products meeting quality specifications.

2. Calibration

a. **Routine Calibration:**

   i. **Purpose:** Ensures that equipment measurements are accurate and within specified limits.

   ii. **Activities:** Regular calibration of equipment such as balances, thermometers, and pH meters using certified standards.

b. **Calibration Schedule:**

   i. **Frequency:** Calibration frequency is determined based on the equipment's usage, manufacturer recommendations, and regulatory requirements.

   ii. **Documentation:** Records of calibration results, including date, results, and any adjustments made, must be maintained.

3. Preventive Maintenance (PM)

a. **Routine Maintenance:**

   i. **Purpose:** Prevents equipment malfunctions and extends the lifespan of the equipment.

   ii. **Activities:** Regular inspection, cleaning, lubrication, and adjustment of equipment to ensure optimal performance.

b. **Maintenance Schedule:**

   i. **Frequency:** Based on equipment type, manufacturer recommendations, and historical performance data.

   ii. **Documentation:** Maintenance logs must be kept, documenting the activities performed, date, and any issues found.

4. Corrective Maintenance (CM)

a. **Problem Resolution:**

   i. **Purpose:** Addresses and corrects equipment malfunctions or failures that occur during operation.

   ii. **Activities:** Diagnosis of the problem, repair or replacement of faulty parts, and verification of proper equipment function post-repair.

b. **Documentation:**

   i. **Records:** Detailed records of the problem, corrective actions taken, and any impact on production must be maintained.

5. Equipment Cleaning

a. **Cleaning Procedures:**

   i. **Purpose:** Prevents contamination and maintains equipment hygiene.

   ii. **Activities:** Regular cleaning of equipment parts, including disassembly, cleaning with appropriate detergents, and reassembly.

b. **Cleaning Validation:**

   i. **Purpose:** Ensures that cleaning procedures are effective and do not leave residues that could affect product quality.

   ii. **Activities:** Validation of cleaning procedures using analytical methods to confirm residue removal.

6. Equipment Documentation

a. **Equipment Logs:**

   i. **Purpose:** Provides a comprehensive record of equipment status, maintenance, and calibration.

   ii. **Activities:** Maintaining logs that include installation details, calibration records, maintenance activities, and repair history.

b. **SOPs (Standard Operating Procedures):**

   i. **Purpose:** Provides detailed instructions for equipment operation, maintenance, and cleaning.

   ii. **Activities:** Creation and regular review of SOPs to ensure they reflect current practices and regulatory requirements.

7. Environmental Control

a. **Temperature and Humidity Monitoring:**

   i. **Purpose:** Ensures that equipment operating conditions are within specified limits to prevent performance issues.

ii. **Activities:** Regular monitoring and recording of temperature and humidity in areas where sensitive equipment is used.

b. **Control Systems:**

i. **Purpose:** Maintains the controlled environment necessary for equipment operation.

ii. **Activities:** Regular calibration and maintenance of environmental control systems, such as HVAC systems.

8. Equipment Qualification and Requalification

a. **Initial Qualification:**

i. **Purpose:** Verifies that newly installed equipment meets all required specifications.

ii. **Activities:** Comprehensive testing and validation upon initial installation.

b. **Periodic Requalification:**

i. **Purpose:** Ensures that equipment continues to perform as expected over time.

ii. **Activities:** Regular requalification based on the criticality of the equipment and changes in operating conditions.

9. Training and Competency

a. **Operator Training:**

i. **Purpose:** Ensures that personnel operating equipment are properly trained and knowledgeable.

ii. **Activities:** Providing training on equipment use, maintenance procedures, and troubleshooting.

b. **Competency Assessment:**

i. **Purpose:** Verifies that personnel can effectively operate and maintain equipment.

ii. **Activities:** Regular assessment of operator skills and knowledge related to equipment operation.

10. Vendor and Supplier Management

a. **Vendor Qualification:**

   i. **Purpose:** Ensures that equipment suppliers meet quality and reliability standards.

   ii. **Activities:** Evaluation of suppliers based on their equipment quality, service, and support capabilities.

b. **Service Contracts:**

   i. **Purpose:** Provides support and maintenance services from equipment manufacturers or specialized service providers.

   ii. **Activities:** Establishing service contracts that outline maintenance schedules, response times, and service levels.

CLASSIFICATION:

The classification of cGMP (current Good Manufacturing Practice) typically refers to different aspects of GMP regulations and practices that are applied to ensure the safety, quality, and efficacy of pharmaceutical products. The classification can be understood through various categories such as GMP guidelines, facilities, equipment, and regulatory compliance. Here's a detailed breakdown with examples:

1. Regulatory Classification

a. **FDA (Food and Drug Administration) GMP:** In the United States, the FDA enforces GMP regulations for pharmaceuticals, biologics, and medical devices.

   i. **Example:** The FDA's 21 CFR Part 210 and Part 211 specify the GMP requirements for the manufacturing, processing, packing, or holding of drugs and their components.

b. **EMA (European Medicines Agency) GMP:** In Europe, the EMA provides guidelines and regulations for GMP compliance in the pharmaceutical industry.

i. **Example:** The EU Guidelines for Good Manufacturing Practice for Medicinal Products for Human and Veterinary Use outline requirements for facilities, quality control, and documentation.

c. **Other Regulatory Bodies:** Similar GMP regulations exist in other countries, such as the TGA (Therapeutic Goods Administration) in Australia, PMDA (Pharmaceuticals and Medical Devices Agency) in Japan, and Health Canada.

    i. **Example:** Health Canada's GMP guidelines are detailed in the "Guidance Document: Good Manufacturing Practices (GMP) for Pharmaceutical Drugs."

2. Facility Classification

a. **Cleanroom Classifications:** Cleanrooms are classified based on their cleanliness and control of airborne particles. This classification is crucial for environments where sensitive products are manufactured.

    i. **Example:** ISO Class 5 clean rooms are used for aseptic processing where the air cleanliness must be extremely high, and ISO Class 8 clean rooms are used for less critical areas where the environment is less controlled.

b. **Controlled Environment Areas:** Facilities are categorized based on environmental control, such as temperature and humidity.

    i. **Example:** Controlled storage areas for raw materials and finished products where temperature and humidity are regulated to prevent degradation.

3. Equipment Classification

a. **Critical Equipment:** Equipment that directly affects the quality of the product and must be meticulously maintained and calibrated.

    i. **Example:** High-Performance Liquid Chromatography (HPLC) systems used for quality control testing.

b. **Non-Critical Equipment:** Equipment that does not directly impact product quality but still requires maintenance and proper operation.

   i. **Example:** Laboratory refrigerators used for storing non-critical reagents.

4. Process Classification

a. **Batch Processing:** Classification of processes based on the batch size and production methods.

   i. **Example:** Large-scale batch processing for tablet production versus small-scale batch processing for clinical trial materials.

b. **Continuous Processing:** A type of manufacturing where materials are continuously fed into the process and products are continuously removed.

   i. **Example:** Continuous manufacturing of oral solid dosage forms like tablets or capsules.

5. Documentation Classification

a. **Records:** Documentation related to production, quality control, and compliance.

   i. **Example:** Batch production records, quality control test results, and equipment maintenance logs.

b. **Standard Operating Procedures (SOPs):** Detailed instructions for conducting operations and procedures.

   i. **Example:** SOPs for equipment cleaning, calibration, and maintenance procedures.

6. Quality Control Classification

a. **In-Process Testing:** Testing conducted during the manufacturing process to ensure that the product meets quality specifications.

   i. **Example:** Testing of in-process materials for potency, purity, and other attributes during tablet compression.

b. **Final Product Testing:** Testing conducted on the finished product to verify it meets all quality and safety standards before release.

i. **Example:** Testing for microbiological contamination, potency, and dissolution of final tablets.

7. Personnel Classification

a. **Qualified Personnel:** Classification of personnel based on their qualifications and training for handling specific GMP-related tasks.

  i. **Example:** Qualified individuals performing critical operations like sterile product manufacturing or quality control testing.

b. **Training Programs:** Programs designed to ensure personnel are adequately trained and competent in GMP practices.

  i. **Example:** Training programs on GMP compliance, equipment operation, and safety procedures.

8. Compliance and Auditing

a. **Internal Audits:** Regular audits conducted to ensure compliance with GMP standards within the facility.

  i. **Example:** Internal audits of production areas, quality control laboratories, and documentation practices.

b. **External Audits:** Audits conducted by regulatory agencies or third-party organizations to verify compliance with GMP regulations.

  i. **Example:** FDA inspections or GMP certification audits by organizations like the British Standards Institution (BSI).

Multiple Choice Questions (MCQs)

1. What enzyme is responsible for synthesizing cGMP from GTP?

   A) Adenylate cyclase

   B) Guanylate cyclase

   C) Phosphodiesterase

   D) Protein kinase G

2. Which type of guanylate cyclase is activated by nitric oxide (NO)?

A) Particulate guanylate cyclase (pGC)

B) Soluble guanylate cyclase (sGC)

C) Membrane-bound guanylate cyclase

D) Cytosolic guanylate cyclase

3. What enzyme degrades cGMP into GMP?

A) Guanylate cyclase

B) Protein kinase G

C) Phosphodiesterase (PDE)

D) Adenylate cyclase

4. What physiological role does cGMP play in smooth muscle cells?

A) Contraction

B) Relaxation

C) Aggregation

D) Proliferation

5. Which drug class works by inhibiting PDE5 to increase cGMP levels?

A) Beta-blockers

B) Calcium channel blockers

C) Phosphodiesterase inhibitors

D) ACE inhibitors

6. What is the primary objective of current Good Manufacturing Practices (cGMP)?

A) Reduce production costs

B) Ensure product quality and safety

C) Improve marketing strategies

D) Enhance product aesthetics

7. Which regulatory body enforces cGMP regulations in the United States?

A) EMA

B) WHO

C) FDA

D) TGA

8. What does the term "process validation" refer to in cGMP?
   A) Ensuring the cleaning process is effective
   B) Confirming that manufacturing processes consistently produce quality products
   C) Conducting market research
   D) Monitoring storage conditions
9. What is the purpose of preventive maintenance in a cGMP facility?
   A) To increase production speed
   B) To prevent equipment malfunctions
   C) To reduce labor costs
   D) To enhance product aesthetics
10. What type of environment is required for cleanrooms in a cGMP facility?
   A) Controlled environment
   B) Open environment
   C) Uncontrolled environment
   D) Outdoor environment
11. What does the acronym SOP stand for in the context of cGMP?
   A) Standard Operating Procedure
   B) Special Operating Plan
   C) Standard Operation Program
   D) Safety Operating Procedure
12. What is the role of HEPA filters in cleanrooms?
   A) To increase room temperature
   B) To filter out high-efficiency particles
   C) To reduce noise levels
   D) To enhance lighting conditions
13. What are Critical Quality Attributes (CQAs)?
   A) Attributes affecting product appearance

B) Attributes that must be controlled to ensure product quality

C) Marketing attributes

D) Cost-related attributes

14. Why are training programs essential in a cGMP facility?

A) To reduce salary expenses

B) To ensure personnel are informed and competent

C) To improve marketing strategies

D) To enhance product packaging

15. What is the primary goal of a Quality Management System (QMS) in a cGMP facility?

A) To increase production volume

B) To ensure product quality and regulatory compliance

C) To enhance product flavor

D) To reduce marketing costs

16. Which type of guanylate cyclase is activated by natriuretic peptides?

A) Soluble guanylate cyclase (sGC)

B) Particulate guanylate cyclase (pGC)

C) Membrane-bound guanylate cyclase

D) Cytosolic guanylate cyclase

17. What does the term "risk management" refer to in cGMP?

A) Identifying and mitigating risks related to marketing

B) Identifying and mitigating risks related to manufacturing processes and product quality

C) Increasing production speed

D) Enhancing product aesthetics

18. What is the purpose of cleanroom classifications in cGMP facilities?

A) To reduce production costs

B) To categorize cleanliness and control of airborne particles

C) To improve marketing strategies

D) To enhance product packaging

19. What does the acronym GMP stand for?

A) Good Marketing Practices

B) Good Manufacturing Practices

C) Great Manufacturing Processes

D) Global Manufacturing Protocols

20. What is the role of phosphodiesterases (PDEs) in the cGMP pathway?

A) Synthesize cGMP from GTP

B) Degrade cGMP into GMP

C) Activate guanylate cyclase

D) Inhibit protein kinase G

Short Answer Type Questions

1. Explain the synthesis of cGMP.
2. What is the role of phosphodiesterases in the cGMP pathway?
3. Describe the mechanism of action of cGMP in smooth muscle cells.
4. How do phosphodiesterase inhibitors like sildenafil work?
5. What are the primary objectives of current Good Manufacturing Practices (cGMP)?
6. Which regulatory body enforces cGMP regulations in Europe?
7. What is process validation and why is it important in cGMP?
8. Why is preventive maintenance essential in a cGMP facility?
9. What are cleanrooms and why are they important in cGMP facilities?
10. Define Standard Operating Procedures (SOPs) in the context of cGMP.
11. What is the purpose of HEPA filters in cleanrooms?
12. Explain the concept of Critical Quality Attributes (CQAs).
13. Why are training programs essential for personnel in a cGMP facility?
14. What is a Quality Management System (QMS) and why is it important?
15. Describe the activation of particulate guanylate cyclase (pGC).

16. What is risk management in the context of cGMP?
17. What are cleanroom classifications and why are they used in cGMP facilities?
18. What does GMP stand for and what does it encompass?
19. Explain the role of guanylate cyclase in the cGMP pathway.
20. Describe the importance of proper documentation and record-keeping in a cGMP facility.

Long Answer Type Questions

1. Discuss the synthesis, degradation, and mechanism of action of cGMP in detail.
2. Explain the primary objectives of current Good Manufacturing Practices (cGMP) and their importance in the pharmaceutical industry.
3. Describe the role and significance of cleanrooms in a cGMP facility.
4. What is process validation? Discuss its importance and the steps involved in ensuring a validated process in a cGMP facility.
5. Explain the various types of preventive maintenance required in a cGMP facility and their importance.
6. Describe the concept and components of a Quality Management System (QMS) in a cGMP facility.
7. Discuss the role of training and competency assessment in ensuring cGMP compliance.
8. Explain the regulatory framework for cGMP in the United States and Europe, highlighting key differences and similarities.
9. Discuss the importance of risk management in a cGMP facility and the strategies used to identify and mitigate risks.
10. Describe the role of phosphodiesterases (PDEs) in the cGMP pathway and the clinical relevance of PDE inhibitors.

Answer Key for MCQs

1. B) Guanylate cyclase
2. B) Soluble guanylate cyclase (sGC)
3. C) Phosphodiesterase (PDE)
4. B) Relaxation
5. C) Phosphodiesterase inhibitors
6. B) Ensure product quality and safety
7. C) FDA
8. B) Confirming that manufacturing processes consistently produce quality products
9. B) To prevent equipment malfunctions
10. A) Controlled environment
11. A) Standard Operating Procedure
12. B) To filter out high-efficiency particles
13. B) Attributes that must be controlled to ensure product quality
14. B) To ensure personnel are informed and competent
15. B) To ensure product quality and regulatory compliance
16. B) Particulate guanylate cyclase (pGC)
17. B) Identifying and mitigating risks related to manufacturing processes and product quality
18. B) To categorize cleanliness and control of airborne particles
19. B) Good Manufacturing Practices
20. B) Degrade cGMP into GMP

CHAPTER – 5

INDUSTRIAL MANAGEMENT

INTRODUCTION:

Industrial Management is a branch of management focused on overseeing and optimizing industrial operations. It involves the planning, organization, control, and execution of production processes in manufacturing and service industries. The goal is to improve efficiency, reduce costs, and ensure high-quality output while meeting organizational goals.

Key Aspects of Industrial Management

1. **Production Planning and Control**:
   a. **Production Planning**: Involves forecasting demand, scheduling production, and coordinating resources. Effective planning ensures that the right quantity of products is produced at the right time.
   b. **Production Control**: Monitoring and controlling the production process to ensure that it adheres to the planned schedule. This includes managing inventory, quality control, and troubleshooting issues.
2. **Operations Management**:
   a. **Process Design**: Designing efficient production processes and workflows to optimize resource use and minimize waste.
   b. **Facility Layout**: Planning the physical arrangement of machinery, equipment, and workstations to enhance productivity and safety.
3. **Supply Chain Management**:
   a. **Procurement**: Acquiring raw materials and components from suppliers.
   b. **Logistics**: Managing the transportation, warehousing, and distribution of products.

c. **Inventory Management**: Balancing inventory levels to meet demand while minimizing holding costs.

4. **Quality Management**:
   a. **Quality Assurance**: Ensuring that products meet established standards and specifications through systematic testing and inspection.
   b. **Quality Improvement**: Implementing continuous improvement programs such as Six Sigma or Total Quality Management (TQM) to enhance product quality and operational efficiency.
5. **Human Resource Management**:
   a. **Workforce Planning**: Recruiting, training, and managing employees to ensure that the organization has the necessary skills and capabilities.
   b. **Performance Management**: Evaluating and improving employee performance through appraisals, feedback, and development programs.
6. **Financial Management**:
   a. **Cost Control**: Monitoring and managing production costs to ensure profitability.
   b. **Budgeting**: Planning and controlling financial resources to align with strategic objectives.
7. **Maintenance Management**:
   a. **Preventive Maintenance**: Performing regular maintenance to prevent equipment failures and extend asset life.
   b. **Corrective Maintenance**: Addressing equipment breakdowns and malfunctions to minimize downtime.
8. **Health and Safety Management**:
   a. **Safety Protocols**: Developing and enforcing safety procedures to protect employees and reduce the risk of accidents.

b. **Compliance**: Ensuring adherence to regulatory standards and environmental guidelines.

9. **Technology and Innovation**:

   a. **Automation**: Implementing automated systems and machinery to improve production efficiency and accuracy.

   b. **Innovation**: Exploring and adopting new technologies and practices to stay competitive and meet changing market demands.

Importance of Industrial Management

1. **Efficiency**: Optimizes production processes to achieve higher efficiency and lower costs.
2. **Quality**: Ensures products meet quality standards, enhancing customer satisfaction and reducing returns.
3. **Competitiveness**: Helps organizations stay competitive by adopting innovative practices and technologies.
4. **Resource Management**: Manages resources effectively to prevent waste and maximize output.

PRODUCTION MANAGEMENT

Production Management is a critical component of Industrial Management that focuses on overseeing the production processes to ensure that goods are produced efficiently, cost-effectively, and to the desired quality standards. It involves the planning, coordination, and control of manufacturing activities, from the procurement of raw materials to the delivery of finished products.

Key Elements of Production Management

1. **Production Planning**:

   a. **Forecasting**: Predicting future demand for products based on historical data, market analysis, and sales trends. Accurate forecasting helps in aligning production schedules with anticipated demand.

b. **Capacity Planning**: Determining the production capacity needed to meet forecasted demand. This involves assessing equipment, labor, and facility requirements.
c. **Scheduling**: Developing detailed schedules for production activities. This includes creating timelines for the completion of tasks, managing work shifts, and setting deadlines for production milestones.

2. **Production Control**:
   a. **Workflow Management**: Designing and managing the sequence of operations in the production process. This ensures that tasks are completed in the most efficient order.
   b. **Inventory Management**: Monitoring and controlling the levels of raw materials, work-in-progress, and finished goods. Effective inventory management prevents shortages and excesses, which can impact production efficiency.
   c. **Quality Control**: Implementing systems to inspect and test products at various stages of production to ensure they meet quality standards. This includes setting quality criteria, conducting inspections, and addressing defects.
3. **Process Design**:
   a. **Process Selection**: Choosing the appropriate production processes (e.g., batch production, continuous production, job shop) based on product requirements and volume.
   b. **Facility Layout**: Designing the physical arrangement of production equipment and workstations to optimize workflow, reduce bottlenecks, and improve safety.
4. **Production Methods**:

a. **Job Production**: Producing custom or one-off items tailored to specific customer requirements. This method is often used for unique or high-value products.
b. **Batch Production**: Producing goods in batches or groups. This method is suitable for products with moderate demand and allows for some flexibility in production.
c. **Continuous Production**: Operating production lines without interruption to produce large volumes of standardized products. This method is used for high-volume, low-variability products.

5. **Resource Management**:
   a. **Material Management**: Ensuring that the necessary raw materials and components are available for production. This involves procurement, storage, and handling of materials.
   b. **Labor Management**: Recruiting, training, and managing workers to ensure they have the skills and motivation to perform their tasks efficiently.
6. **Technology and Automation**:
   a. **Automation**: Implementing automated systems and machinery to enhance production efficiency, precision, and consistency. Automation can reduce labor costs and minimize human error.
   b. **Technology Integration**: Utilizing advanced technologies such as Computer-Aided Design (CAD), Computer-Aided Manufacturing (CAM), and Enterprise Resource Planning (ERP) systems to streamline production processes.
7. **Cost Management**:
   a. **Cost Estimation**: Calculating the costs associated with production, including materials, labor, and overhead. Accurate cost estimation helps in pricing products competitively.

b. **Cost Control**: Monitoring and controlling production costs to ensure they align with budgeted figures. This involves identifying and reducing cost variances.

8. **Lean Production**:
   a. **Principles**: Adopting lean production principles to eliminate waste, improve efficiency, and enhance value to customers. This includes techniques such as Just-In-Time (JIT) production and Kaizen (continuous improvement).
   b. **Waste Reduction**: Identifying and minimizing various types of waste, such as overproduction, excess inventory, and defects.
9. **Performance Measurement**:
   a. **Key Performance Indicators (KPIs)**: Tracking metrics such as production output, efficiency, quality, and downtime to evaluate the performance of production operations.
   b. **Benchmarking**: Comparing production performance against industry standards or best practices to identify areas for improvement.

Importance of Production Management

1. **Efficiency**: Ensures that production processes are optimized for maximum efficiency and minimal waste.
2. **Quality**: Maintains high standards of product quality through effective quality control measures.
3. **Cost-effectiveness**: Helps in managing production costs and maximizing profitability.
4. **Customer Satisfaction**: Aligns production with customer demand to ensure timely delivery and product availability.

PRODUCTION ORGANIZATION

Production Organization in Industrial Management refers to the structured arrangement of roles, responsibilities, and processes involved in managing and executing production activities within a company. It encompasses the design of the organizational structure, coordination of production functions, and implementation of processes to ensure efficient and effective manufacturing operations.

Key Aspects of Production Organization

1. **Organizational Structure**:
    a. **Hierarchical Structure**: Traditional structure with a clear chain of command, including roles such as Production Manager, Supervisors, and Workers. Each level has specific responsibilities and authority.
    b. **Functional Structure**: Organizes employees based on their specialized functions (e.g., Production, Quality Control, Maintenance). Each function is managed separately but must work together to achieve production goals.
    c. **Matrix Structure**: Combines elements of both functional and project-based structures. Employees report to both a functional manager and a project manager, allowing for flexibility and better coordination across projects.
2. **Production Roles and Responsibilities**:
    a. **Production Manager**: Oversees the overall production process, including planning, scheduling, and resource allocation. Ensures that production targets are met and quality standards are maintained.
    b. **Production Supervisors**: Manage day-to-day operations on the shop floor. They supervise workers, coordinate activities, and address any issues that arise during production.
    c. **Production Workers**: Operate machinery, assemble products, and perform various tasks required for production. Their performance directly impacts production efficiency and quality.

d. **Quality Control Inspectors**: Monitor and inspect products to ensure they meet quality standards. They report defects and collaborate with production teams to resolve quality issues.
e. **Maintenance Personnel**: Responsible for the upkeep and repair of machinery and equipment to prevent downtime and ensure smooth operations.

3. **Production Planning and Coordination**:
   a. **Production Planning**: Involves creating production schedules, estimating resource needs, and coordinating with procurement and logistics to ensure timely availability of materials and equipment.
   b. **Coordination**: Ensures effective communication and collaboration between different departments (e.g., Production, Supply Chain, Quality) to align production activities with overall business objectives.
4. **Production Processes**:
   a. **Process Design**: Developing efficient workflows and layouts for production processes. This includes deciding on equipment setup, task sequences, and handling methods to optimize production.
   b. **Standard Operating Procedures (SOPs)**: Documented procedures that outline the steps for performing production tasks. SOPs ensure consistency and adherence to quality standards.
5. **Resource Management**:
   a. **Material Management**: Ensuring that raw materials, components, and supplies are available when needed. This involves inventory control, procurement, and supplier management.
   b. **Human Resource Management**: Recruiting, training, and managing production staff. Ensures that workers have the necessary skills and motivation to perform their roles effectively.
6. **Production Control**:

a. **Monitoring**: Tracking production progress, equipment performance, and worker output. Use of real-time data and performance metrics to manage and adjust production processes.
b. **Problem Solving**: Addressing issues such as equipment failures, quality defects, and delays. Implementing corrective actions and continuous improvement practices.

7. **Technology and Automation**:
   a. **Automation Integration**: Incorporating automated systems and machinery to enhance production efficiency, reduce labor costs, and improve consistency.
   b. **Technology Management**: Managing the implementation and maintenance of production technologies such as Manufacturing Execution Systems (MES) and Computer-Aided Manufacturing (CAM).
8. **Safety and Compliance**:
   a. **Safety Management**: Implementing safety protocols and practices to ensure a safe working environment. This includes training, safety equipment, and adherence to regulatory standards.
   b. **Compliance**: Ensuring that production activities comply with industry regulations, environmental laws, and quality standards.
9. **Performance Evaluation**:
   a. **Key Performance Indicators (KPIs)**: Measuring production performance through metrics such as output rates, defect rates, and efficiency. KPIs help in assessing the effectiveness of production processes and identifying areas for improvement.
   b. **Continuous Improvement**: Implementing initiatives to enhance production processes, reduce waste, and improve overall performance. Techniques such as Lean Manufacturing and Six Sigma are commonly used.

Importance of Production Organization

1. **Efficiency**: An effective production organization ensures streamlined operations, optimal resource utilization, and reduced waste.
2. **Quality**: Proper organization and management of production processes contribute to high product quality and consistency.
3. **Cost Control**: Helps in managing production costs by optimizing resource use and minimizing downtime.
4. **Coordination**: Facilitates effective communication and collaboration between different departments, leading to better alignment with organizational goals.

MATERIALS MANAGEMENT

Materials Management is a crucial aspect of Industrial Management that involves overseeing the acquisition, storage, and utilization of materials required for production. Effective materials management ensures that the right materials are available at the right time, in the right quantities, and at the right cost. This function plays a key role in optimizing production efficiency, minimizing costs, and maintaining product quality.

Key Aspects of Materials Management

1. **Material Planning**:
    a. **Demand Forecasting**: Predicting the future demand for materials based on production schedules, sales forecasts, and historical data. Accurate forecasting helps in planning the procurement of materials and avoiding shortages or excess inventory.
    b. **Material Requirements Planning (MRP)**: A systematic approach to determine the quantities and timing of material requirements based on the production schedule. MRP systems help in planning and controlling inventory levels.
2. **Procurement**:

a. **Supplier Selection**: Identifying and selecting suppliers who can provide materials that meet quality, cost, and delivery requirements. This involves evaluating potential suppliers based on criteria such as price, reliability, and service.
b. **Purchasing**: Placing orders for materials from selected suppliers. This includes negotiating terms and conditions, managing contracts, and ensuring timely delivery of materials.
c. **Vendor Management**: Building and maintaining strong relationships with suppliers. Effective vendor management includes monitoring supplier performance, resolving issues, and fostering collaboration.

3. **Inventory Management**:
   a. **Inventory Control**: Managing the levels of raw materials, work-in-progress, and finished goods to ensure that inventory is maintained at optimal levels. This involves tracking inventory levels, reordering materials, and minimizing carrying costs.
   b. **Stock Replenishment**: Implementing systems to replenish stock as it is consumed. This includes setting reorder points and managing safety stock to prevent stockouts.
   c. **Inventory Valuation**: Determining the value of inventory using methods such as First-In-First-Out (FIFO), Last-In-First-Out (LIFO), or Weighted Average Cost. Accurate inventory valuation is important for financial reporting and cost management.
4. **Storage and Handling**:
   a. **Warehouse Management**: Organizing and managing storage facilities to ensure efficient handling and retrieval of materials. This includes optimizing warehouse layout, implementing inventory tracking systems, and ensuring proper storage conditions.

b. **Material Handling**: Managing the movement of materials within the warehouse and production facility. This includes using equipment such as forklifts, conveyors, and automated systems to handle materials efficiently and safely.

5. **Quality Control**:
   a. **Material Inspection**: Inspecting incoming materials to ensure they meet quality standards and specifications. This includes conducting tests and inspections to verify material quality.
   b. **Supplier Quality Assurance**: Working with suppliers to ensure that materials consistently meet quality requirements. This may involve setting quality standards, conducting audits, and addressing quality issues.
6. **Cost Management**:
   a. **Cost Analysis**: Analyzing the costs associated with acquiring and managing materials. This includes evaluating material costs, transportation costs, and storage costs.
   b. **Cost Control**: Implementing measures to control and reduce material costs. This includes negotiating better terms with suppliers, optimizing inventory levels, and reducing waste.
7. **Logistics**:
   a. **Transportation Management**: Coordinating the transportation of materials from suppliers to the production facility. This includes selecting transportation methods, managing shipping schedules, and ensuring timely delivery.
   b. **Distribution**: Managing the distribution of finished products to customers. This involves planning distribution routes, managing shipping logistics, and coordinating with distribution partners.
8. **Technology and Systems**:

   a. **Materials Management Systems**: Implementing software solutions such as Enterprise Resource Planning (ERP) and Warehouse Management Systems (WMS) to streamline materials management processes. These systems help in tracking inventory, managing procurement, and improving overall efficiency.
   b. **Automation**: Utilizing automated systems for inventory tracking, order processing, and material handling to enhance accuracy and reduce manual labor.
9. **Sustainability and Compliance**:
   a. **Sustainable Sourcing**: Implementing practices to source materials responsibly and reduce environmental impact. This includes selecting suppliers who adhere to environmental and ethical standards.
   b. **Regulatory Compliance**: Ensuring that materials management practices comply with relevant regulations and standards, such as safety, environmental, and industry-specific requirements.

Importance of Materials Management

1. **Efficiency**: Ensures that materials are available when needed, reducing production delays and improving operational efficiency.
2. **Cost Control**: Helps in managing material costs and minimizing excess inventory, leading to cost savings and improved profitability.
3. **Quality Assurance**: Maintains high product quality by ensuring that materials meet required standards and specifications.
4. **Customer Satisfaction**: Ensures timely availability of products by managing materials effectively, leading to improved customer satisfaction and on-time delivery.

HANDLING AND TRANSPORTATION

Handling and Transportation are critical components of Industrial Management, focused on the efficient movement and management of materials and products within and between facilities. These processes are essential for ensuring that materials are available where and when needed, minimizing costs, and maintaining product quality.

Key Aspects of Handling and Transportation

1. Material Handling

Material Handling involves the movement, protection, and storage of materials and products throughout the production process. It includes the following aspects:

a. **Handling Equipment**: Utilization of various equipment to move materials safely and efficiently. Common types of equipment include:
    i. **Forklifts**: Used for lifting and transporting heavy materials.
    ii. **Conveyors**: Automated systems for moving materials along production lines.
    iii. **Cranes**: Used for lifting and moving large or heavy items.
    iv. **Pallet Jacks**: For moving pallets within a warehouse or production facility.

b. **Handling Techniques**:
    i. **Manual Handling**: Involves human effort for lifting, carrying, and moving materials. It requires proper ergonomics and safety practices to prevent injuries.
    ii. **Mechanical Handling**: Utilizes machines and equipment to move materials, reducing manual labor and increasing efficiency.

c. **Safety and Ergonomics**: Ensuring safe handling practices to prevent accidents and injuries. This includes proper training for personnel, using appropriate protective equipment, and adhering to safety guidelines.

d. **Storage Systems**:
    i. **Racking Systems**: Shelving and racking solutions for organizing materials and products in storage areas.

ii. **Automated Storage and Retrieval Systems (AS/RS)**: Automated systems for efficiently storing and retrieving materials from warehouses.

e. **Inventory Management**: Accurate tracking of inventory levels and locations to ensure materials are available when needed and to prevent stockouts or overstocking.

2. Transportation:

Transportation refers to the movement of materials and products from one location to another, whether within a facility, between facilities, or to customers. It includes the following aspects:

a. **Transportation Modes**:

i. **Road Transportation**: Includes trucks, lorries, and vans for transporting goods overland. It is versatile and commonly used for short to medium distances.

ii. **Rail Transportation**: Uses trains for transporting large quantities of goods over long distances. It is cost-effective for bulk shipments.

iii. **Air Transportation**: Provides fast delivery for high-value or time-sensitive goods. It is more expensive compared to other modes but offers speed and reliability.

iv. **Sea Transportation**: Utilizes ships for transporting goods across oceans and seas. It is cost-effective for international shipping of bulk goods.

b. **Logistics Management**:

i. **Routing and Scheduling**: Planning and optimizing transportation routes and schedules to ensure timely delivery and minimize transportation costs.

ii. **Fleet Management**: Managing and maintaining a fleet of vehicles or carriers to ensure they are in good working condition and efficiently utilized.

c. **Loading and Unloading**:

i. **Loading**: Ensuring that goods are properly loaded onto transportation vehicles or containers. This includes securing items to prevent damage during transit.

ii. **Unloading**: Safely removing goods from transportation vehicles or containers upon arrival at their destination.

d. **Packaging**:

i. **Packaging Design**: Creating packaging that protects products during transportation and handling. It should be sturdy, secure, and suitable for the type of product.

ii. **Labeling**: Properly labeling packages with information such as handling instructions, destination, and contents to facilitate efficient handling and transportation.

e. **Documentation**:

i. **Shipping Documents**: Preparing and managing documents such as bills of lading, invoices, and customs paperwork to ensure smooth transportation and compliance with regulations.

ii. **Tracking and Visibility**: Using tracking systems to monitor the location and status of shipments in real-time. This helps in providing updates to customers and managing potential delays.

f. **Cost Management**:

i. **Cost Analysis**: Evaluating transportation costs and identifying opportunities for cost savings, such as optimizing routes, consolidating shipments, and negotiating with carriers.

ii. **Cost Control**: Implementing measures to manage and reduce transportation expenses, including fuel management and maintenance of transportation assets.

g. **Sustainability**:

i. **Eco-friendly Practices**: Adopting sustainable practices in transportation, such as using energy-efficient vehicles, reducing emissions, and optimizing routes to minimize environmental impact.

ii. **Green Logistics**: Implementing strategies to reduce the carbon footprint of logistics operations, including improving packaging materials and reducing waste.

Importance of Handling and Transportation

1. **Efficiency**: Effective handling and transportation processes streamline operations, reduce delays, and improve overall efficiency in the supply chain.
2. **Cost Control**: Proper management of handling and transportation reduces costs associated with labor, equipment, and transportation services.
3. **Product Quality**: Ensures that materials and products are transported and handled in a way that maintains their quality and prevents damage.
4. **Customer Satisfaction**: Timely and accurate delivery of products enhances customer satisfaction and supports reliable service.

INVENTORY MANAGEMENT AND CONTROL

Inventory Management and Control are essential aspects of Industrial Management that involve overseeing and optimizing inventory levels to ensure that materials and products are available when needed, while minimizing costs and avoiding excess stock. Effective inventory management is crucial for maintaining operational efficiency, reducing costs, and meeting customer demands.

Key Aspects of Inventory Management and Control

1. Inventory Planning

a. **Demand Forecasting**: Predicting future demand for products based on historical data, market trends, and sales projections. Accurate forecasting helps in planning the right inventory levels to meet customer needs without overstocking or understocking.

b. **Inventory Models**: Utilizing inventory management models to determine optimal stock levels and reorder points. Common models include:

   i. **Economic Order Quantity (EOQ)**: Calculates the optimal order quantity that minimizes the total cost of ordering and holding inventory.

   ii. **Just-In-Time (JIT)**: Aims to reduce inventory levels by ordering materials only when needed, reducing holding costs and minimizing waste.

2. Inventory Control

a. **Inventory Tracking**: Monitoring inventory levels in real-time using systems such as barcodes, RFID (Radio-Frequency Identification), or inventory management software. Accurate tracking ensures that inventory levels are up-to-date and helps in preventing stockouts or overstocking.

b. **Reorder Points**: Setting predetermined inventory levels at which new orders should be placed. Reorder points are calculated based on lead times, demand variability, and safety stock levels.

c. **Safety Stock**: Maintaining a buffer stock of inventory to account for uncertainties in demand or supply. Safety stock helps prevent stockouts and ensures that production and customer orders can be fulfilled even during unexpected disruptions.

3. Inventory Valuation

a. **Valuation Methods**: Determining the value of inventory using various accounting methods. Common valuation methods include:

i. **First-In-First-Out (FIFO)**: Assumes that the oldest inventory items are sold first. This method is useful for perishable goods and ensures that older inventory is used before newer stock.

ii. **Last-In-First-Out (LIFO)**: Assumes that the most recent inventory items are sold first. This method can be used for non-perishable goods and may help in managing inflation impacts.

iii. **Weighted Average Cost**: Calculates the average cost of inventory items based on the total cost of goods available for sale. This method smooths out price fluctuations over time.

4. Inventory Optimization

a. **Inventory Turnover Ratio**: Measuring how quickly inventory is sold and replaced over a specific period. A higher turnover ratio indicates efficient inventory management and better sales performance.

b. **ABC Analysis**: Classifying inventory items into categories (A, B, and C) based on their importance and value. Category A items are high-value and require close monitoring, while Category C items are lower value and can be managed with less frequent reviews.

c. **Cycle Counting**: Conducting periodic physical counts of inventory to verify accuracy and reconcile discrepancies with inventory records. Cycle counting helps maintain inventory accuracy without disrupting operations.

5. Inventory Replenishment

a. **Order Quantities**: Determining the appropriate order quantities based on factors such as demand, lead time, and storage capacity. Replenishment orders should align with inventory planning and control strategies.

b. **Supplier Management**: Working with suppliers to ensure timely delivery of materials and maintaining good relationships to support reliable and consistent supply.

6. Technology and Systems

a. **Inventory Management Software**: Implementing software solutions to automate and streamline inventory management processes. These systems provide features such as real-time tracking, reporting, and analytics.
b. **Automated Systems**: Utilizing technologies such as automated storage and retrieval systems (AS/RS), warehouse management systems (WMS), and enterprise resource planning (ERP) systems to improve inventory management efficiency.

7. Cost Management

a. **Carrying Costs**: Managing the costs associated with holding inventory, including storage, insurance, and obsolescence. Minimizing carrying costs helps improve overall profitability.
b. **Order Costs**: Controlling costs related to placing and receiving inventory orders. This includes purchasing, shipping, and handling costs.

8. Compliance and Risk Management

a. **Regulatory Compliance**: Ensuring that inventory management practices comply with relevant regulations and industry standards. This includes adhering to safety, environmental, and quality requirements.
b. **Risk Management**: Identifying and mitigating risks associated with inventory, such as supply chain disruptions, obsolescence, and inventory shrinkage. Implementing risk management strategies helps maintain inventory integrity and operational continuity.

Importance of Inventory Management and Control

a. **Efficiency**: Optimizes inventory levels to meet demand while minimizing holding costs and reducing stockouts or excess inventory.
b. **Cost Savings**: Reduces carrying costs, ordering costs, and potential losses from obsolescence or spoilage.
c. **Customer Satisfaction**: Ensures timely availability of products to meet customer orders and improve service levels.

d. **Operational Performance**: Enhances overall operational efficiency by maintaining accurate inventory records and improving supply chain coordination.

PRODUCTION AND PLANNING CONTROL

Production and Planning Control (PPC) is a vital component of Industrial Management that focuses on coordinating and managing production activities to ensure efficient, timely, and cost-effective manufacturing processes. It involves planning, scheduling, controlling, and monitoring production operations to meet organizational goals and customer demands.

Key Aspects of Production and Planning Control

1. Production Planning

Production Planning involves determining the necessary resources, schedules, and procedures required to produce goods efficiently. Key elements include:

a. **Forecasting**: Predicting future demand for products based on historical data, market trends, and sales projections. Accurate forecasting helps in creating realistic production plans.

b. **Master Production Schedule (MPS)**: A detailed plan that outlines what products need to be produced, in what quantities, and when. It serves as a guide for the production process and aligns with overall business goals.

c. **Resource Planning**: Identifying and allocating the resources required for production, including raw materials, machinery, labor, and facilities. This ensures that resources are available and used efficiently.

d. **Capacity Planning**: Determining the production capacity needed to meet forecasted demand. It involves assessing equipment capabilities, workforce availability, and facility constraints to ensure that production goals can be achieved.

e. **Material Requirements Planning (MRP)**: A system used to calculate the quantities of raw materials and components needed for production.

MRP helps in scheduling material procurement and inventory management.

2. Production Scheduling

Production Scheduling involves creating a timeline for production activities to ensure that products are manufactured on time and in the right quantities. Key elements include:

a. **Detailed Scheduling**: Developing a schedule that specifies the sequence of production activities, machine usage, and labor assignments. This includes setting start and end times for each production task.
b. **Work Orders**: Generating work orders that provide instructions for production tasks, including the materials to be used, production processes, and quality standards.
c. **Gantt Charts**: Using visual tools like Gantt charts to represent the production schedule, showing task durations, dependencies, and progress. This helps in tracking production timelines and identifying potential delays.
d. **Priority Setting**: Establishing priorities for production tasks based on factors such as customer orders, product urgency, and resource availability. This ensures that critical tasks are completed on time.

3. Production Control

Production Control involves monitoring and managing production processes to ensure they are carried out as planned. Key elements include:

a. **Real-Time Monitoring**: Tracking production progress in real-time to ensure that operations are running smoothly and according to schedule. This includes monitoring equipment performance, labor productivity, and material usage.
b. **Quality Control**: Implementing quality control measures to ensure that products meet specified standards and requirements. This includes inspecting products, conducting tests, and addressing quality issues.

c. **Problem Resolution**: Identifying and resolving production issues such as equipment breakdowns, material shortages, and process deviations. Effective problem resolution helps minimize production disruptions and maintain efficiency.

d. **Performance Metrics**: Measuring production performance using key performance indicators (KPIs) such as production output, cycle time, defect rates, and efficiency. KPIs provide insights into production performance and areas for improvement.

4. Inventory Management

Inventory Management is closely related to production planning and control, involving the management of raw materials, work-in-progress, and finished goods. Key elements include:

a. **Inventory Levels**: Maintaining optimal inventory levels to ensure that materials and products are available when needed, while minimizing carrying costs and avoiding excess inventory.

b. **Reorder Points**: Setting reorder points for materials to trigger procurement orders when inventory levels fall below a specified threshold. This helps in preventing stockouts and ensuring timely availability of materials.

c. **Stock Audits**: Conducting regular stock audits to verify inventory accuracy and reconcile discrepancies between physical counts and inventory records.

5. Production Optimization

Production Optimization involves improving production processes to enhance efficiency, reduce costs, and improve product quality. Key elements include:

a. **Lean Manufacturing**: Implementing lean principles to eliminate waste, streamline processes, and enhance overall production efficiency. Lean techniques include value stream mapping, 5S, and continuous improvement.

b. **Six Sigma**: Utilizing Six Sigma methodologies to improve production quality and reduce defects by identifying and addressing process variations. This involves using statistical tools and techniques to drive process improvements.
c. **Capacity Utilization**: Maximizing the utilization of production resources, including machinery, labor, and facilities, to achieve optimal production output and efficiency.

6. Communication and Coordination

Communication and Coordination are essential for effective production and planning control, involving:

a. **Cross-Functional Collaboration**: Coordinating between different departments such as production, procurement, quality control, and sales to align production activities with overall business objectives.
b. **Information Flow**: Ensuring timely and accurate information flow between production teams, management, and other stakeholders. Effective communication helps in coordinating activities and addressing issues promptly.

7. Technology and Systems

Technology and Systems play a significant role in production and planning control:

a. **Production Management Software**: Implementing software solutions for managing production planning, scheduling, and control. These systems provide features such as real-time monitoring, reporting, and analytics.
b. **Automation**: Utilizing automation technologies such as robotics, automated production lines, and process control systems to enhance production efficiency and consistency.

c. **ERP Systems**: Integrating production planning and control processes with Enterprise Resource Planning (ERP) systems to streamline operations and improve data visibility.

Importance of Production and Planning Control

a. **Efficiency**: Ensures that production processes are optimized, minimizing delays and resource wastage while maximizing output.

b. **Cost Management**: Helps in managing production costs, including labor, materials, and overhead, by optimizing resource utilization and minimizing waste.

c. **Product Quality**: Maintains high product quality by implementing quality control measures and addressing issues promptly.

d. **Customer Satisfaction**: Ensures timely delivery of products and meets customer demands by aligning production schedules with market requirements.

SALES FORECASTING

Sales Forecasting is a critical aspect of Industrial Management that involves predicting future sales based on historical data, market analysis, and other relevant factors. Accurate sales forecasting is essential for effective planning, resource allocation, and decision-making in various areas such as production, inventory management, and financial planning.

Key Aspects of Sales Forecasting

1. Importance of Sales Forecasting

a. **Demand Planning**: Helps in predicting future demand for products, enabling companies to plan production schedules, manage inventory levels, and align supply chain activities.

b. **Resource Allocation**: Assists in allocating resources such as labor, materials, and equipment based on anticipated sales volumes.

c. **Financial Planning**: Provides insights into future revenue and cash flow, aiding in budgeting, financial forecasting, and investment decisions.

d. **Strategic Planning**: Supports long-term strategic planning by providing a basis for setting business goals, identifying growth opportunities, and assessing market potential.

2. Sales Forecasting Methods

Sales forecasting methods can be broadly categorized into quantitative and qualitative approaches:

a. **Quantitative Methods**: Rely on historical sales data and statistical techniques to predict future sales. Common quantitative methods include:

   i. **Time Series Analysis**: Analyzing historical sales data over time to identify patterns and trends. Techniques include:

      1. **Moving Averages**: Calculating the average sales over a specific time period to smooth out fluctuations and identify trends.

      2. **Exponential Smoothing**: Applying weighted averages to recent sales data, giving more weight to recent observations to predict future sales.

   ii. **Regression Analysis**: Using statistical methods to model the relationship between sales and one or more independent variables (e.g., marketing spend, economic indicators). Regression models help in understanding how changes in independent variables impact sales.

   iii. **Sales Trend Analysis**: Identifying long-term trends in sales data and using them to project future sales. This includes analyzing growth rates, seasonality, and cyclic patterns.

b. **Qualitative Methods**: Based on expert judgment, market research, and subjective analysis. Common qualitative methods include:

   i. **Expert Judgment**: Relying on the knowledge and experience of sales managers, industry experts, and key stakeholders to make forecasts based on their insights and understanding of market conditions.

ii. **Market Research**: Conducting surveys, interviews, and focus groups to gather information about customer preferences, market trends, and competitive dynamics. Market research helps in understanding potential demand and market opportunities.

iii. **Delphi Method**: Using a structured process to obtain consensus forecasts from a panel of experts. The Delphi method involves multiple rounds of questioning and feedback to refine and converge on a forecast.

iv. **Sales Force Composite**: Collecting input from the sales team on their expectations and insights regarding future sales. Salespeople's knowledge of customer behavior and market conditions can provide valuable input for forecasting.

3. Sales Forecasting Process

a. **Data Collection**: Gathering historical sales data, market information, and other relevant data sources. Accurate data collection is crucial for developing reliable forecasts.

b. **Data Analysis**: Analyzing historical data to identify patterns, trends, and correlations. This involves using statistical tools and techniques to process and interpret data.

c. **Forecast Development**: Applying forecasting methods to develop sales projections. This includes selecting appropriate methods, building forecasting models, and generating forecasts.

d. **Validation and Adjustment**: Evaluating the accuracy of forecasts by comparing them with actual sales data. Adjustments may be needed based on new information, changing market conditions, or feedback from stakeholders.

e. **Communication and Implementation**: Sharing forecasts with relevant departments, such as production, marketing, and finance, to ensure alignment with operational and strategic plans. Implementing actions based on forecasted sales, such as adjusting production schedules or inventory levels.

4. Challenges in Sales Forecasting

a. **Data Accuracy**: Ensuring the accuracy and reliability of historical sales data and other inputs used for forecasting. Inaccurate data can lead to flawed forecasts.

b. **Market Uncertainty**: Accounting for external factors such as economic conditions, market trends, and competitive actions that can impact sales. Unpredictable events and changes in the market can affect forecast accuracy.

c. **Forecast Bias**: Avoiding biases in forecasting, such as overestimating or underestimating sales based on subjective opinions or optimistic assumptions.

d. **Changing Trends**: Adapting forecasts to reflect changes in consumer behavior, technological advancements, and industry dynamics. Staying updated with market trends is essential for accurate forecasting.

5. Best Practices in Sales Forecasting

a. **Regular Review**: Continuously reviewing and updating forecasts based on new data, market conditions, and business performance. Regular adjustments help maintain forecast accuracy.

b. **Cross-Functional Collaboration**: Collaborating with different departments, such as sales, marketing, and finance, to gather diverse perspectives and insights for more accurate forecasts.

c. **Scenario Planning**: Developing multiple forecast scenarios based on different assumptions and potential outcomes. Scenario planning helps in preparing for various possibilities and managing uncertainties.

d. **Leverage Technology**: Utilizing advanced forecasting tools and software that offer predictive analytics, machine learning, and data visualization capabilities. Technology can enhance the accuracy and efficiency of the forecasting process.

BUDGET AND COST CONTROL

Budget and Cost Control are crucial components of Industrial Management that focus on managing financial resources effectively to achieve organizational goals, maintain profitability, and ensure efficient operations. Effective budgeting and cost control help in planning financial activities, monitoring expenditures, and making informed decisions.

Key Aspects of Budget and Cost Control

1. Budgeting

Budgeting involves creating a detailed financial plan that outlines expected revenues, expenses, and capital investments for a specific period. Key aspects of budgeting include:

a. **Types of Budgets**:

   i. **Operational Budget**: Covers day-to-day expenses related to production, sales, and administrative activities. It includes revenues, direct costs (materials and labor), and overheads.

   ii. **Capital Budget**: Focuses on long-term investments in assets such as machinery, facilities, and technology. It evaluates the cost, benefits, and return on investment (ROI) of capital projects.

   iii. **Cash Flow Budget**: Projects cash inflows and outflows to ensure sufficient liquidity for operational needs and to manage cash flow effectively.

   iv. **Flexible Budget**: Adjusts budgeted figures based on changes in activity levels or operational conditions. It helps in comparing actual performance against flexible targets.

b. **Budget Preparation Process**:

i. **Setting Objectives**: Defining financial goals and objectives aligned with the organization's strategic plan.
ii. **Gathering Data**: Collecting historical financial data, market trends, and forecasts to inform the budgeting process.
iii. **Developing Assumptions**: Making assumptions about future revenues, costs, and economic conditions. These assumptions form the basis for budget projections.
iv. **Creating the Budget**: Developing detailed budget plans for different departments or cost centers. This includes estimating revenues, expenses, and investments.
v. **Approval and Implementation**: Reviewing and approving the budget at various organizational levels before implementation. Communicating the budget to relevant departments and stakeholders.

c. **Budget Variance Analysis**:

i. **Variance Analysis**: Comparing actual financial performance against the budgeted figures to identify deviations or variances. Variance analysis helps in understanding the reasons for deviations and taking corrective actions.
ii. **Types of Variances**: Analyzing different types of variances, such as favorable (actual costs are lower than budgeted) or unfavorable (actual costs exceed budgeted amounts).

2. Cost Control:

Cost Control involves monitoring and managing costs to ensure they align with the budget and organizational objectives. Key aspects of cost control include:

a. **Cost Classification**:

i. **Fixed Costs**: Costs that remain constant regardless of production levels, such as rent, salaries, and insurance.

ii. **Variable Costs**: Costs that vary with production levels, such as raw materials, direct labor, and utility expenses.

iii. **Semi-Variable Costs**: Costs that have both fixed and variable components, such as maintenance expenses and certain utilities.

b. **Cost Management Techniques**:

i. **Standard Costing**: Establishing standard costs for materials, labor, and overhead based on historical data and industry benchmarks. Comparing actual costs with standard costs to identify variances and inefficiencies.

ii. **Activity-Based Costing (ABC)**: Allocating costs based on activities and resource consumption rather than traditional cost allocation methods. ABC provides a more accurate understanding of cost drivers and profitability.

iii. **Cost-Volume-Profit (CVP) Analysis**: Analyzing the relationship between costs, sales volume, and profits to make informed decisions about pricing, production levels, and profitability.

c. **Cost Reduction Strategies**:

i. **Cost Benchmarking**: Comparing costs with industry standards or competitors to identify areas for improvement and cost-saving opportunities.

ii. **Process Improvement**: Implementing process improvement techniques such as Lean Manufacturing or Six Sigma to reduce waste, enhance efficiency, and lower costs.

iii. **Supplier Management**: Negotiating with suppliers for better terms, prices, or bulk discounts to reduce procurement costs.

d. **Monitoring and Reporting**:

i. **Cost Tracking**: Continuously monitoring actual costs against budgeted amounts to ensure adherence to financial plans. This involves tracking expenses, reviewing financial statements, and using cost control tools.

ii. **Cost Reports**: Generating regular cost reports to provide insights into spending patterns, cost drivers, and areas requiring attention. Reports help in evaluating cost control performance and making data-driven decisions.

e. **Performance Measurement**:

i. **Key Performance Indicators (KPIs)**: Using KPIs to measure cost control effectiveness and operational efficiency. Common KPIs include cost per unit, return on investment (ROI), and cost variance percentages.

ii. **Cost Control Audits**: Conducting periodic audits to review cost control processes, identify weaknesses, and ensure compliance with financial policies.

Importance of Budget and Cost Control

a. **Financial Management**: Helps in managing financial resources effectively, ensuring that expenditures are within budgetary limits and aligned with organizational goals.

b. **Profitability**: Supports maintaining or improving profitability by controlling costs and optimizing resource utilization.

c. **Decision Making**: Provides valuable financial information for making informed decisions regarding investments, pricing, and operational strategies.

d. **Operational Efficiency**: Enhances operational efficiency by identifying cost-saving opportunities and improving cost management practices.

INDUSTRIAL AND PERSONAL RELATIONSHIP

Industrial and Personal Relationships in Industrial Management focus on the interactions between individuals and groups within an organization and between the organization and its external stakeholders. Effective management of these relationships is crucial for fostering a positive work environment, enhancing employee satisfaction, and achieving organizational goals.

Key Aspects of Industrial and Personal Relationships

1. Industrial Relations

Industrial Relations involve the relationship between employers, employees, and trade unions. It encompasses the systems, policies, and practices that govern workplace interactions and employment conditions.

a. **Employee Relations**:

   i. **Communication**: Establishing effective channels of communication between employees and management. Open communication helps in addressing concerns, sharing information, and fostering a collaborative work environment.

   ii. **Employee Engagement**: Creating a work environment that motivates employees and encourages their active participation in achieving organizational goals. Employee engagement initiatives include recognition programs, feedback mechanisms, and opportunities for professional development.

   iii. **Conflict Resolution**: Implementing mechanisms to address and resolve conflicts between employees and management. This includes grievance procedures, mediation, and negotiation to find mutually acceptable solutions.

b. **Trade Unions**:

   i. **Collective Bargaining**: Engaging in negotiations with trade unions to establish terms and conditions of employment, such as wages, working hours, and benefits. Collective bargaining agreements (CBAs) define the rights and responsibilities of both parties.

   ii. **Labor Law Compliance**: Adhering to labor laws and regulations governing employment practices, worker rights, and working conditions. Compliance helps in avoiding legal disputes and maintaining a fair work environment.

c. **Workplace Policies**:

   i. **Human Resource Policies**: Developing and implementing policies related to recruitment, training, performance management, and employee welfare. Clear HR policies help in maintaining consistency and fairness in employee management.

   ii. **Health and Safety**: Ensuring a safe and healthy work environment by adhering to occupational health and safety standards. Implementing safety protocols, providing training, and conducting regular inspections contribute to a safe workplace.

2. Personal Relationships:

Personal Relationships within the workplace focus on the interpersonal dynamics between individuals, including relationships with colleagues, supervisors, and subordinates.

a. **Team Dynamics**:

   i. **Team Building**: Fostering collaboration and cooperation among team members through team-building activities, workshops, and collaborative projects. Strong team dynamics enhance productivity and job satisfaction.

   ii. **Leadership**: Effective leadership involves building positive relationships with team members, providing guidance, support, and feedback. Leaders play a crucial role in shaping team culture and motivating employees.

b. **Employee Well-being**:

   i. **Work-Life Balance**: Supporting employees in balancing their professional and personal lives. Offering flexible work arrangements, wellness programs, and support services contributes to employee well-being and job satisfaction.

ii. **Stress Management**: Providing resources and support for managing work-related stress. Stress management programs, counseling services, and workload adjustments help in maintaining employee health and productivity.

c. **Recognition and Motivation**:

i. **Recognition Programs**: Implementing programs to acknowledge and reward employee achievements and contributions. Recognition boosts morale, enhances motivation, and reinforces positive behaviors.

ii. **Career Development**: Offering opportunities for career growth and advancement. Providing training, mentorship, and clear career paths helps employees achieve their professional goals and enhances job satisfaction.

3. Organizational Culture:

Organizational Culture refers to the shared values, beliefs, and practices that shape behavior within an organization. It influences industrial and personal relationships by defining the work environment and interpersonal interactions.

a. **Culture Building**:

i. **Values and Mission**: Defining and communicating the organization's core values, mission, and vision. Aligning employee behavior and practices with organizational values fosters a cohesive culture.

ii. **Cultural Norms**: Establishing norms and practices that guide behavior and interactions within the organization. Cultural norms influence how employees communicate, collaborate, and resolve conflicts.

b. **Diversity and Inclusion**:

i. **Promoting Diversity**: Encouraging a diverse workforce by recruiting and supporting employees from various backgrounds.

Diversity enhances creativity, problem-solving, and decision-making.

ii. **Fostering Inclusion**: Creating an inclusive work environment where all employees feel valued and respected. Implementing inclusion initiatives, such as training programs and support networks, helps in building a positive workplace culture.

4. External Relationships:

External Relationships involve interactions with stakeholders outside the organization, including customers, suppliers, partners, and the community.

a. **Customer Relations**:

i. **Customer Service**: Providing high-quality customer service to build and maintain positive relationships with customers. Effective customer service includes addressing inquiries, resolving issues, and ensuring customer satisfaction.

ii. **Customer Feedback**: Collecting and analyzing customer feedback to improve products, services, and processes. Feedback mechanisms help in understanding customer needs and enhancing customer experience.

b. **Supplier and Partner Relations**:

i. **Supplier Management**: Building and maintaining strong relationships with suppliers to ensure reliable and cost-effective procurement of materials and services. Effective supplier management includes negotiating terms, monitoring performance, and fostering collaboration.

ii. **Strategic Partnerships**: Developing partnerships with other organizations to achieve mutual benefits. Strategic partnerships can enhance capabilities, expand market reach, and drive innovation.

c. **Community Engagement**:

i. **Corporate Social Responsibility (CSR)**: Engaging in CSR activities to contribute to the well-being of the community and address social and environmental issues. CSR initiatives include philanthropy, environmental sustainability, and community development projects.

ii. **Stakeholder Communication**: Maintaining open and transparent communication with external stakeholders. Effective communication helps in managing relationships, addressing concerns, and building trust.

Multiple-Choice Questions (Objective)

1. What is the primary goal of Industrial Management?
   a) To increase production speed
   b) To reduce costs while ensuring high-quality output
   c) To automate all industrial processes
   d) To manage financial resources
2. Which aspect of Industrial Management involves forecasting demand and scheduling production?
   a) Operations Management
   b) Supply Chain Management
   c) Production Planning
   d) Quality Management
3. What does Production Control focus on?
   a) Forecasting demand
   b) Monitoring and controlling the production process
   c) Designing efficient workflows
   d) Managing procurement
4. What is the main objective of Quality Management?

a) Ensuring products meet established standards and specifications
b) Optimizing resource use and minimizing waste
c) Managing logistics and transportation
d) Planning financial resources

5. Which aspect of Industrial Management deals with acquiring raw materials and components?
   a) Operations Management
   b) Supply Chain Management
   c) Financial Management
   d) Maintenance Management
6. What is the purpose of Preventive Maintenance in Maintenance Management?
   a) Addressing equipment breakdowns
   b) Extending asset life by performing regular maintenance
   c) Managing financial resources
   d) Improving employee performance
7. What is included in the scope of Health and Safety Management?
   a) Developing and enforcing safety procedures
   b) Managing procurement processes
   c) Planning production schedules
   d) Designing efficient workflows
8. Which of the following is NOT a key element of Production Management?
   a) Production Planning
   b) Process Design
   c) Cost Estimation
   d) Marketing Strategy
9. What is the purpose of Inventory Management?
   a) Balancing inventory levels to meet demand while minimizing holding costs

b) Managing financial resources
c) Developing new products
d) Designing efficient workflows

10. What does Facility Layout focus on?
    a) Forecasting demand
    b) Planning the physical arrangement of machinery and workstations
    c) Managing procurement processes
    d) Ensuring product quality

11. Which technique is commonly used in Lean Production to improve efficiency?
    a) Just-In-Time (JIT)
    b) Regression Analysis
    c) FIFO (First-In-First-Out)
    d) Last-In-First-Out (LIFO)

12. What is the main goal of Production Organization?
    a) Developing marketing strategies
    b) Structuring and managing production activities
    c) Planning financial resources
    d) Conducting market research

13. What is the primary purpose of Material Requirements Planning (MRP)?
    a) Managing financial resources
    b) Calculating quantities and timing of material requirements
    c) Forecasting demand
    d) Ensuring product quality

14. Which of the following is a key aspect of Handling and Transportation?
    a) Marketing Strategy
    b) Inventory Valuation
    c) Material Handling
    d) Financial Planning

15. What is the purpose of Safety and Ergonomics in material handling?

a) Ensuring safe handling practices to prevent accidents and injuries
b) Managing financial resources
c) Designing efficient workflows
d) Forecasting demand

16. Which method of inventory valuation assumes that the oldest inventory items are sold first?

a) LIFO (Last-In-First-Out)
b) FIFO (First-In-First-Out)
c) Weighted Average Cost
d) Just-In-Time (JIT)

17. What is the focus of Production and Planning Control (PPC)?

a) Conducting market research
b) Coordinating and managing production activities
c) Developing new products
d) Managing financial resources

18. Which technique is used to analyze the relationship between costs, sales volume, and profits?

a) Activity-Based Costing (ABC)
b) Cost-Volume-Profit (CVP) Analysis
c) Regression Analysis
d) Economic Order Quantity (EOQ)

19. What is a key aspect of Industrial Relations?

a) Managing procurement processes
b) Engaging in collective bargaining with trade unions
c) Planning financial resources
d) Designing efficient workflows

20. What does Employee Engagement focus on?

a) Balancing inventory levels

b) Motivating employees and encouraging active participation

c) Managing procurement processes

d) Developing new products

Short Answer Type Questions (Subjective)

1. Define Industrial Management and explain its primary goal.
2. What are the key elements of Production Planning?
3. Describe the role of Quality Management in Industrial Management.
4. Explain the purpose of Supply Chain Management.
5. What is Preventive Maintenance and why is it important?
6. Describe the scope of Health and Safety Management.
7. What are the main objectives of Production Control?
8. Explain the concept of Facility Layout and its importance.
9. What is Lean Production and what techniques are commonly used in it?
10. Define Production Organization and its primary purpose.
11. What is Material Requirements Planning (MRP) and how does it work?
12. Describe the key aspects of Handling and Transportation.
13. Explain the importance of Safety and Ergonomics in material handling.
14. What is FIFO (First-In-First-Out) inventory valuation method?
15. Define Production and Planning Control (PPC) and its focus.
16. Describe the purpose of Cost-Volume-Profit (CVP) Analysis.
17. What is Industrial Relations and its key aspects?
18. Explain the concept of Employee Engagement and its importance.
19. Describe the role of Inventory Management in Industrial Management.
20. What is the significance of Performance Measurement in production?

Long Answer Type Questions (Subjective)

1. Discuss the importance of Industrial Management in modern manufacturing and service industries, focusing on its key aspects.

2. Explain the process and importance of Production Planning and Control (PPC) in Industrial Management.
3. Describe the key elements and significance of Quality Management in ensuring high product standards.
4. Discuss the role of Supply Chain Management in optimizing industrial operations and maintaining product quality.
5. Explain the various techniques used in Lean Production and their impact on efficiency and waste reduction.
6. Describe the process of Material Requirements Planning (MRP) and its importance in production management.
7. Discuss the key aspects of Handling and Transportation and their role in maintaining efficient industrial operations.
8. Explain the importance of Health and Safety Management in the workplace and the measures used to ensure compliance.
9. Describe the relationship between Budget and Cost Control in Industrial Management and their significance in financial planning.
10. Discuss the importance of Industrial and Personal Relationships in fostering a positive work environment and achieving organizational goals.

Answer Key for MCQ Questions

1. b) To reduce costs while ensuring high-quality output
2. c) Production Planning
3. b) Monitoring and controlling the production process
4. a) Ensuring products meet established standards and specifications
5. b) Supply Chain Management
6. b) Extending asset life by performing regular maintenance
7. a) Developing and enforcing safety procedures
8. d) Marketing Strategy

9. a) Balancing inventory levels to meet demand while minimizing holding costs
10. b) Planning the physical arrangement of machinery and workstations
11. a) Just-In-Time (JIT)
12. b) Structuring and managing production activities
13. b) Calculating quantities and timing of material requirements
14. c) Material Handling
15. a) Ensuring safe handling practices to prevent accidents and injuries
16. b) FIFO (First-In-First-Out)
17. b) Coordinating and managing production activities
18. b) Cost-Volume-Profit (CVP) Analysis
19. b) Engaging in collective bargaining with trade unions
20. b) Motivating employees and encouraging active participation

CHAPTER – 6

CONCEPT OF TOTAL QUALITY MANAGEMENT

INTRODUCTION:

Total Quality Management (TQM) is a comprehensive management approach that focuses on improving quality and performance in all areas of an organization through the active involvement of all employees. Here's a detailed introduction to TQM:

1. Definition of TQM

TQM is a management philosophy that seeks to enhance the quality of products and services, ensuring customer satisfaction, and fostering continuous improvement. It involves the collective efforts of all members of an organization to improve processes, products, and services.

2. Core Principles of TQM

a. **Customer Focus:** The primary goal of TQM is to meet or exceed customer expectations. This involves understanding customer needs, seeking feedback, and ensuring high levels of satisfaction.

b. **Leadership Commitment:** Effective leadership is crucial for the successful implementation of TQM. Leaders must set a clear vision, provide direction, and support the quality improvement initiatives.

c. **Employee Involvement:** TQM emphasizes the importance of involving all employees in the quality improvement process. This includes fostering a culture of teamwork, encouraging employee suggestions, and providing training and development.

d. **Process Approach:** TQM focuses on improving processes to enhance quality. This involves identifying, mapping, and analyzing processes to find and address inefficiencies or areas for improvement.

e. **Continuous Improvement:** TQM advocates for ongoing improvements in all aspects of the organization. This includes incremental changes as well as breakthrough innovations to enhance performance and quality.
f. **Data-Driven Decision Making:** Decisions should be based on data and factual information rather than intuition. TQM relies on statistical tools and methods to analyze performance and guide improvements.
g. **Integrated System:** TQM integrates various quality management practices and systems into a cohesive framework. It ensures that all processes and functions are aligned with the organization's quality goals.

3. Key Components of TQM

a. **Quality Planning:** Establishing quality objectives and defining processes to achieve them. This includes setting standards, developing quality policies, and creating plans to meet customer requirements.
b. **Quality Control:** Monitoring and measuring processes to ensure they meet the established quality standards. This involves inspection, testing, and using control charts to track performance.
c. **Quality Assurance:** Ensuring that processes and procedures are consistently followed to meet quality standards. This includes implementing quality management systems and conducting audits.
d. **Quality Improvement:** Continuously seeking ways to enhance quality and performance. This involves using tools like Six Sigma, Lean, and Kaizen to drive improvements.

4. Tools and Techniques

TQM employs various tools and techniques to facilitate quality management, including:

a. **Statistical Process Control (SPC):** Using statistical methods to monitor and control processes.
b. **Failure Mode and Effects Analysis (FMEA):** Identifying potential failures and their impact on quality.

c. **Cause and Effect Diagram:** Analyzing the root causes of quality problems.

d. **Pareto Analysis:** Identifying the most significant factors contributing to quality issues.

e. **Benchmarking:** Comparing performance with industry standards or best practices.

5. Benefits of TQM

a. **Improved Quality:** Enhanced products and services that meet or exceed customer expectations.

b. **Increased Customer Satisfaction:** Higher levels of customer loyalty and retention.

c. **Enhanced Efficiency:** Streamlined processes and reduced waste.

d. **Employee Morale:** Greater job satisfaction and engagement due to involvement in improvement efforts.

e. **Competitive Advantage:** Better quality and customer service leading to a stronger market position.

6. Challenges of TQM

a. **Resistance to Change:** Employees and management may resist adopting new practices.

b. **Resource Allocation:** Implementing TQM requires time, effort, and financial resources.

c. **Sustaining Efforts:** Maintaining a culture of continuous improvement can be challenging.

7. Implementation Steps

a. **Commitment from Top Management:** Ensure that leadership is fully committed to TQM.

b. **Establish a TQM Team:** Form a team to lead and coordinate TQM efforts.

c. **Develop a TQM Plan:** Create a detailed plan outlining objectives, strategies, and actions.
d. **Provide Training:** Train employees in quality management principles and tools.
e. **Monitor Progress:** Regularly assess progress and make necessary adjustments.
f. **Foster a Quality Culture:** Promote a culture that values quality and continuous improvement.

CLASSIFICATION:

The concept of Total Quality Management (TQM) can be classified into several key categories, each with specific principles and practices aimed at improving overall quality in an organization. Here's a detailed classification of TQM concepts with examples:

1. Core Principles of TQM:

A. Customer Focus:

Customer Focus is a fundamental principle in Total Quality Management (TQM) and involves orienting the organization's efforts toward meeting or exceeding customer expectations. Here's a detailed look at Customer Focus within the core principles of TQM:

Definition and Importance:

Customer Focus means understanding and addressing the needs and expectations of customers in every aspect of the organization's operations. It is based on the premise that the ultimate goal of any organization is to create value for its customers, thereby ensuring their satisfaction and loyalty.

Importance:

a. **Enhances Satisfaction:** By focusing on customer needs, organizations can deliver products and services that meet or exceed expectations, leading to higher customer satisfaction.

b. **Drives Business Success:** Satisfied customers are more likely to become repeat buyers, recommend the company to others, and contribute to the organization's long-term success.
c. **Encourages Innovation:** Understanding customer preferences and pain points can drive innovation, leading to the development of new products and services that better meet market demands.

Key Aspects of Customer Focus:

a. **Understanding Customer Needs:**
    i. **Description:** Identifying and analyzing customer requirements through various methods such as surveys, feedback, and market research.
    ii. **Example: Netflix** uses data analytics and customer feedback to understand viewing preferences and tailor its content recommendations to individual users.
b. **Customer Feedback Mechanisms:**
    i. **Description:** Implementing systems to collect and analyze customer feedback to gain insights into their experiences and expectations.
    ii. **Example: Apple** gathers customer feedback through online reviews, customer support interactions, and surveys to improve its products and services.
c. **Customer Service Excellence:**
    i. **Description:** Providing high-quality customer service that addresses customer inquiries, resolves issues, and enhances their overall experience.
    ii. **Example: Zappos** is renowned for its exceptional customer service, including free shipping and a generous return policy, which contributes to high customer satisfaction.

Customer-Centric Culture:

iii. **Description:** Creating a company culture that prioritizes customer needs and encourages employees to think from the customer's perspective.

iv. **Example:** **Amazon** fosters a customer-centric culture by incorporating customer feedback into decision-making processes and training employees to focus on delivering a superior customer experience.

d. **Measuring Customer Satisfaction:**

i. **Description:** Using metrics and tools to assess customer satisfaction levels and identify areas for improvement.

ii. **Example:** **Toyota** uses customer satisfaction surveys and Net Promoter Scores (NPS) to measure and enhance customer satisfaction with its vehicles and services.

Strategies for Implementing Customer Focus:

a. **Developing Customer Personas:**

i. **Description:** Creating detailed profiles of different customer segments to better understand their needs and preferences.

ii. **Example:** **Nike** develops customer personas based on demographic, behavioral, and psychographic data to design targeted marketing campaigns and product offerings.

b. **Implementing Quality Standards:**

i. **Description:** Establishing and adhering to quality standards that align with customer expectations.

ii. **Example:** **ISO 9001** certification requires organizations to meet customer requirements and continually improve their quality management systems.

c. **Continuous Improvement Based on Customer Feedback:**

i. **Description:** Regularly updating processes, products, and services based on customer feedback to ensure ongoing improvement.

ii. **Example: Adobe** frequently updates its software products based on user feedback to enhance functionality and user experience.

d. **Training and Empowering Employees:**

i. **Description:** Providing employees with the skills and authority to address customer needs effectively.

ii. **Example: The Ritz-Carlton** empowers its employees to make decisions that enhance guest experiences and resolve issues promptly.

B. Leadership:

Leadership is a critical core principle of Total Quality Management (TQM) and plays a fundamental role in guiding and sustaining quality improvement efforts across an organization. Here's a detailed look at Leadership within the context of TQM:

Definition and Importance:

Leadership in TQM refers to the role of leaders in creating and maintaining a quality-focused culture, setting strategic directions, and supporting continuous improvement initiatives. Effective leadership is essential for aligning the organization's vision with quality goals and fostering a culture that values and strives for excellence.

Importance:

a. **Direction and Vision:** Leaders provide a clear vision and strategic direction for quality initiatives, ensuring that all efforts are aligned with organizational goals.

b. **Motivation and Engagement:** Leaders inspire and motivate employees to commit to quality goals, enhancing their engagement and participation in improvement activities.

c. **Resource Allocation:** Leaders ensure that adequate resources, including time, budget, and training, are allocated to support quality initiatives.

Key Aspects of Leadership in TQM:

a. **Setting a Clear Vision and Direction:**

   i. **Description:** Establishing a vision for quality and communicating it effectively throughout the organization.

   ii. **Example: Satya Nadella** at Microsoft revitalized the company's focus on innovation and customer-centricity, guiding the organization through a cultural transformation towards quality and excellence.

b. **Creating a Quality-Centric Culture:**

   i. **Description:** Fostering a culture that prioritizes quality and encourages continuous improvement.

   ii. **Example: Paul Polman** at Unilever promoted a sustainability-focused culture, embedding quality and social responsibility into the company's core values and practices.

c. **Empowering Employees:**

   i. **Description:** Providing employees with the authority, resources, and support to contribute to quality improvements.

   ii. **Example: Starbucks** empowers its baristas to make decisions that enhance customer experiences and address issues promptly.

d. **Providing Support and Resources:**

   i. **Description:** Ensuring that the necessary resources, including training and technology, are available to support quality initiatives.

ii. **Example: Google** invests heavily in employee development and innovation resources to foster a culture of continuous improvement and high-quality output.

e. **Leading by Example:**

i. **Description:** Demonstrating a commitment to quality through personal actions and behaviors.

ii. **Example: Jeff Bezos** at Amazon is known for his relentless focus on customer satisfaction and operational excellence, setting a high standard for the organization's quality practices.

f. **Communicating Effectively:**

i. **Description:** Ensuring clear and open communication about quality goals, expectations, and progress.

ii. **Example: Richard Branson** at Virgin Group emphasizes transparent communication and regularly engages with employees to share updates on quality initiatives and company performance.

g. **Driving Strategic Alignment:**

i. **Description:** Aligning quality objectives with the organization's overall strategy and goals.

ii. **Example: Indra Nooyi** at PepsiCo aligned the company's strategic goals with a focus on healthier products and sustainability, integrating quality and corporate responsibility into the business strategy.

Strategies for Effective Leadership in TQM:

a. **Developing and Communicating a Quality Vision:**

i. **Description:** Crafting a compelling vision for quality and ensuring it is communicated clearly to all levels of the organization.

ii. **Example: IBM**'s leadership communicates its commitment to innovation and quality through its strategic vision and continuous investment in research and development.

b. **Building a Quality-Driven Leadership Team:**
    i. **Description:** Assembling a team of leaders who are committed to quality and capable of driving improvement efforts.
    ii. **Example: Toyota**'s leadership team includes members who are deeply committed to the principles of Lean manufacturing and continuous improvement.

c. **Encouraging Employee Participation:**
    i. **Description:** Involving employees in decision-making and improvement processes to enhance their engagement and commitment.
    ii. **Example: Toyota**'s use of "Kaizen" encourages all employees to contribute to continuous improvement efforts, leading to innovations and enhanced quality.

d. **Implementing Recognition and Reward Systems:**
    i. **Description:** Recognizing and rewarding employees who contribute to quality improvements and demonstrate excellence.
    ii. **Example: General Electric (GE)** uses performance-based rewards and recognition to motivate employees and reinforce a culture of quality.

C. Employee Involvement:

Employee Involvement is a key principle of Total Quality Management (TQM) that emphasizes the active participation of employees at all levels in quality improvement efforts. It recognizes that employees are crucial to the success of quality initiatives and that their engagement, ideas, and contributions can drive significant improvements in products, services, and processes. Here's a detailed look at Employee Involvement within the context of TQM:

Definition and Importance:

Employee Involvement refers to engaging employees in the quality management process by involving them in decision-making, problem-solving, and continuous improvement activities. It is based on the belief that employees, being directly involved in the operational aspects of the organization, have valuable insights and ideas for enhancing quality.

Importance:

a. **Enhances Problem-Solving:** Employees who are involved in decision-making processes are better positioned to identify problems and propose effective solutions.

b. **Increases Commitment:** When employees are engaged and have a sense of ownership, they are more likely to be committed to the organization's quality goals.

c. **Fosters Innovation:** Employee involvement encourages creativity and innovation by leveraging diverse perspectives and experiences.

Key Aspects of Employee Involvement

a. **Empowerment:**

   i. **Description:** Granting employees the authority and responsibility to make decisions and take actions related to quality.

   ii. **Example: The Ritz-Carlton** empowers its employees to make on-the-spot decisions to resolve customer issues and enhance service quality.

b. **Training and Development:**

   i. **Description:** Providing employees with the skills and knowledge necessary to contribute effectively to quality improvement efforts.

   ii. **Example: Toyota** offers continuous training programs to ensure employees have the expertise to identify and address quality issues in their roles.

c. **Encouraging Suggestions and Feedback:**

i. **Description:** Creating mechanisms for employees to submit ideas and feedback on improving processes and quality.

ii. **Example: 3M** has a "Innovation Time Off" policy that encourages employees to explore new ideas and submit them through formal channels for review and implementation.

d. **Teamwork and Collaboration:**

i. **Description:** Promoting teamwork and collaborative efforts to solve quality-related problems and implement improvements.

ii. **Example: Google** fosters a collaborative environment where cross-functional teams work together to develop and refine products and services.

e. **Recognition and Reward:**

i. **Description:** Acknowledging and rewarding employees for their contributions to quality improvement and excellence.

ii. **Example: Southwest Airlines** recognizes employees with awards and incentives for exceptional customer service and contributions to operational excellence.

Strategies for Implementing Employee Involvement:

a. **Creating Quality Circles:**

i. **Description:** Forming small groups of employees who meet regularly to discuss and solve quality-related issues.

ii. **Example: Ford Motor Company** uses quality circles to engage employees in identifying problems and developing solutions to improve manufacturing processes.

b. **Implementing Suggestion Schemes:**

i. **Description:** Establishing systems for employees to submit suggestions for quality improvements, with a structured process for evaluating and implementing them.

ii. **Example: General Electric (GE)** has a formal suggestion system that encourages employees to contribute ideas for improving processes and products.

c. **Encouraging Continuous Improvement Initiatives:**

i. **Description:** Supporting and promoting continuous improvement efforts, such as Kaizen, across all levels of the organization.

ii. **Example: Toyota** uses Kaizen principles to involve employees in making small, incremental improvements to processes and reducing waste.

d. **Facilitating Open Communication:**

i. **Description:** Ensuring open channels of communication between employees and management to discuss quality issues and improvement opportunities.

ii. **Example: Facebook** encourages open communication through regular team meetings and feedback sessions, allowing employees to share ideas and concerns.

D. Process Approach:

Process Approach is a fundamental principle of Total Quality Management (TQM) that focuses on managing and improving processes to achieve consistent and predictable results. It emphasizes understanding, controlling, and improving the processes that contribute to the creation of products or services. Here's a detailed look at the Process Approach within the context of TQM:

Definition and Importance:

Process Approach refers to managing processes in a systematic way to achieve desired outcomes and continuously improve efficiency and effectiveness. By focusing on processes rather than just individual tasks or functions, organizations can better understand how different activities interrelate and impact overall quality.

Importance:

a. **Consistency:** Helps ensure that processes are performed consistently, leading to predictable and reliable outcomes.
b. **Efficiency:** Identifies and eliminates inefficiencies, reducing waste and improving resource utilization.
c. **Improvement:** Provides a framework for continuous improvement by analyzing and optimizing processes over time.

Key Aspects of Process Approach:

a. **Understanding Processes:**
    i. **Description:** Identifying and mapping out the processes involved in producing products or delivering services.
    ii. **Example: McDonald's** uses detailed process maps to ensure that each step in the food preparation process is standardized and efficient, leading to consistent quality across all locations.
b. **Defining Process Inputs and Outputs:**
    i. **Description:** Clearly defining the inputs (resources, information, materials) and outputs (products, services) of each process to ensure clarity and accountability.
    ii. **Example: Intel** defines the inputs and outputs for its semiconductor manufacturing processes, ensuring precise control and high quality in the final products.
c. **Process Performance Measurement:**
    i. **Description:** Establishing metrics and indicators to measure process performance and effectiveness.
    ii. **Example: Amazon** uses performance metrics like order fulfillment time and delivery accuracy to monitor and improve its logistics and supply chain processes.
d. **Process Control:**

i. **Description:** Implementing controls and procedures to maintain process consistency and quality.

ii. **Example: Toyota** uses standard operating procedures and control charts to monitor and maintain the quality of its manufacturing processes.

e. **Process Improvement:**

i. **Description:** Continuously analyzing and improving processes to enhance performance and achieve better results.

ii. **Example: General Electric (GE)** uses Six Sigma methodologies to identify and improve inefficient processes, leading to significant cost savings and quality improvements.

Strategies for Implementing the Process Approach:

a. **Process Mapping and Documentation:**

i. **Description:** Creating detailed maps and documentation of processes to understand and manage them effectively.

ii. **Example: Boeing** uses process mapping to document its complex aircraft manufacturing processes, ensuring clarity and efficiency.

b. **Establishing Clear Process Objectives:**

i. **Description:** Setting specific objectives for each process to align them with overall organizational goals.

ii. **Example: Procter & Gamble** sets objectives for its manufacturing processes to achieve high production efficiency and product quality.

c. **Implementing Standard Operating Procedures (SOPs):**

i. **Description:** Developing and enforcing SOPs to standardize processes and ensure consistent performance.

ii. **Example: Coca-Cola** uses SOPs to ensure consistent quality and safety in its beverage production processes.

d. **Conducting Regular Process Reviews:**

   i. **Description:** Periodically reviewing processes to identify areas for improvement and ensure they are meeting performance objectives.
   ii. **Example: Dell Technologies** conducts regular reviews of its supply chain processes to identify and address inefficiencies.

e. **Utilizing Process Improvement Methodologies:**
   i. **Description:** Applying methodologies such as Lean, Six Sigma, and Kaizen to enhance process performance.
   ii. **Example: Toyota** employs Lean manufacturing principles to streamline its production processes and reduce waste.

E. Continuous Improvement:

Continuous Improvement is a core principle of Total Quality Management (TQM) and is essential for sustaining and enhancing quality over time. It involves ongoing efforts to improve products, services, and processes through incremental changes and innovations. Here's a detailed exploration of Continuous Improvement within the context of TQM:

Core Principles of Continuous Improvement in TQM:

1. **Commitment to Quality:**
   a. **Principle:** Achieve a company-wide commitment to quality and continuous improvement.
   b. **Details:** Quality should be embedded in the organization's culture and be a shared responsibility. Leaders and employees must be committed to quality and support continuous improvement initiatives.
2. **Customer Focus:**
   a. **Principle:** Prioritize customer satisfaction and align improvements with customer needs and expectations.

b. **Details:** Regularly gather and analyze customer feedback to identify areas for improvement. Ensure that improvement efforts are driven by the goal of enhancing customer satisfaction.

3. **Data-Driven Decision Making:**
   a. **Principle:** Use data and evidence to identify improvement opportunities and measure the impact of changes.
   b. **Details:** Collect and analyze performance data, customer feedback, and process metrics to inform decision-making. Use statistical tools and techniques to identify trends, problems, and opportunities for improvement.
4. **Employee Involvement:**
   a. **Principle:** Engage employees at all levels in the continuous improvement process.
   b. **Details:** Encourage and empower employees to contribute ideas for improvement. Foster a collaborative environment where employees can share their insights and participate in problem-solving.
5. **Process Management:**
   a. **Principle:** Focus on improving processes to enhance overall performance and quality.
   b. **Details:** Map and analyze existing processes to identify inefficiencies, bottlenecks, and areas for improvement. Implement process improvements and monitor their effectiveness.
6. **Leadership and Support:**
   a. **Principle:** Ensure strong leadership and support for continuous improvement efforts.
   b. **Details:** Leaders should champion continuous improvement initiatives, allocate resources, and provide the necessary support to drive change. Leadership commitment is crucial for sustaining improvement efforts.

7. **Innovation and Creativity:**
    a. **Principle:** Foster a culture of innovation and creativity to drive continuous improvement.
    b. **Details:** Encourage experimentation and creative problem-solving. Explore new technologies, methodologies, and practices to enhance processes and achieve better results.
8. **Systematic Approach:**
    a. **Principle:** Apply a systematic approach to continuous improvement.
    b. **Details:** Use structured methodologies such as Plan-Do-Check-Act (PDCA), Six Sigma, or Lean to guide improvement efforts. Follow a systematic process to plan, implement, and evaluate changes.

Implementation of Continuous Improvement in TQM:

1. **Identify Improvement Areas:**
    a. **Principle:** Regularly assess performance and identify areas for improvement.
    b. **Details:** Use performance metrics, customer feedback, and internal audits to pinpoint areas where improvements can be made. Prioritize areas based on impact and feasibility.
2. **Set Improvement Goals:**
    a. **Principle:** Define clear, measurable goals for improvement initiatives.
    b. **Details:** Establish specific, achievable objectives that align with overall business goals. Ensure that goals are measurable and can be tracked to evaluate progress.
3. **Develop Action Plans:**
    a. **Principle:** Create detailed action plans for implementing improvements.

b. **Details:** Outline the steps required to achieve the improvement goals, assign responsibilities, and set timelines. Include resources needed and potential risks.

4. **Implement Improvements:**
   a. **Principle:** Execute the action plans and apply changes to processes, products, or services.
   b. **Details:** Carry out the planned improvements, ensuring that changes are implemented effectively. Communicate changes to all relevant stakeholders and provide necessary training.
5. **Monitor and Measure:**
   a. **Principle:** Track the performance of implemented improvements to assess their effectiveness.
   b. **Details:** Use performance metrics and feedback to monitor the results of changes. Measure progress against the defined goals and analyze the impact on quality and performance.
6. **Review and Refine:**
   a. **Principle:** Continuously review and refine improvement efforts.
   b. **Details:** Regularly evaluate the results of improvements and identify opportunities for further enhancement. Make adjustments as needed based on performance data and feedback.
7. **Share Best Practices:**
   a. **Principle:** Share successful improvement practices and learnings across the organization.
   b. **Details:** Document and disseminate best practices and lessons learned from improvement initiatives. Encourage other teams and departments to adopt successful practices.
8. **Celebrate Successes:**
   a. **Principle:** Recognize and celebrate achievements and improvements.

b. **Details:** Acknowledge and reward individuals and teams for their contributions to continuous improvement. Celebrating successes helps maintain motivation and reinforces the value of improvement efforts.

Tools and Techniques for Continuous Improvement:

1. **Plan-Do-Check-Act (PDCA) Cycle:**
    a. A systematic approach for implementing and evaluating improvements.
2. **Kaizen:**
    a. Continuous, incremental improvements involving all employees.
3. **Six Sigma:**
    a. A data-driven methodology for reducing defects and variation.
4. **Lean:**
    a. Focus on eliminating waste and improving process efficiency.
5. **Root Cause Analysis (RCA):**
    a. Identifying and addressing the underlying causes of problems.
6. **Benchmarking:**
    a. Comparing performance against industry best practices.
7. **Statistical Process Control (SPC):**
    a. Monitoring and controlling processes using statistical methods.
8. **Failure Mode and Effects Analysis (FMEA):**
    a. Assessing potential failure modes and their impact.

F. **Data-Driven Decision Making:**

Data-Driven Decision Making (DDDM) is a core principle of Total Quality Management (TQM) and is crucial for making informed and effective decisions that drive continuous improvement and quality enhancement. It involves using data and evidence to guide decision-making processes, rather than relying on intuition or anecdotal information. Here's a detailed look at Data-Driven Decision Making within the context of TQM:

Core Principles of Data-Driven Decision Making in TQM:

1. **Collect Accurate and Relevant Data:**
    a. **Principle:** Gather data that is accurate, reliable, and pertinent to the decision-making process.
    b. **Details:** Ensure that data collection methods are robust and that data sources are credible. Collect data that directly relates to the areas being analyzed and the decisions being made.
2. **Analyze Data Systematically:**
    a. **Principle:** Use systematic methods to analyze data and extract meaningful insights.
    b. **Details:** Employ statistical tools and techniques to analyze data. Techniques such as regression analysis, hypothesis testing, and trend analysis can help identify patterns, correlations, and causations.
3. **Base Decisions on Evidence:**
    a. **Principle:** Make decisions based on empirical evidence and data rather than assumptions or opinions.
    b. **Details:** Use the results of data analysis to inform decision-making. Ensure that decisions are supported by objective data and evidence.
4. **Establish Metrics and KPIs:**
    a. **Principle:** Define and use key performance indicators (KPIs) and metrics to measure performance and progress.
    b. **Details:** Identify relevant KPIs and metrics that align with organizational goals and objectives. Use these indicators to track performance, set targets, and evaluate success.
5. **Monitor and Evaluate:**
    a. **Principle:** Continuously monitor performance and evaluate the impact of decisions.

b. **Details:** Track performance against established metrics and KPIs. Regularly review data to assess the effectiveness of decisions and make necessary adjustments.

6. **Foster a Data-Driven Culture:**
   a. **Principle:** Promote a culture that values data and evidence in decision-making processes.
   b. **Details:** Encourage employees to use data in their decision-making and problem-solving activities. Provide training and resources to support data-driven decision-making practices.
7. **Utilize Data Visualization:**
   a. **Principle:** Use data visualization tools to present data in a clear and understandable manner.
   b. **Details:** Employ charts, graphs, and dashboards to make data more accessible and easier to interpret. Effective visualization helps in communicating insights and facilitating decision-making.
8. **Ensure Data Quality and Integrity:**
   a. **Principle:** Maintain high standards of data quality and integrity.
   b. **Details:** Implement data governance practices to ensure data accuracy, consistency, and reliability. Regularly audit data for errors and address any issues promptly.

Implementation of Data-Driven Decision Making in TQM:

1. **Identify Data Needs:**
   a. **Principle:** Determine the type of data required for making informed decisions.
   b. **Details:** Identify key areas of interest and decision-making needs. Define the data sources and types of data that will provide the necessary insights.
2. **Develop Data Collection Methods:**
   a. **Principle:** Establish effective methods for collecting data.

b. **Details:** Use surveys, databases, sensors, and other data collection tools to gather relevant information. Ensure that data collection methods are consistent and reliable.

3. **Analyze Data:**
    a. **Principle:** Apply analytical methods to interpret data and generate insights.
    b. **Details:** Use statistical software and analytical techniques to process and analyze data. Interpret the results to understand trends, correlations, and implications.
4. **Make Informed Decisions:**
    a. **Principle:** Use data insights to guide decision-making.
    b. **Details:** Base decisions on data analysis and evidence. Consider multiple data sources and perspectives to ensure well-rounded decision-making.
5. **Implement Decisions and Monitor Outcomes:**
    a. **Principle:** Execute decisions and track their impact on performance.
    b. **Details:** Implement the decisions and monitor performance metrics to assess their effectiveness. Use data to evaluate the outcomes and make adjustments as needed.
6. **Review and Refine Data Practices:**
    a. **Principle:** Continuously review and improve data collection and analysis practices.
    b. **Details:** Evaluate the effectiveness of data-driven decision-making processes. Refine data collection methods, analysis techniques, and reporting practices to enhance decision-making.
7. **Provide Training and Support:**
    a. **Principle:** Equip employees with the skills and knowledge needed for data-driven decision-making.

b. **Details:** Offer training programs on data analysis, interpretation, and visualization. Provide tools and resources to support employees in using data effectively.

8. **Ensure Data Accessibility:**
   a. **Principle:** Make data readily accessible to those involved in decision-making.
   b. **Details:** Implement systems and tools that allow easy access to data for relevant stakeholders. Ensure that data is available in a user-friendly format.

Tools and Techniques for Data-Driven Decision Making:

1. **Statistical Analysis Software:**
   a. Tools like SPSS, SAS, and R for advanced statistical analysis.
2. **Data Visualization Tools:**
   a. Software like Tableau, Power BI, and QlikView for creating interactive dashboards and visualizations.
3. **Business Intelligence (BI) Systems:**
   a. Tools that integrate and analyze data from various sources to support decision-making.
4. **Data Warehousing:**
   a. Systems for storing and managing large volumes of data to ensure easy access and analysis.
5. **Predictive Analytics:**
   a. Techniques for forecasting future trends and outcomes based on historical data.
6. **Benchmarking Tools:**
   a. Tools for comparing organizational performance with industry standards and best practices.

G. **Integrated System:**

In the context of Total Quality Management (TQM), an **Integrated System** is a fundamental principle that emphasizes the coordination and alignment of various processes and functions within an organization to achieve comprehensive quality improvements. An Integrated System ensures that all parts of the organization work together harmoniously to meet quality objectives and enhance overall performance. Here's a detailed exploration of the Integrated System principle in TQM:

Core Principles of an Integrated System in TQM:

1. **Alignment with Organizational Goals:**
    a. **Principle:** Ensure that all processes and functions are aligned with the organization's strategic goals and objectives.
    b. **Details:** Integrate quality management practices with overall business strategies. Ensure that quality objectives support and drive organizational goals and that all departments understand their role in achieving these goals.
2. **Cross-Functional Collaboration:**
    a. **Principle:** Foster collaboration across different departments and functions.
    b. **Details:** Promote teamwork and communication among various departments such as production, marketing, finance, and customer service. Encourage cross-functional teams to work together on quality improvement initiatives and problem-solving.
3. **Unified Quality Management System (QMS):**
    a. **Principle:** Implement a comprehensive and unified QMS that encompasses all aspects of the organization.
    b. **Details:** Develop and maintain a QMS that integrates quality policies, procedures, standards, and practices across the organization. Ensure that the QMS is consistent and supports all areas of operations.

4. **Standardization of Processes:**
    a. **Principle:** Standardize processes to ensure consistency and efficiency.
    b. **Details:** Establish standardized procedures and practices to ensure uniformity in operations. Use process documentation, guidelines, and best practices to maintain consistency and reduce variability.
5. **Data Integration and Sharing:**
    a. **Principle:** Integrate data from various sources and ensure its availability across the organization.
    b. **Details:** Use integrated information systems to collect, manage, and share data. Ensure that data from different functions, such as customer feedback, production metrics, and financial performance, is accessible and utilized for decision-making.
6. **Holistic Approach to Problem Solving:**
    a. **Principle:** Address problems and opportunities from a holistic perspective.
    b. **Details:** Analyze issues and opportunities across the entire organization rather than in isolation. Use cross-functional teams to develop and implement solutions that consider all aspects of the organization.
7. **Continuous Feedback and Improvement:**
    a. **Principle:** Use feedback from various sources to drive continuous improvement.
    b. **Details:** Collect feedback from customers, employees, and other stakeholders. Integrate this feedback into the improvement process to refine and enhance processes and practices continuously.
8. **Resource Optimization:**
    a. **Principle:** Optimize the use of resources across the organization.

b. **Details:** Ensure that resources, including human, financial, and material resources, are allocated and utilized efficiently. Integrate resource management practices to avoid duplication and waste.

Implementation of an Integrated System in TQM:

1. **Develop a Quality Management Framework:**
   a. **Principle:** Create a framework that outlines the structure and components of the QMS.
   b. **Details:** Define the scope, objectives, and components of the QMS. Develop policies, procedures, and guidelines that integrate quality management practices across the organization.
2. **Establish Cross-Functional Teams:**
   a. **Principle:** Form teams that represent various functions and departments.
   b. **Details:** Create cross-functional teams to work on quality improvement projects, problem-solving, and process optimization. Ensure that teams have clear objectives and roles.
3. **Implement Integrated Information Systems:**
   a. **Principle:** Use technology to integrate and manage data.
   b. **Details:** Deploy enterprise resource planning (ERP) systems, customer relationship management (CRM) systems, and other integrated tools to collect, manage, and analyze data from various sources.
4. **Standardize Processes and Procedures:**
   a. **Principle:** Develop and implement standardized processes.
   b. **Details:** Document and standardize processes and procedures to ensure consistency and efficiency. Communicate standards and provide training to ensure adherence.
5. **Monitor and Evaluate Performance:**
   a. **Principle:** Track performance across integrated systems.

b. **Details:** Use performance metrics and indicators to monitor the effectiveness of integrated processes. Evaluate performance data to identify areas for improvement.

6. **Facilitate Communication and Collaboration:**
   a. **Principle:** Enhance communication and collaboration among departments.
   b. **Details:** Implement communication channels and collaboration tools to facilitate interaction between departments. Promote a culture of open communication and teamwork.
7. **Review and Update the Integrated System:**
   a. **Principle:** Regularly review and update the integrated system.
   b. **Details:** Conduct periodic reviews of the QMS and integrated systems to ensure their effectiveness and relevance. Make updates based on performance data, feedback, and changes in organizational goals.
8. **Promote a Unified Quality Culture:**
   a. **Principle:** Cultivate a culture that values quality and integration.
   b. **Details:** Encourage a shared commitment to quality across the organization. Promote the understanding that quality is the responsibility of all employees and that integration supports overall success.

Tools and Techniques for Implementing an Integrated System:

1. **Enterprise Resource Planning (ERP) Systems:**
   a. Integrated software solutions for managing various business processes and data.
2. **Customer Relationship Management (CRM) Systems:**
   a. Tools for managing customer interactions and data.
3. **Process Mapping:**

a. Visual representation of processes to understand and optimize workflows.

4. **Business Process Management (BPM) Tools:**
    a. Tools for designing, modeling, and optimizing business processes.
5. **Balanced Scorecard:**
    a. A performance management framework that integrates financial and non-financial metrics.
6. **Integrated Performance Metrics:**
    a. Metrics that encompass various aspects of performance, such as quality, cost, and efficiency.

2. Quality Management Systems:

A. Quality Planning:

Quality planning is a crucial aspect of Quality Management Systems (QMS) within the framework of Total Quality Management (TQM). It involves outlining how an organization will achieve its quality objectives and ensuring that processes, resources, and activities are in place to meet or exceed customer expectations. Here's a detailed look at quality planning in the context of TQM:

Key Components of Quality Planning

1. **Define Quality Objectives:**
    a. **Principle:** Establish clear, measurable quality objectives aligned with the organization's strategic goals.
    b. **Details:** Objectives should be specific, measurable, achievable, relevant, and time-bound (SMART). They should address customer requirements, regulatory compliance, and internal performance targets.
2. **Develop Quality Policies:**
    a. **Principle:** Create policies that define the organization's commitment to quality and its approach to managing quality.

   b. **Details:** Quality policies should articulate the organization's quality vision, values, and standards. They guide decision-making and actions across the organization.
3. **Identify Customer Requirements:**
   a. **Principle:** Understand and document customer needs and expectations to ensure that products and services meet these requirements.
   b. **Details:** Engage with customers through surveys, feedback, and market research. Use this information to define quality requirements and standards for products and services.
4. **Establish Quality Standards:**
   a. **Principle:** Define specific standards and criteria that products, services, and processes must meet to ensure quality.
   b. **Details:** Standards may include technical specifications, performance metrics, and compliance with industry regulations. Develop clear criteria for evaluating quality at different stages of the product or service lifecycle.
5. **Design Quality Processes:**
   a. **Principle:** Plan and design processes that will be used to produce quality products and services.
   b. **Details:** Create process maps, flowcharts, and procedures that outline how each process will be executed. Ensure that processes are designed to be efficient, effective, and capable of meeting quality standards.
6. **Resource Planning:**
   a. **Principle:** Identify and allocate the necessary resources to support quality objectives and processes.
   b. **Details:** This includes human resources, technology, equipment, materials, and financial resources. Ensure that resources are

available, properly trained, and equipped to perform quality-related tasks.

7. **Risk Management:**
    a. **Principle:** Assess and address potential risks that could impact quality.
    b. **Details:** Identify risks related to processes, suppliers, and external factors. Develop contingency plans and preventive measures to mitigate these risks and ensure that quality objectives can be achieved.
8. **Develop a Quality Plan:**
    a. **Principle:** Create a comprehensive quality plan that integrates all aspects of quality management and outlines how quality objectives will be achieved.
    b. **Details:** The quality plan should include objectives, policies, standards, processes, resource requirements, timelines, and responsibilities. It serves as a roadmap for implementing and monitoring quality management activities.
9. **Communication and Training:**
    a. **Principle:** Ensure that all stakeholders are informed about the quality plan and their roles in achieving quality objectives.
    b. **Details:** Provide training and development programs to enhance employees' skills and understanding of quality requirements. Communicate the quality plan clearly and regularly to all relevant parties.
10. **Monitoring and Evaluation:**
    a. **Principle:** Establish mechanisms to monitor and evaluate the effectiveness of the quality plan.
    b. **Details:** Use performance metrics, audits, and reviews to assess how well the quality plan is being implemented and whether

quality objectives are being met. Make adjustments to the plan as needed based on evaluation results.

Implementation of Quality Planning:

1. **Develop a Quality Management Team:**
   a. Assemble a team responsible for quality planning and management. This team should include representatives from various departments and levels within the organization.
2. **Create a Quality Plan Document:**
   a. Document the quality planning process, including objectives, policies, standards, processes, resources, and responsibilities. Ensure that the plan is accessible and communicated to all stakeholders.
3. **Integrate Quality Planning with Strategic Planning:**
   a. Align the quality plan with the organization's overall strategic plan. Ensure that quality objectives support the strategic goals and that quality management is integrated into all aspects of organizational planning.
4. **Review and Update the Quality Plan:**
   a. Regularly review and update the quality plan to ensure that it remains relevant and effective. Incorporate feedback from stakeholders and lessons learned from previous quality initiatives.
5. **Foster a Culture of Quality:**
   a. Promote a culture that values quality and encourages continuous improvement. Recognize and reward contributions to quality planning and achievement of quality objectives.

B. **Quality Control:**

Quality Control (QC) is a critical component of Quality Management Systems (QMS) within the framework of Total Quality Management (TQM). It focuses on identifying defects and ensuring that products and services meet predefined quality standards. Here's a detailed look at Quality Control in the context of TQM:

Key Components of Quality Control:

1. **Establishing Quality Standards:**
    a. **Principle:** Define clear, measurable quality standards for products, services, and processes.
    b. **Details:** Standards should be based on customer requirements, regulatory requirements, and industry best practices. They serve as benchmarks against which quality can be assessed.
2. **Quality Measurement:**
    a. **Principle:** Implement methods to measure and evaluate quality against established standards.
    b. **Details:** Use various measurement tools and techniques to assess product and process performance. This may include physical measurements, inspections, and testing. Measurement should be accurate and reliable to ensure meaningful results.
3. **Inspection and Testing:**
    a. **Principle:** Conduct inspections and tests to detect defects and ensure that products and services meet quality standards.
    b. **Details:** Inspections can be performed at various stages, such as during production, before shipment, or after delivery. Testing can include functional, durability, and safety tests. Both methods help identify non-conformities and prevent defective products from reaching customers.
4. **Statistical Process Control (SPC):**
    a. **Principle:** Use statistical methods to monitor and control processes.
    b. **Details:** Apply SPC tools such as control charts, histograms, and Pareto analysis to track process performance and detect variations.

SPC helps in identifying trends, understanding process behavior, and making data-driven decisions.

5. **Root Cause Analysis:**
   a. **Principle:** Identify and address the underlying causes of quality issues.
   b. **Details:** Use techniques like the 5 Whys, Fishbone diagrams (Ishikawa), and Failure Mode and Effects Analysis (FMEA) to investigate and determine the root causes of defects. Addressing these root causes helps in preventing recurrence and improving overall quality.
6. **Corrective and Preventive Actions (CAPA):**
   a. **Principle:** Implement actions to correct defects and prevent future occurrences.
   b. **Details:** Corrective actions address immediate issues, while preventive actions focus on eliminating the causes of potential problems. Develop and implement CAPA plans to resolve quality issues and enhance processes.
7. **Documentation and Record Keeping:**
   a. **Principle:** Maintain comprehensive records of quality control activities.
   b. **Details:** Document inspection results, test reports, non-conformance reports, and CAPA actions. Proper record keeping ensures traceability, accountability, and compliance with regulatory requirements.
8. **Training and Competence:**
   a. **Principle:** Ensure that personnel involved in quality control are properly trained and competent.
   b. **Details:** Provide training on quality control procedures, measurement techniques, and problem-solving skills. Regularly

assess and update training programs to keep pace with changes in technology and standards.

9. **Continuous Improvement:**
    a. **Principle:** Focus on ongoing improvement in quality control processes.
    b. **Details:** Use feedback from inspections, tests, and performance metrics to identify opportunities for improvement. Implement initiatives to enhance quality control practices and drive continuous improvement.

Implementation of Quality Control in TQM:

1. **Develop a Quality Control Plan:**
    a. Create a detailed plan outlining the quality control procedures, standards, measurement methods, and responsibilities. Ensure that the plan aligns with the overall quality management strategy.
2. **Integrate QC with Other Quality Management Activities:**
    a. Ensure that quality control is integrated with quality planning, quality assurance, and continuous improvement activities. Coordination between these elements helps in achieving comprehensive quality management.
3. **Utilize Quality Control Tools and Techniques:**
    a. Implement tools such as control charts, process capability analysis, and failure analysis to monitor and control quality. Use these tools to identify trends, diagnose issues, and make informed decisions.
4. **Monitor and Review Quality Control Performance:**
    a. Regularly assess the effectiveness of quality control activities. Review performance metrics, inspection results, and non-conformance data to evaluate the impact of quality control measures.
5. **Foster a Quality Culture:**

a. Promote a culture that values quality and supports quality control efforts. Encourage employees to take ownership of quality and participate actively in quality control activities.

6. **Engage in Supplier Quality Management:**
    a. Collaborate with suppliers to ensure that incoming materials and components meet quality standards. Implement supplier quality control measures such as audits, inspections, and performance evaluations.
7. **Review and Update Quality Control Procedures:**
    a. Regularly review and update quality control procedures to ensure their effectiveness and relevance. Incorporate feedback from stakeholders and lessons learned from quality control activities.

3. Quality Improvement Tools and Techniques

a. **Statistical Process Control (SPC):**
    i. **Description:** Using statistical methods to monitor and control processes.
    ii. **Example:** A **manufacturing plant** uses control charts to monitor production lines and ensure they remain within specified quality limits.

b. **Failure Mode and Effects Analysis (FMEA):**
    i. **Description:** Identifying and analyzing potential failure modes and their effects.
    ii. **Example:** An **automotive company** conducts FMEA to assess potential risks in vehicle design and implement preventive measures.

c. **Root Cause Analysis (RCA):**
    i. **Description:** Identifying the underlying causes of quality problems and addressing them.

   ii. **Example:** A **software company** performs RCA to determine the root cause of a recurring bug and implement a fix to prevent future occurrences.

4. Cultural and Behavioral Aspects

a. **Quality Culture:**
   i. **Description:** Fostering a culture that values quality and continuous improvement.
   ii. **Example: The Ritz-Carlton** Hotel Company emphasizes exceptional customer service and quality through rigorous training and employee empowerment.

b. **Teamwork and Collaboration:**
   i. **Description:** Encouraging teamwork and collaboration to achieve quality goals.
   ii. **Example:** In the **pharmaceutical industry**, cross-functional teams work together to ensure drug development processes adhere to the highest quality standards.

5. Strategic TQM Initiatives

a. **Benchmarking:**
   i. **Description:** Comparing performance against best practices or industry standards.
   ii. **Example:** A **retail chain** benchmarks its customer service practices against leading competitors to identify areas for improvement.

b. **Six Sigma:**
   i. **Description:** A data-driven methodology aimed at reducing defects and variability in processes.
   ii. **Example: Motorola** implemented Six Sigma to improve manufacturing processes, achieving significant cost savings and quality improvements.

c. **Lean Management:**
   i. **Description:** Eliminating waste and improving efficiency in processes.
   ii. **Example:** A **logistics company** uses Lean principles to streamline its supply chain operations and reduce lead times.

Multiple-Choice Questions (Objective)

1. What is the primary goal of Total Quality Management (TQM)?
   a) To increase production speed
   b) To ensure customer satisfaction through continuous improvement
   c) To automate all industrial processes
   d) To manage financial resources
2. Which principle of TQM focuses on understanding and meeting customer needs?
   a) Employee Involvement
   b) Process Approach
   c) Customer Focus
   d) Integrated System
3. What role do leaders play in TQM?
   a) Implementing control charts
   b) Setting a clear vision and supporting quality initiatives
   c) Performing root cause analysis
   d) Managing inventory levels
4. What is a key component of Quality Planning in TQM?
   a) Conducting internal audits
   b) Establishing quality objectives and defining processes to achieve them
   c) Implementing corrective actions
   d) Measuring customer satisfaction

5. Which tool is used in TQM to monitor and control processes statistically?
    a) Failure Mode and Effects Analysis (FMEA)
    b) Root Cause Analysis (RCA)
    c) Statistical Process Control (SPC)
    d) Benchmarking
6. What does Quality Assurance focus on in TQM?
    a) Detecting and correcting defects
    b) Ensuring processes are consistently followed to meet quality standards
    c) Analyzing customer feedback
    d) Reducing production costs
7. Which TQM principle involves the continuous enhancement of processes, products, and services?
    a) Customer Focus
    b) Leadership
    c) Continuous Improvement
    d) Data-Driven Decision Making
8. What is the purpose of a Cause and Effect Diagram in TQM?
    a) To measure process performance
    b) To identify and analyze root causes of quality problems
    c) To establish quality standards
    d) To implement corrective actions
9. What is the main benefit of employee involvement in TQM?
    a) Increased production speed
    b) Higher job satisfaction and engagement
    c) Reduced inventory costs
    d) Enhanced marketing strategies
10. Which aspect of TQM focuses on aligning all processes and functions with organizational quality goals?
    a) Process Approach

b) Integrated System
c) Quality Control
d) Quality Improvement

11. What is the purpose of Quality Control in TQM?
a) To plan quality objectives
b) To monitor and measure processes to ensure they meet quality standards
c) To involve employees in quality improvement
d) To integrate quality management practices

12. Which tool is used to compare performance against industry standards or best practices in TQM?
a) Pareto Analysis
b) Benchmarking
c) Control Charts
d) Six Sigma

13. What does the Plan-Do-Check-Act (PDCA) cycle focus on?
a) Implementing statistical control charts
b) Monitoring customer satisfaction
c) Continuous improvement through iterative steps
d) Managing financial resources

14. What is a key aspect of Supplier Quality Assurance in TQM?
a) Reducing inventory costs
b) Ensuring suppliers meet quality requirements
c) Analyzing customer feedback
d) Implementing automation

15. What is the main objective of Failure Mode and Effects Analysis (FMEA)?
a) To monitor process performance
b) To identify and analyze potential failure modes and their impact
c) To develop quality standards

d) To measure customer satisfaction

16. Which TQM principle emphasizes using data and evidence to guide decision-making?
    a) Employee Involvement
    b) Continuous Improvement
    c) Data-Driven Decision Making
    d) Quality Control
17. What does the term "Quality Culture" refer to in TQM?
    a) A culture that prioritizes financial performance
    b) A culture that values quality and continuous improvement
    c) A culture focused on marketing and sales
    d) A culture that emphasizes rapid production
18. What is a key challenge in implementing TQM?
    a) Increasing production speed
    b) Ensuring compliance with financial regulations
    c) Overcoming resistance to change
    d) Reducing employee engagement
19. Which TQM tool is used to visually represent processes and identify inefficiencies?
    a) Pareto Analysis
    b) Control Charts
    c) Process Mapping
    d) Failure Mode and Effects Analysis (FMEA)
20. What is the purpose of training and competence development in TQM?
    a) To increase production speed
    b) To ensure employees are properly trained to perform quality-related tasks effectively
    c) To reduce inventory costs
    d) To enhance marketing strategies

Short Answer Type Questions (Subjective)

1. Define Total Quality Management (TQM) and explain its primary goal.
2. What are the core principles of TQM?
3. Describe the role of leadership in TQM.
4. Explain the concept of employee involvement in TQM.
5. What is the purpose of quality planning in TQM?
6. How does Statistical Process Control (SPC) contribute to quality management?
7. Define Quality Assurance and its significance in TQM.
8. What is the role of Continuous Improvement in TQM?
9. Describe the use of a Cause and Effect Diagram in TQM.
10. What are the benefits of having an Integrated System in TQM?
11. Explain the purpose of Quality Control in TQM.
12. How does Benchmarking help in improving quality in TQM?
13. Describe the Plan-Do-Check-Act (PDCA) cycle and its importance in TQM.
14. What is Supplier Quality Assurance and why is it important in TQM?
15. Explain the process and purpose of Failure Mode and Effects Analysis (FMEA).
16. What does Data-Driven Decision Making entail in the context of TQM?
17. Define Quality Culture and its impact on an organization.
18. Discuss the challenges faced in implementing TQM.
19. How is Process Mapping used in TQM?
20. What is the significance of training and competence development in TQM?

Long Answer Type Questions (Subjective)

1. Discuss the core principles of Total Quality Management (TQM) and their significance in achieving organizational goals.
2. Explain the role of leadership in TQM and how leaders can foster a quality-centric culture.

3. Describe the process of quality planning in TQM and its importance in ensuring consistent quality.
4. Discuss the role of employee involvement in TQM and its impact on organizational performance and quality improvement.
5. Explain the concept of an Integrated System in TQM and how it helps in aligning organizational processes and functions.
6. Describe the various tools and techniques used in TQM for quality improvement and provide examples of their application.
7. Discuss the challenges in implementing TQM and suggest strategies to overcome them.
8. Explain the importance of Quality Assurance in TQM and the steps involved in implementing a robust QA system.
9. Describe the process and benefits of using Statistical Process Control (SPC) in TQM.
10. Discuss the significance of Continuous Improvement in TQM and how organizations can implement and sustain it.

Answer Key for MCQ Questions

1. b) To ensure customer satisfaction through continuous improvement
2. c) Customer Focus
3. b) Setting a clear vision and supporting quality initiatives
4. b) Establishing quality objectives and defining processes to achieve them
5. c) Statistical Process Control (SPC
6. b) Ensuring processes are consistently followed to meet quality standards
7. c) Continuous Improvement: "Continuous Improvement
8. b) To identify and analyze root causes of quality problems
9. b) Higher job satisfaction and engagement
10. b) Integrated System

11.b) To monitor and measure processes to ensure they meet quality standards

12.b) Benchmarking

13.c) Continuous improvement through iterative steps

14.b) Ensuring suppliers meet quality requirements

15.b) To identify and analyze potential failure modes and their impact

16.c) Data-Driven Decision Making

17.b) A culture that values quality and continuous improvement

18.c) Overcoming resistance to change

19.c) Process Mapping

20.b) To ensure employees are properly trained to perform quality-related tasks effectively

CHAPTER – 7

COMPRESSION AND COMPACTION

INTRODUCTION:

Compression and compaction are critical processes in pharmaceutical manufacturing, particularly in the production of solid dosage forms like tablets. Here's a detailed introduction to both:

Compression:

1. Definition: Compression refers to the process of applying pressure to powders or granules to form solid tablets. This process reduces the volume of the material and binds the particles together to create a cohesive solid mass.

2. Purpose:

a. **Uniform Dosage:** Ensures that each tablet contains a consistent amount of active pharmaceutical ingredient (API) and excipients.

b. **Stability:** Helps in forming a stable dosage form that can withstand handling and environmental conditions.

c. **Bioavailability:** Can influence the release rate of the drug from the tablet.

3. Process:

a. **Powder Blending:** Before compression, powders or granules are mixed to ensure uniform distribution of the active ingredient and excipients.

b. **Granulation:** Powders are often granulated to improve flowability and compressibility. This can be done via wet granulation, dry granulation, or direct compression.

c. **Tablet Compression:** The granules or powders are then fed into a tablet press where they are subjected to high pressure. The tablet press consists of upper and lower punches that compress the powder into tablet form.

4. Types of Compression:

a. **Direct Compression:** Involves compressing powders directly into tablets without prior granulation. Suitable for powders with good flow properties and compressibility.

b. **Wet Granulation:** Powders are granulated with a liquid binder before compression. This process improves flow and compressibility.

c. **Dry Granulation:** Involves compacting powders into large slugs or briquettes, which are then broken down and compressed into tablets. Used when powders are sensitive to moisture.

5. Equipment:

a. **Single-Punch Press:** For small-scale production.

b. **Rotary Press:** For large-scale production, with multiple stations for continuous tablet formation.

Compaction:

1. Definition: Compaction is the process of compressing powders or granules into a solid form. It is similar to compression but can refer to the broader concept of increasing the density of the powder bed.

2. Purpose:

a. **Enhanced Flowability:** Reduces the volume of the powder bed, improving the handling and processing characteristics.

b. **Density Improvement:** Increases the bulk density of the powder, which is important for tablet formulation.

3. Process:

a. **Powder Compaction:** Powders are compressed between two rollers or within a compaction chamber to form tablets or compacted granules.

b. **Pre-Compaction:** Involves compressing powders before the final tablet formation to improve flowability and reduce segregation.

4. Types of Compaction:

a. **Roller Compaction:** Uses two counter-rotating rollers to compress powders into sheets or ribbons, which are then milled into granules.

b. **Tableting Compaction:** Refers specifically to the compression of powders into tablets using tablet presses.

5. Equipment:

a. **Roller Compactor:** For producing granules from powders.

b. **Tablet Press:** For final tablet formation after initial compaction or granulation.

Factors Affecting Compression and Compaction

a. **Powder Characteristics:** Particle size, shape, and distribution influence compressibility and tablet quality.

b. **Formulation:** The choice of excipients (binders, fillers, lubricants) affects the flow, compressibility, and tablet hardness.

c. **Process Parameters:** Pressure, speed, and temperature during compression and compaction impact the final product's quality.

PHYSICS OF TABLET COMPRESSION

The physics of tablet compression involves the application of mechanical principles to convert powders or granules into solid tablets. Understanding these principles is crucial for optimizing tablet quality, consistency, and performance. Here's a detailed look at the physics behind tablet compression:

1. Fundamental Principles:

1.1. Granular Mechanics:

a. **Particle Size and Shape:** The size and shape of the particles influence how they pack together during compression. Smaller particles tend to pack more tightly, while irregular shapes can cause poor flow and uneven compression.

b. **Interparticle Forces:** Forces such as van der Waals forces, electrostatic forces, and mechanical interlocking play a role in how particles bond together. Effective compression relies on these forces to create a cohesive tablet.

1.2. Compressibility and Flowability:

a. **Compressibility:** The ability of the powder to decrease in volume under pressure. This depends on factors such as particle size, distribution, and the presence of lubricants. Compressible powders can form tablets with fewer defects.
b. **Flowability:** Good flow properties are essential for consistent tablet weight and uniformity. Poor flow can lead to uneven filling of tablet dies and inconsistent tablet properties.

2. Compression Mechanics:

2.1. Tablet Formation:

a. **Die and Punch System:** The tablet press consists of upper and lower punches and a die cavity. The powder or granules are compressed between these punches to form a tablet.
b. **Pressure Application:** As the punches move together, they apply pressure to the powder bed. This pressure must be sufficient to cause plastic deformation and bonding of the particles to form a solid tablet.

2.2. Deformation and Bonding:

a. **Elastic Deformation:** Initially, particles may deform elastically, meaning they return to their original shape when the pressure is released.
b. **Plastic Deformation:** Under sufficient pressure, particles undergo plastic deformation, where they permanently change shape and bond together. This is crucial for tablet formation.
c. **Elastic Recovery:** After the compression force is removed, some elastic recovery can occur, potentially causing tablet expansion. This needs to be accounted for in the formulation and compression process.

3. Compaction Dynamics:

3.1. Powder Bed Density:

a. **Bulk Density:** The density of the powder bed before compression. Higher bulk density often indicates better flow properties.

b. **Tapped Density:** The density of the powder bed after tapping or vibration, reflecting how tightly the powder can be packed.

3.2. Compaction Pressure:

a. **Pressure Profiles:** During compression, pressure changes can affect tablet hardness and friability. Higher pressures generally result in harder tablets but can also increase the risk of capping or lamination.

b. **Compaction Curves:** These curves plot tablet hardness against applied pressure, helping to identify optimal compression settings.

3.3. Force Transmission:

a. **Punch and Die Interaction:** Forces applied by the punches are transmitted to the powder bed through the die walls. Uniform pressure distribution is essential for consistent tablet quality.

b. **Frictional Forces:** Friction between the powder and the die walls or punches can affect tablet ejection and cause surface defects.

4. Tablet Properties and Quality Control

4.1. Tablet Hardness and Friability:

a. **Hardness:** The mechanical strength of the tablet, influenced by the compaction pressure and formulation. Hard tablets resist breaking and crumbling.

b. **Friability:** The tendency of the tablet to crumble or break into smaller pieces. High friability indicates poor tablet cohesion.

4.2. Tablet Uniformity:

a. **Weight Variation:** Ensuring that each tablet contains the correct amount of API and excipients. Consistent tablet weight is critical for dosage accuracy.

b. **Content Uniformity:** Variability in API content among tablets can affect therapeutic efficacy. Proper compression ensures uniform distribution of the API.

5. Challenges and Considerations

5.1. Tool Wear and Maintenance:

a. **Wear and Tear:** Over time, punches and dies can wear out, affecting compression quality. Regular maintenance and replacement are necessary to maintain tablet consistency.

b. **Cleaning:** Residual powders or contaminants can affect the next batch's quality, so cleaning protocols are essential.

5.2. Environmental Factors:

a. **Humidity and Temperature:** These can affect the flow and compressibility of powders. Controlling environmental conditions helps maintain consistent tablet quality.

COMPRESSION, CONSOLIDATION

Compression and consolidation are key processes in tablet manufacturing that involve transforming powders or granules into solid tablets. Here's a detailed look at both concepts:

Compression:

1. Definition: Compression in tablet manufacturing refers to the process of applying pressure to a powder or granule mixture to form a solid tablet. It involves reducing the volume of the material and binding the particles together to produce a cohesive tablet.

2. Process of Compression:

2.1. Powder Blending: Before compression, powders or granules are blended to ensure uniform distribution of the active pharmaceutical ingredient (API) and excipients. This step is critical for ensuring consistent tablet content and performance.

2.2. Granulation (if applicable):

a. **Wet Granulation:** Powders are mixed with a liquid binder to form granules. This improves flowability and compressibility.

b. **Dry Granulation:** Powders are compacted into large slugs or briquettes, which are then broken down into granules. This method is used for powders sensitive to moisture.

c. **Direct Compression:** Powders or granules are compressed directly into tablets without prior granulation, suitable for powders with good flow properties.

2.3. Tablet Compression:

a. **Die and Punch Mechanism:** In a tablet press, the powder or granules are placed into a die cavity. Upper and lower punches apply pressure to compress the material into tablet form.

b. **Pressure Application:** The pressure applied must be sufficient to cause plastic deformation and bonding of particles. This pressure is crucial for tablet hardness and integrity.

2.4. Parameters Influencing Compression:

a. **Compression Force:** The amount of pressure applied to the powder mixture, affecting tablet hardness and density.

b. **Tablet Geometry:** The shape and size of the tablet are determined by the die and punches.

c. **Speed of Compression:** The rate at which tablets are compressed, which can influence the consistency and quality of the tablets.

Consolidation:

1. Definition: Consolidation refers to the process by which particles in a powder or granule bed are compacted and bonded together under pressure to form a solid structure. It involves the reduction of void spaces between particles and the formation of a cohesive mass.

2. Process of Consolidation:

2.1. Particle Packing:

a. **Initial Packing:** When powders are initially packed, particles arrange themselves in a certain structure with interparticle voids.

b. **Compaction:** During compression, particles are pressed together, reducing these voids and increasing the density of the powder bed.

2.2. Mechanisms of Consolidation:

a. **Plastic Deformation:** Under compression, particles deform plastically, which helps in creating strong bonds between them.

b. **Elastic Deformation:** Initially, particles may deform elastically, but with increased pressure, they transition to plastic deformation.

c. **Bond Formation:** Particle bonds form through mechanisms such as van der Waals forces, mechanical interlocking, or solid-state bonding, depending on the material and pressure applied.

2.3. Consolidation Phases:

a. **Loose Powder Bed:** The powder bed starts in a loose, low-density state.

b. **Compacted Bed:** As pressure is applied, the powder bed densifies, and particles start to bond together.

c. **Fully Consolidated Tablet:** At sufficient pressure, the particles form a solid, cohesive tablet with minimal voids.

2.4. Factors Affecting Consolidation:

a. **Particle Size and Shape:** Smaller particles and those with regular shapes tend to consolidate more easily and uniformly.

b. **Powder Flow Properties:** Powders with good flow properties generally consolidate more effectively, resulting in more consistent tablets.

c. **Formulation Additives:** Excipients such as binders and lubricants affect the consolidation process by improving particle bonding and flowability.

Differences Between Compression and Consolidation

a. **Compression:** Primarily refers to the process of applying mechanical force to form tablets. It involves the transformation of loose powders into a solid dosage form.

b. **Consolidation:** Refers to the process of densifying and bonding particles together within the powder bed. It is a broader concept that encompasses the mechanisms leading to a cohesive solid mass.

Applications and Importance

a. **Tablet Quality:** Proper compression and consolidation are crucial for ensuring that tablets have the desired hardness, disintegration, and dissolution characteristics.

b. **Uniform Dosage:** Consistent compression and consolidation processes ensure that each tablet contains the correct amount of API and excipients.

c. **Manufacturing Efficiency:** Optimizing compression and consolidation parameters improves production efficiency and reduces the likelihood of defects such as capping or lamination.

EFFECT OF FRICTION

Friction plays a significant role in the compression and compaction of powders and granules during tablet manufacturing. It affects various aspects of the process, including powder flow, tablet quality, and equipment performance. Here's a detailed look at how friction impacts these processes:

1. Friction in Tablet Compression:

1.1. Role of Friction:

a. **Powder Flow:** Friction between powder particles and between the powder and equipment surfaces can affect the flowability of the powder. High friction can lead to poor flow, causing inconsistent filling of the tablet die and uneven tablet weight.

b. **Particle Interaction:** Friction between particles during compression can influence how they interact and bond together. Excessive friction may impede particle deformation and bonding.

1.2. Impact on Compression:

a. **Tablet Ejection:** Friction between the tablet and the die walls can affect the ease of tablet ejection. High friction can cause sticking or binding of the tablet to the die, leading to defects like surface imperfections or incomplete ejection.

b. **Compression Force:** High friction can require higher compression forces to achieve the desired tablet hardness, potentially leading to increased wear on the tablet press and variability in tablet quality.

c. **Uniformity:** Variations in friction can cause inconsistencies in tablet hardness and weight. For example, if friction is uneven across the die surface, it can lead to non-uniform compression and tablet defects.

2. Friction in Powder Compaction:

2.1. Role of Friction:

a. **Compaction Efficiency:** Friction affects the efficiency of powder compaction. High friction between powder particles or between powder and compaction rollers can hinder the compaction process, affecting the density and uniformity of the compacted material.

b. **Roller Interaction:** In roller compaction, friction between the powder and the rollers can influence the formation of compacted ribbons or flakes. Excessive friction can lead to uneven compaction and reduced granule quality.

2.2. Impact on Compaction:

a. **Density and Cohesion:** Friction affects the extent to which particles are compressed and bonded together. High friction can impede the formation of a uniform, dense compact, leading to variations in granule density and cohesion.

b. **Compaction Force:** Increased friction may require higher forces for compaction, which can affect equipment performance and increase the risk of damage or excessive wear.

3. Managing Friction

3.1. Powder Formulation:

a. **Particle Size and Shape:** Optimizing particle size and shape can reduce friction and improve flowability. Smaller, more spherical particles generally exhibit lower friction and better flow properties.
b. **Lubricants and Glidants:** Adding lubricants (e.g., magnesium stearate) and glidants (e.g., talc) can reduce friction between particles and between particles and equipment surfaces, improving powder flow and tablet ejection.

3.2. Equipment Design:

a. **Die and Punch Surface:** Smooth die and punch surfaces can reduce friction and improve tablet ejection. Regular maintenance and polishing of these surfaces help maintain their effectiveness.
b. **Roller Compaction Settings:** Adjusting the settings on roller compactors, such as roller speed and gap, can help manage friction and optimize compaction performance.

3.3. Process Optimization:

a. **Compression Pressure:** Adjusting compression pressure to balance the effects of friction and achieve the desired tablet hardness and quality.
b. **Compaction Speed:** Modifying the speed of the compaction process can help manage friction and improve the consistency of compacted material.

4. Effects on Tablet Quality and Production:

4.1. Tablet Defects:

a. **Capping and Lamination:** High friction can contribute to capping (separation of the tablet top) and lamination (separation of the tablet into layers), leading to defects in tablet appearance and performance.
b. **Surface Imperfections:** Excessive friction can cause surface imperfections, such as roughness or pitting, affecting the tablet's visual and functional quality.

4.2. Equipment Wear:

a. **Increased Wear:** High friction can accelerate wear and tear on tablet press components and roller compaction equipment, leading to increased maintenance needs and potential downtime.

DISTRIBUTION OF FORCES

In tablet manufacturing, the distribution of forces during compression and compaction is crucial for ensuring the formation of high-quality tablets and efficient production processes. Here's a detailed look at how forces are distributed and their impact:

1. Distribution of Forces in Tablet Compression:

1.1. Tablet Press Mechanism:

a. **Die and Punch System:** A tablet press typically has an upper punch, a lower punch, and a die cavity. The upper punch moves downward, and the lower punch moves upward to compress the powder between them.

b. **Force Application:** As the punches move together, they apply a compressive force to the powder bed. This force is intended to compact the powder and bond particles together to form a tablet.

1.2. Force Distribution:

a. **Uniformity:** Ideally, the applied force should be distributed uniformly across the die cavity to ensure even tablet compression. However, non-uniform force distribution can lead to inconsistencies in tablet hardness and weight.

b. **Edge Effects:** Forces at the edges of the die cavity may be different from those in the center. This can lead to variations in tablet density and hardness, particularly in tablets with irregular shapes or large diameters.

1.3. Factors Affecting Force Distribution:

a. **Die Fill:** Inconsistent die fill can lead to uneven force distribution. Proper die filling is essential for uniform compression.

b. **Powder Characteristics:** The flowability and compressibility of the powder affect how forces are transmitted through the powder bed.

Powders with poor flow properties may result in uneven force distribution.

c. **Tablet Press Design:** The design of the tablet press, including the alignment of punches and the condition of the die, affects how forces are distributed. Worn or misaligned parts can lead to uneven compression.

1.4. Impact on Tablet Quality:

a. **Hardness Variability:** Non-uniform force distribution can cause variations in tablet hardness, leading to problems with tablet disintegration and dissolution.

b. **Defects:** Uneven compression forces can result in tablet defects such as capping, lamination, or uneven surfaces.

2. Distribution of Forces in Powder Compaction:

2.1. Compaction Process:

a. **Roller Compaction:** In roller compaction, powder is fed between two counter-rotating rollers. The forces applied by the rollers compress the powder to form ribbons or flakes.

b. **Force Application:** The forces applied by the rollers are intended to densify the powder and improve granule formation.

2.2. Force Distribution:

a. **Roller Surface Contact:** The distribution of force between the rollers and the powder bed affects the quality of the compacted material. Uneven roller surfaces or inconsistent feed rates can lead to uneven compaction.

b. **Compaction Pressure:** The pressure exerted by the rollers on the powder bed influences the density and cohesion of the compacted material. Uniform pressure distribution is essential for producing consistent granules.

2.3. Factors Affecting Force Distribution:

a. **Roller Design:** The design of the rollers, including their surface texture and alignment, affects how forces are applied to the powder. Smooth, properly aligned rollers ensure even force distribution.
b. **Powder Feed Rate:** Variations in the feed rate can lead to uneven force application and inconsistent compaction.

2.4. Impact on Granule Quality:

a. **Density Consistency:** Uneven force distribution can result in inconsistent granule density, affecting the quality of the final tablet.
b. **Granule Size and Shape:** Inconsistent compaction forces can lead to variations in granule size and shape, which can impact the flowability and compressibility of the powder.

3. Managing Force Distribution:

3.1. Equipment Calibration and Maintenance:

a. **Regular Maintenance:** Ensuring that tablet press and compaction equipment are well-maintained and calibrated helps in achieving uniform force distribution.
b. **Alignment Checks:** Regular checks for alignment and wear on punches, dies, and rollers are crucial for maintaining consistent force application.

3.2. Process Optimization:

a. **Uniform Die Filling:** Ensuring consistent die filling helps in achieving uniform force distribution and tablet quality.
b. **Powder Preparation:** Properly prepared powders with good flow and compressibility characteristics contribute to more uniform force distribution.

3.3. Design Considerations:

a. **Die and Punch Design:** Using high-quality dies and punches with smooth surfaces and precise alignment helps in achieving uniform force distribution.

b. **Roller Design:** Roller compactors with well-designed rollers and consistent surface textures ensure even force application.

4. Effects on Tablet Quality and Production:

4.1. Tablet Uniformity:

a. **Consistent Hardness:** Uniform force distribution helps in achieving consistent tablet hardness and weight.

b. **Reduced Defects:** Proper force distribution reduces the likelihood of defects such as capping, lamination, or uneven surfaces.

4.2. Manufacturing Efficiency:

a. **Reduced Downtime:** Consistent force distribution minimizes equipment wear and reduces the need for maintenance or adjustments.

b. **Improved Productivity:** Efficient force application enhances the overall productivity of the tablet manufacturing process.

COMPACTION PROFILES

Compaction profiles are critical for understanding how powders behave under pressure during the compression and compaction processes. They provide insights into the relationship between applied pressure and the resulting physical properties of the compacted material. Here's a detailed look at compaction profiles:

1. Definition of Compaction Profiles

1.1. Compaction Profile: A compaction profile is a graphical representation that shows how various properties of the powder change as a function of applied compaction pressure. These profiles help in understanding the behavior of powders during the compaction process.

1.2. Key Parameters:

a. **Pressure:** The amount of force applied to the powder during compaction.

b. **Density:** The bulk density or tapped density of the powder before and after compaction.

c. **Tablet Hardness:** The strength or hardness of the tablets formed under different pressures.
d. **Compaction Force:** The force applied by the compaction equipment (e.g., roller compactor, tablet press).

2. Types of Compaction Profiles:

2.1. Density vs. Pressure Profile:

a. **Initial Density:** The bulk density of the powder before compaction.
b. **Compacted Density:** The density of the powder after compaction at various pressure levels.
c. **Profile Characteristics:** The profile typically shows a curve where density increases with applied pressure. At higher pressures, the curve often flattens out, indicating that further increases in pressure result in smaller changes in density.

2.2. Hardness vs. Pressure Profile:

a. **Tablet Hardness:** The mechanical strength of the tablets formed at different compaction pressures.
b. **Profile Characteristics:** This profile often shows that tablet hardness increases with applied pressure. At higher pressures, the rate of increase in hardness may slow down, and the tablets may reach a point where further pressure does not significantly enhance hardness.

2.3. Compaction Force vs. Pressure Profile:

a. **Force Application:** The force exerted by the compaction equipment on the powder.
b. **Profile Characteristics:** This profile illustrates how the force required for compaction changes with applied pressure. It often shows a linear or exponential increase in force as pressure increases, reflecting the increased resistance of the powder to compression.

3. Key Concepts in Compaction Profiles:

3.1. Elastic Deformation:

a. **Definition:** The reversible deformation that occurs when pressure is applied. Powders initially deform elastically, which means they return to their original shape when the pressure is removed.
b. **Profile Impact:** In the early stages of compaction, the profile shows a significant increase in density with pressure due to elastic deformation.

3.2. Plastic Deformation:

a. **Definition:** Permanent deformation that occurs when the applied pressure exceeds a certain threshold. Powders undergo plastic deformation and bond together to form a solid structure.
b. **Profile Impact:** As pressure increases, the profile shows a more pronounced increase in density and hardness due to plastic deformation.

3.3. Compaction Limits:

a. **Compression Limits:** The maximum pressure at which the powder can be compacted effectively. Beyond this point, further increases in pressure may not significantly enhance density or hardness.
b. **Profile Characteristics:** The profiles often plateau at high pressures, indicating that additional pressure does not result in substantial improvements in tablet properties.

4. Applications of Compaction Profiles:

4.1. Formulation Development:

a. **Optimizing Formulation:** Compaction profiles help in optimizing tablet formulations by identifying the appropriate pressure ranges for achieving desired tablet properties.
b. **Material Selection:** Profiles aid in selecting suitable excipients and active ingredients based on their compaction behavior.

4.2. Process Optimization:

a. **Equipment Calibration:** Compaction profiles assist in calibrating compaction equipment to ensure consistent and efficient tablet production.

b. **Quality Control:** Monitoring compaction profiles helps in maintaining tablet quality and consistency during production.

4.3. Troubleshooting:

a. **Identifying Issues:** Deviations from expected compaction profiles can indicate problems such as inconsistent powder properties, equipment malfunctions, or formulation issues.

5. Example Profiles:

5.1. Density Profile Example:

a. **Low Pressure:** Initial steep slope indicating rapid increase in density.

b. **Mid Pressure:** Gradual flattening of the curve as the powder becomes more densely packed.

c. **High Pressure:** Plateau indicating that further increases in pressure have minimal effect on density.

5.2. Hardness Profile Example:

a. **Low Pressure:** Gradual increase in tablet hardness with applied pressure.

b. **Mid Pressure:** Steeper slope showing significant increases in hardness.

c. **High Pressure:** Flattening of the curve as hardness reaches its maximum limit.

SOLUBILITY

Solubility is an important factor in the formulation of tablets and the compaction process. It influences the dissolution and bioavailability of the active pharmaceutical ingredient (API) in the final tablet. Here's a detailed look at how solubility impacts compression and compaction:

1. Solubility and Its Importance:

1.1. Definition:

a. **Solubility** refers to the ability of a substance (typically the API) to dissolve in a solvent, usually water, to form a solution. For tablets, it's crucial because it determines how quickly and effectively the API can be released and absorbed in the body.

1.2. Impact on Tablet Formulation:

a. **Dissolution Rate:** The rate at which the API dissolves affects its bioavailability and therapeutic efficacy. APIs with poor solubility may lead to slower drug release and absorption.

b. **Formulation Strategy:** Solubility influences the choice of excipients and the design of the tablet formulation to enhance drug release and performance.

2. Solubility and Compression:

2.1. Influence on Powder Flow:

a. **Poorly Soluble APIs:** Powders with poorly soluble APIs may have different flow properties compared to those with highly soluble APIs. Poor solubility can lead to issues such as poor flowability and difficulty in achieving uniform die fill during compression.

b. **Granulation:** Granulating poorly soluble powders can improve flowability and compressibility, making them easier to compress into tablets.

2.2. Impact on Tablet Compression:

a. **Compaction Behavior:** APIs with low solubility may affect the compaction behavior. These APIs might require higher compression forces to achieve the desired tablet hardness and density.

b. **Tablet Integrity:** Poorly soluble APIs may influence the tablet's physical integrity, potentially leading to issues such as capping or lamination.

2.3. Solubility Enhancement Techniques:

a. **Use of Excipients:** Excipients such as solubilizers, surfactants, and solubilizing agents can be added to improve the solubility of the API and facilitate compression.

b. **Formulation Modifications:** Techniques such as particle size reduction, the use of salts, and the formation of solid dispersions can enhance the solubility of poorly soluble APIs.

3. Solubility and Compaction:

3.1. Effect on Granule Formation:

a. **Compaction of Granules:** The solubility of the API affects the formation and quality of granules. Granules formed with poorly soluble APIs might have different characteristics compared to those with highly soluble APIs.

b. **Binder Selection:** Soluble binders can be used in granulation to enhance the cohesion of granules and improve compaction.

3.2. Impact on Granule Properties:

a. **Granule Density:** Solubility affects the density and porosity of the granules. Poorly soluble APIs may lead to lower-density granules, affecting compaction and tablet quality.

b. **Granule Flowability:** The solubility of the API can influence the flowability of granules. Granules with poorly soluble APIs may have different flow properties, affecting the consistency of tablet production.

3.3. Solubility-Driven Compaction Strategies:

a. **Pre-Compaction Treatments:** Pre-treating powders or granules to enhance solubility can improve the compaction process and tablet quality.

b. **Compaction Aids:** Using compaction aids or modifiers can help manage the effects of solubility on the compaction process, ensuring consistent tablet formation.

4. Solubility Enhancement Methods:

4.1. Physical Modifications:

a. **Particle Size Reduction:** Reducing the particle size of the API increases its surface area and can enhance its solubility.

b. **Solid Dispersions:** Forming solid dispersions with polymers can improve the solubility of poorly soluble APIs.

4.2. Chemical Modifications:

a. **Salt Formation:** Converting the API into a salt form can enhance its solubility.

b. **Complexation:** Using complexing agents such as cyclodextrins to improve solubility.

4.3. Formulation Techniques:

a. **Use of Surfactants:** Incorporating surfactants into the formulation can enhance the solubility of the API.

b. **Hydrophilic Excipients:** Using hydrophilic excipients in the formulation to improve solubility and drug release.

5. Practical Considerations:

5.1. Solubility Testing:

a. **Pre-Formulation Studies:** Conducting solubility studies during the pre-formulation phase to understand how the API behaves in different solvents and conditions.

b. **In-Vitro Dissolution Testing:** Testing the dissolution rate of tablets to ensure that the solubility of the API is sufficient for therapeutic efficacy.

5.2. Tablet Quality Control:

a. **Uniformity:** Ensuring uniform distribution of the API and excipients in the tablet to achieve consistent dissolution and solubility.

b. **Dissolution Testing:** Regularly testing the dissolution characteristics of tablets to ensure that the API is released as intended.

Solubility plays a crucial role in the compression and compaction processes, influencing the flowability, compressibility, and final quality of the tablets. By understanding and addressing solubility issues, pharmaceutical scientists can develop effective formulations and optimize tablet manufacturing processes.

CLASSIFICATION:

1. Compression:

1.1. **Direct Compression:**

a. **Definition:** A process where powders or granules are compressed directly into tablets without any intermediate granulation step.

b. **Characteristics:**

i. Suitable for powders with good flow and compressibility properties.
ii. Simpler and more cost-effective compared to other methods.
iii. Minimal use of excipients, which may include lubricants, disintegrants, and binders.

c. **Example: Paracetamol Tablets:** Paracetamol tablets are often manufactured by direct compression because paracetamol has suitable flow and compressibility properties.

1.2. **Wet Granulation:**

a. **Definition:** A process where powders are mixed with a liquid binder to form a wet mass, which is then dried, milled, and compressed into tablets.

b. **Characteristics:**

i. Enhances the flowability and compressibility of powders that are difficult to compress directly.
ii. Helps in granulating poorly compressible materials and improving uniformity.
iii. Involves multiple steps: mixing, granulating, drying, and milling.

c. **Example: Aspirin Tablets:** Aspirin may require wet granulation to ensure uniformity and improve the compressibility of the powder blend.

1.3. **Dry Granulation:**

a. **Definition:** A process where powders are compacted into large tablets (or slugs) and then milled into granules before being compressed into tablets.

b. **Characteristics:**

i. Used for powders that are sensitive to moisture or heat.
ii. Involves slugging (compacting powder into large tablets) and milling the slugs into granules.
iii. Suitable for materials that cannot withstand wet granulation.

c. **Example: Caffeine Tablets:** Caffeine, which is sensitive to moisture, can be processed using dry granulation to avoid exposure to moisture.

1.4. **Roller Compaction:**

a. **Definition:** A process where powders are fed between two counter-rotating rollers to form compacted ribbons or flakes, which are then milled and compressed into tablets.

b. **Characteristics:**

i. Used for powders with poor flowability or compressibility.

ii. Produces granules with consistent size and density.

iii. Suitable for high-volume production.

c. **Example: Antacid Tablets:** Antacid formulations that require uniform granules for consistent tablet properties may use roller compaction.

2. Compaction:

2.1. **Single Punch Compaction:**

a. **Definition:** A process where powder or granules are compressed into tablets using a single set of punches in a tablet press.

b. **Characteristics:**

i. Suitable for small-scale or laboratory-scale tablet production.

ii. Simple and easy to set up, but not ideal for high-volume manufacturing.

c. **Example: Experimental Tablets:** Small batches of experimental formulations are often compressed using single-punch tablet presses in research settings.

2.2. **Rotary Tablet Press Compaction:**

a. **Definition:** A process where powders are compressed into tablets using a rotary press with multiple sets of punches and dies.

b. **Characteristics:**

i. Suitable for large-scale, high-speed tablet production.

ii. Allows for continuous operation and high output.

iii. Equipped with features for controlling tablet weight, thickness, and hardness.

c. **Example: Over-the-Counter (OTC) Tablets:** High-volume production of OTC tablets, such as cold medications or pain relievers, typically uses rotary tablet presses.

2.3. **Hydraulic Press Compaction:**

a. **Definition:** A process where powders are compressed into tablets using a hydraulic press, which applies pressure using hydraulic cylinders.

b. **Characteristics:**

i. Suitable for small to medium-scale production and for manufacturing tablets with high compression forces.

ii. Allows for precise control of compression force and tablet density.

c. **Example: Nutraceutical Tablets:** Specialty tablets, such as those containing high doses of vitamins or minerals, may be manufactured using hydraulic presses.

2.4. **Isostatic Compaction:**

a. **Definition:** A process where powders are compressed using uniform pressure applied from all directions (isostatic pressure) to form tablets or pellets.

b. **Characteristics:**

i. Used for high-density and high-strength tablets or pellets.

ii. Provides uniform compaction and minimizes particle segregation.

c. **Example: Advanced Ceramic Tablets:** Isostatic compaction is used in the production of advanced ceramic tablets and materials used in high-tech applications.

3. Other Methods:

3.1. **Tableting by Compression Molding:**

a. **Definition:** A method where powders are compressed in a mold under pressure to form tablets, often used for specialized or custom shapes.

b. **Characteristics:**

i. Allows for precise control of tablet shape and size.

ii. Used for tablets requiring unique designs or high precision.

c. **Example: Specialty Tablets:** Custom-shaped or embossed tablets used for specific applications or branding.

3.2. **Extrusion and Spheronization:**

a. **Definition:** A process where powders are extruded into long cylinders or rods, which are then spheronized into spherical granules before compression into tablets.

b. **Characteristics:**

i. Produces uniform granules with controlled size and shape.

ii. Often used for controlled-release formulations.

c. **Example: Controlled-Release Tablets:** Tablets designed for controlled drug release may use extrusion and spheronization to ensure consistent granule size.

A. Paracetamol Tablets:

1. **Paracetamol (Acetaminophen) Overview:**

a. **Chemical Name:** N-acetyl-p-aminophenol

b. **Mechanism of Action:** Paracetamol primarily exerts its analgesic (pain-relieving) and antipyretic (fever-reducing) effects through inhibition of cyclooxygenase (COX) enzymes, particularly COX-3, in the central nervous system. Unlike non-steroidal anti-inflammatory drugs (NSAIDs), it has minimal anti-inflammatory effects.

c. **Uses:** Commonly used to relieve mild to moderate pain (e.g., headaches, muscle aches) and reduce fever.

2. **Paracetamol Tablets in Compression and Compaction:**

2.1. **Compression:**

a. **Direct Compression:**

i. **Powder Properties:** Paracetamol powder is generally suitable for direct compression due to its good flowability and compressibility.

ii. **Formulation:** Involves mixing paracetamol with excipients like fillers (e.g., microcrystalline cellulose), binders (e.g., starch), and lubricants (e.g., magnesium stearate).

iii. **Tablet Characteristics:** Directly compressed tablets of paracetamol are typically smooth and uniform in size, with consistent hardness and dissolution characteristics.

b. **Granulation:**

i. **Wet Granulation:** If paracetamol powder exhibits poor flow properties or compressibility, wet granulation might be used. This involves creating granules from the powder using a liquid binder, followed by drying and milling.

ii. **Dry Granulation:** This method may be used if moisture-sensitive excipients are involved. Powder is compacted into slugs or ribbons and then granulated.

2.2. **Compaction:**

a. **Single Punch Press:**

i. **Application:** Often used in research and small-scale production. Paracetamol tablets can be compressed using single-punch presses, which apply force to compact the powder into tablets.

b. **Rotary Tablet Press:**

i. **Application:** Used in large-scale production. Provides high-speed compression with multiple dies and punches, suitable for producing large batches of paracetamol tablets with consistent quality.

c. **Roller Compaction:**

i. **Application:** Less common for paracetamol, but can be used if granulation is necessary. Powder is compacted between rollers to form granules before tableting.

3. **Pharmacokinetics and Pharmacodynamics:**

a. **Absorption:** Paracetamol is well absorbed from the gastrointestinal tract. Peak plasma concentrations are usually achieved within 30 minutes to 2 hours after oral administration.
b. **Distribution:** Distributed throughout most body tissues, with high concentrations in the liver.
c. **Metabolism:** Mainly metabolized in the liver to non-toxic metabolites. Some is conjugated to sulfate and glucuronide.
d. **Excretion:** Primarily excreted via the kidneys as conjugated metabolites.

B. Aspirin Tablets:

1. **Aspirin (Acetylsalicylic Acid) Overview:**
   a. **Chemical Name:** 2-acetoxybenzoic acid
   b. **Mechanism of Action:** Aspirin works by irreversibly inhibiting cyclooxygenase (COX) enzymes (COX-1 and COX-2), leading to reduced synthesis of prostaglandins. This results in analgesic, antipyretic, and anti-inflammatory effects. Additionally, aspirin has antiplatelet effects by inhibiting thromboxane A2 production.
   c. **Uses:** Used to relieve pain, reduce inflammation, lower fever, and as an antiplatelet agent to prevent cardiovascular events.

2. **Aspirin Tablets in Compression and Compaction:**

2.1. **Compression:**

a. **Direct Compression:**
   i. **Powder Properties:** Aspirin powder can be compressed directly into tablets but may require additional excipients to enhance flowability and compressibility.
   ii. **Formulation:** Typically includes fillers (e.g., calcium carbonate), binders (e.g., cellulose derivatives), and lubricants (e.g., stearic acid).

iii. **Tablet Characteristics:** Directly compressed aspirin tablets are effective for standard formulations, but may need careful control to avoid issues like capping or lamination.

b. **Granulation:**

i. **Wet Granulation:** Aspirin may be granulated to improve powder flow and compressibility. The process involves mixing with a liquid binder, drying, and milling.

ii. **Dry Granulation:** Suitable for aspirin, especially when dealing with moisture-sensitive formulations. Powders are compacted into larger units and then granulated.

2.2. **Compaction:**

a. **Single Punch Press:**

i. **Application:** Utilized for small-scale or laboratory-scale tablet production. Aspirin tablets can be effectively compressed using single-punch presses.

b. **Rotary Tablet Press:**

i. **Application:** Ideal for large-scale production. Aspirin tablets produced using rotary presses benefit from high-speed and high-efficiency manufacturing.

c. **Roller Compaction:**

i. **Application:** Used when granulation is necessary. Aspirin powder is compacted between rollers to form granules before compression into tablets.

3. **Pharmacokinetics and Pharmacodynamics:**

a. **Absorption:** Aspirin is rapidly absorbed from the gastrointestinal tract, with peak plasma levels usually reached within 1-2 hours after oral administration.

b. **Distribution:** Aspirin is widely distributed throughout the body and crosses the blood-brain barrier.

c. **Metabolism:** Aspirin is hydrolyzed to salicylic acid, which is then further metabolized in the liver.

d. **Excretion:** Mainly excreted in the urine as salicylate and its conjugates.

C. Caffeine Tablets:

1. **Caffeine Overview:**

   a. **Chemical Name:** 1,3,7-Trimethylxanthine

   b. **Mechanism of Action:** Caffeine is a central nervous system stimulant. It works primarily by blocking adenosine receptors (particularly A1 and A2A receptors), which prevents the inhibitory effects of adenosine on neurotransmitter release. This leads to increased release of excitatory neurotransmitters such as dopamine and norepinephrine, resulting in enhanced alertness and wakefulness.

   c. **Uses:** Caffeine is commonly used to treat fatigue, improve mental alertness, and as a diuretic. It is also included in some pain relief medications for its synergistic effects with analgesics.

2. **Caffeine Tablets in Compression and Compaction:**

2.1. **Compression:**

   a. **Direct Compression:**

      i. **Powder Properties:** Caffeine powder is generally suitable for direct compression due to its good flowability and compressibility.

      ii. **Formulation:** The formulation may include excipients such as fillers (e.g., microcrystalline cellulose), binders (e.g., hydroxypropyl cellulose), and lubricants (e.g., magnesium stearate).

      iii. **Tablet Characteristics:** Tablets produced by direct compression are typically uniform in size and hardness, with consistent release profiles.

   b. **Granulation:**

i. **Wet Granulation:** If caffeine exhibits poor flow properties or compressibility, wet granulation may be used. This process involves adding a liquid binder to form granules, which are then dried and milled before compression.

ii. **Dry Granulation:** Suitable for caffeine tablets when moisture-sensitive excipients are involved. Powder is compacted into slugs or ribbons, then milled into granules.

2.2. **Compaction:**

a. **Single Punch Press:**

i. **Application:** Used in research or small-scale production. Single punch presses can effectively compress caffeine tablets, especially for initial formulations or small batches.

b. **Rotary Tablet Press:**

i. **Application:** Ideal for large-scale production. Rotary presses provide high-speed and high-efficiency tablet compression for caffeine tablets, ensuring consistent quality and production volume.

c. **Roller Compaction:**

i. **Application:** Used when granulation is needed. Caffeine powders are compacted between rollers to form granules before compression into tablets. This method is helpful for powders with poor flowability.

3. **Pharmacokinetics and Pharmacodynamics:**

a. **Absorption:** Rapidly absorbed from the gastrointestinal tract, with peak plasma concentrations reached within 1-2 hours after ingestion.

b. **Distribution:** Widely distributed throughout the body, including the brain.

c. **Metabolism:** Primarily metabolized in the liver by cytochrome P450 enzymes (mainly CYP1A2) into metabolites such as paraxanthine, theobromine, and theophylline.

d. **Excretion:** Mainly excreted in the urine as metabolites.

D. Antacid Tablets:

1. **Antacids Overview:**

a. **Common Active Ingredients:**

i. **Calcium Carbonate:** Acts as a neutralizing agent by reacting with gastric acid to form calcium chloride, water, and carbon dioxide.

ii. **Magnesium Hydroxide:** Neutralizes stomach acid by reacting to form magnesium chloride and water.

iii. **Aluminum Hydroxide:** Neutralizes stomach acid and forms aluminum chloride and water.

b. **Mechanism of Action:** Antacids work by neutralizing excess stomach acid (hydrochloric acid) to provide symptomatic relief from heartburn and indigestion. They do not inhibit acid secretion but rather neutralize it directly.

c. **Uses:** Used to relieve symptoms of heartburn, acid indigestion, and upset stomach.

2. **Antacid Tablets in Compression and Compaction:**

2.1. **Compression:**

a. **Direct Compression:**

i. **Powder Properties:** Antacid powders (e.g., calcium carbonate, magnesium hydroxide) are often directly compressed into tablets. These powders generally have good flow properties but may require additional excipients to ensure proper tablet formation.

ii. **Formulation:** Excipient choices may include fillers (e.g., lactose), binders (e.g., starch), and lubricants (e.g., magnesium stearate).

iii. **Tablet Characteristics:** Tablets must be carefully compressed to ensure they are not too soft or too hard, which could affect their dissolution and efficacy.

b. **Granulation:**

i. **Wet Granulation:** If the powder blend shows poor compressibility or flowability, wet granulation may be used. This process involves mixing with a binder to form granules, drying them, and then milling before compression.

ii. **Dry Granulation:** For moisture-sensitive antacid components, dry granulation might be used. Powders are compacted into slugs or ribbons and then granulated.

2.2. **Compaction:**

a. **Single Punch Press:**

i. **Application:** Used for small-scale production or experimental batches of antacid tablets. Single punch presses can handle the compression of antacid formulations with proper control over tablet properties.

b. **Rotary Tablet Press:**

i. **Application:** Suitable for large-scale production. Rotary presses efficiently compress antacid tablets, ensuring uniform size, hardness, and dissolution characteristics.

c. **Roller Compaction:**

i. **Application:** Used for granulating antacid powders that have poor flow properties. Compaction between rollers forms granules, which are then compressed into tablets.

3. **Pharmacokinetics and Pharmacodynamics:**

a. **Absorption:** Antacids are not absorbed in significant amounts through the gastrointestinal tract. Their action is localized to the stomach.

b. **Distribution:** Since antacids do not get absorbed, they do not have systemic distribution.

c. **Metabolism:** Not applicable, as antacids act locally and are not metabolized.

d. **Excretion:** Antacids are excreted in the feces or urine depending on their formulation and the extent of systemic absorption (e.g., calcium carbonate).

E. Over-the-Counter (OTC) Tablets:

1. **OTC Tablets Overview:**

a. **Definition:** OTC tablets are medications available without a prescription, used to treat a variety of common ailments such as pain, cold symptoms, allergies, and digestive issues.

b. **Examples:** Common OTC tablets include ibuprofen (analgesic/anti-inflammatory), diphenhydramine (antihistamine), and loperamide (antidiarrheal).

2. **Pharmacology of Specific OTC Tablets:**

2.1. **Ibuprofen Tablets:**

a. **Chemical Name:** (RS)-2-(4-(2-Methylpropyl)phenyl)propanoic acid

b. **Mechanism of Action:** Ibuprofen is a nonsteroidal anti-inflammatory drug (NSAID) that inhibits cyclooxygenase (COX-1 and COX-2) enzymes, leading to reduced synthesis of prostaglandins, which are responsible for inflammation, pain, and fever.

c. **Uses:** Used for pain relief (e.g., headaches, menstrual cramps), inflammation reduction, and fever lowering.

2.2. **Diphenhydramine Tablets:**

a. **Chemical Name:** 2-(Diphenylmethoxy)-N,N-dimethylethanamine

b. **Mechanism of Action:** Diphenhydramine is an antihistamine that blocks H1 receptors in the histaminergic pathways, thereby reducing allergic reactions and symptoms such as itching, sneezing, and runny nose.

c. **Uses:** Used for relief from allergy symptoms, insomnia, and motion sickness.

2.3. **Loperamide Tablets:**

a. **Chemical Name:** 4-(p-Chlorophenyl)-4-hydroxy-N,N-dimethyl-α-methylphenethylamine
b. **Mechanism of Action:** Loperamide works by acting on opioid receptors in the gut wall to decrease gastrointestinal motility, thereby reducing the frequency of bowel movements and increasing stool consistency.
c. **Uses:** Used to treat diarrhea by slowing down the movement of the intestines.

3. **Compression and Compaction of OTC Tablets:**

3.1. **Compression:**

a. **Direct Compression:**
   i. **Formulation:** OTC tablets like ibuprofen and diphenhydramine are often formulated for direct compression. This involves mixing the active pharmaceutical ingredient (API) with excipients such as fillers (e.g., lactose), binders (e.g., cellulose derivatives), and lubricants (e.g., magnesium stearate).
   ii. **Characteristics:** Direct compression yields tablets with uniform size and hardness, which is crucial for consistency in dosing and performance.

b. **Granulation:**
   i. **Wet Granulation:** If the API or excipients have poor flow or compressibility, wet granulation may be used to form granules, which are then dried and compressed into tablets.
   ii. **Dry Granulation:** For APIs sensitive to moisture, dry granulation is preferred. Powders are compacted into slugs or ribbons and then granulated before compression.

3.2. **Compaction:**

a. **Single Punch Press:**

i. **Application:** Used for small-scale or laboratory production of OTC tablets. Single-punch presses are suitable for experimental formulations and initial trials.

b. **Rotary Tablet Press:**

i. **Application:** Ideal for large-scale production of OTC tablets. Rotary presses provide high-speed and efficient compression, ensuring consistent quality across large batches.

c. **Roller Compaction:**

i. **Application:** Used if granulation is required. Roller compaction can handle powders with poor flowability, producing granules that are then compressed into tablets.

4. **Pharmacokinetics and Pharmacodynamics:**

- **Absorption:** Varies by API; generally, OTC tablets are designed for rapid absorption to ensure quick relief of symptoms.
- **Distribution:** APIs are distributed throughout the body; specifics depend on the individual drug.
- **Metabolism:** Typically metabolized in the liver, but specifics vary by API.
- **Excretion:** Generally excreted via the urine, with some variability based on the API.

F. Nutraceutical Tablets:

1. **Nutraceutical Tablets Overview:**

a. **Definition:** Nutraceutical tablets are dietary supplements containing nutrients, vitamins, minerals, herbs, or other bioactive compounds intended to provide health benefits beyond basic nutrition.

b. **Examples:** Common nutraceuticals include multivitamin tablets, fish oil capsules, and probiotics.

2. **Pharmacology of Specific Nutraceutical Tablets:**

2.1. **Multivitamin Tablets:**

a. **Composition:** Typically contain a blend of essential vitamins and minerals such as vitamins A, C, D, E, B-complex, and minerals like calcium, magnesium, and zinc.

b. **Mechanism of Action:** Vitamins and minerals play various roles in supporting bodily functions, including metabolism, immune function, and cellular repair. They do not have a single pharmacological mechanism but contribute to overall health and well-being.

c. **Uses:** Used to supplement dietary intake and prevent deficiencies.

2.2. **Fish Oil Tablets:**

a. **Active Ingredient:** Omega-3 fatty acids (e.g., EPA and DHA)

b. **Mechanism of Action:** Omega-3 fatty acids have anti-inflammatory properties and support cardiovascular health by reducing triglyceride levels and improving endothelial function.

c. **Uses:** Used for cardiovascular health, cognitive support, and joint health.

2.3. **Probiotic Tablets:**

a. **Active Ingredient:** Live microorganisms (e.g., Lactobacillus, Bifidobacterium)

b. **Mechanism of Action:** Probiotics promote a healthy balance of gut microbiota, enhance gut barrier function, and support immune function by interacting with the gut-associated lymphoid tissue (GALT).

c. **Uses:** Used to support digestive health, improve gut flora, and enhance immune function.

3. **Compression and Compaction of Nutraceutical Tablets:**

3.1. **Compression:**

a. **Direct Compression:**

i. **Formulation:** Nutraceutical tablets often use direct compression if the powders have good flow and compressibility. Formulation includes active ingredients (nutrients) and excipients such as binders (e.g., cellulose), fillers (e.g., microcrystalline cellulose), and lubricants (e.g., stearates).

ii. **Characteristics:** Direct compression ensures uniformity and consistency in nutraceutical tablets, which is crucial for effective dosing.

b. **Granulation:**

i. **Wet Granulation:** Used when powders have poor flowability or compressibility. Nutrients are mixed with a binder to form granules, dried, and then compressed.

ii. **Dry Granulation:** Suitable for moisture-sensitive ingredients. Powders are compacted into slugs or ribbons, then granulated.

3.2. **Compaction:**

a. **Single Punch Press:**

i. **Application:** Used for smaller batches or experimental nutraceutical formulations. Single-punch presses are suitable for initial trials and small-scale production.

b. **Rotary Tablet Press:**

i. **Application:** Used for large-scale production. Rotary presses ensure high-speed and efficient compression of nutraceutical tablets, crucial for consistent quality in commercial production.

c. **Roller Compaction:**

i. **Application:** Used when granulation is necessary. Produces uniform granules from powders with poor flowability, which are then compressed into tablets.

4. **Pharmacokinetics and Pharmacodynamics:**

a. **Absorption:** Nutraceuticals are absorbed through the gastrointestinal tract; absorption rates depend on the specific ingredient and formulation.

b. **Distribution:** Generally distributed throughout the body; specifics depend on the nutrient.

c. **Metabolism:** Metabolized differently based on the type of nutrient (e.g., vitamins are often stored in the liver, while fatty acids may be incorporated into cell membranes).

d. **Excretion:** Excreted via urine or feces, depending on the nutrient type and body needs.

Multiple-Choice Questions (Objective)

1. What is the primary goal of compression in tablet manufacturing?
   a) To increase the weight of the tablet
   b) To bind powders or granules together to form a solid mass
   c) To decrease the dissolution rate of the tablet
   d) To improve the taste of the tablet
2. Which process involves compacting powders into large slugs or briquettes before compressing them into tablets?
   a) Wet Granulation
   b) Direct Compression
   c) Dry Granulation
   d) Roller Compaction
3. What equipment is used for large-scale tablet production with multiple stations for continuous tablet formation?
   a) Single-Punch Press
   b) Rotary Press
   c) Hydraulic Press
   d) Isostatic Press
4. What is the primary purpose of wet granulation in tablet manufacturing?
   a) To increase the weight of the tablet
   b) To improve the flowability and compressibility of powders
   c) To reduce the size of the tablet
   d) To increase the dissolution rate of the tablet

5. Which principle describes the irreversible deformation that particles undergo under sufficient pressure to form a solid tablet?
   a) Elastic Deformation
   b) Plastic Deformation
   c) Compaction Force
   d) Force Transmission
6. What is the main benefit of using lubricants in powder formulation?
   a) To increase tablet weight
   b) To improve powder flow and reduce friction
   c) To enhance tablet taste
   d) To decrease tablet hardness
7. Which method is suitable for high-volume production of tablets with consistent quality?
   a) Single Punch Press Compaction
   b) Rotary Tablet Press Compaction
   c) Hydraulic Press Compaction
   d) Isostatic Compaction
8. What does a compaction profile typically plot in tablet manufacturing?
   a) Density vs. Pressure
   b) Hardness vs. Temperature
   c) Weight vs. Time
   d) Dissolution vs. Volume
9. Which factor primarily affects the uniform distribution of forces during tablet compression?
   a) Powder Color
   b) Die Fill
   c) Tablet Shape
   d) Lubricant Type
10. What role does particle size reduction play in enhancing solubility?

a) It decreases the surface area of the particles
b) It increases the surface area of the particles
c) It changes the chemical composition of the particles
d) It improves the taste of the particles

11. Which compaction method involves applying uniform pressure from all directions?
a) Single Punch Compaction
b) Rotary Tablet Press Compaction
c) Hydraulic Press Compaction
d) Isostatic Compaction

12. How does the addition of glidants affect powder properties?
a) It decreases flowability
b) It improves flowability
c) It increases compressibility
d) It reduces compressibility

13. What is the primary mechanism of action of aspirin?
a) Inhibiting adenosine receptors
b) Blocking H1 receptors
c) Inhibiting cyclooxygenase enzymes
d) Decreasing gastrointestinal motility

14. Which excipient is commonly used as a filler in tablet formulations?
a) Magnesium Stearate
b) Microcrystalline Cellulose
c) Talc
d) Hydroxypropyl Cellulose

15. What is the main function of binders in tablet formulation?
a) To improve powder flowability
b) To bind powders together
c) To lubricate the tablet press

d) To enhance the taste of the tablet

16. Which process involves reducing the void spaces between particles and forming a cohesive mass?

a) Compression
b) Consolidation
c) Lubrication
d) Granulation

17. What impact does high friction have on tablet ejection?

a) It improves tablet ejection
b) It causes sticking or binding of the tablet to the die
c) It decreases tablet weight
d) It enhances tablet hardness

18. What type of deformation do particles initially undergo during tablet compression?

a) Plastic Deformation
b) Elastic Deformation
c) Compaction Force
d) Force Transmission

19. Which equipment is used for producing granules from powders?

a) Roller Compactor
b) Tablet Press
c) Single-Punch Press
d) Hydraulic Press

20. How does the addition of surfactants enhance solubility?

a) By decreasing the surface tension between particles and solvent
b) By increasing the surface tension between particles and solvent
c) By reducing the particle size
d) By changing the chemical composition of the particles

Short Answer Type Questions (Subjective)

1. Define compression in the context of tablet manufacturing.
2. What are the main purposes of compression in tablet production?
3. Describe the process of direct compression.
4. Explain the role of granulation in improving powder flowability and compressibility.
5. What is the difference between wet granulation and dry granulation?
6. Describe the principle of plastic deformation in tablet compression.
7. How do lubricants improve powder flow in tablet manufacturing?
8. What is the purpose of a compaction profile?
9. How does uniform die filling affect tablet quality?
10. Explain the impact of particle size reduction on solubility.
11. Describe the process of isostatic compaction.
12. How do glidants affect powder properties in tablet formulation?
13. What is the mechanism of action of aspirin?
14. What role do fillers play in tablet formulations?
15. How do binders contribute to tablet formulation?
16. Define consolidation in the context of tablet manufacturing.
17. What are the effects of high friction on tablet ejection?
18. Explain the concept of elastic deformation in tablet compression.
19. What is the function of a roller compactor in tablet manufacturing?
20. How do surfactants enhance the solubility of an API?

Long Answer Type Questions (Subjective)

1. Discuss the fundamental principles of tablet compression and the importance of understanding these principles for optimizing tablet quality.
2. Explain the processes of wet granulation and dry granulation, highlighting their advantages and disadvantages in tablet manufacturing.

3. Describe the equipment used for tablet compression and compaction, including single-punch presses, rotary tablet presses, and roller compactors.
4. Discuss the impact of friction in tablet manufacturing, including its effects on powder flow, tablet quality, and equipment performance.
5. Explain the concept of compaction profiles and their applications in optimizing tablet formulations and manufacturing processes.
6. Describe the role of solubility in tablet formulation, including techniques for enhancing the solubility of poorly soluble APIs.
7. Discuss the differences between compression and consolidation in tablet manufacturing, including the processes and factors affecting each.
8. Explain the pharmacokinetics and pharmacodynamics of paracetamol tablets, including their mechanism of action, absorption, metabolism, and excretion.
9. Describe the formulation, compression, and compaction processes of aspirin tablets, including the role of excipients and equipment used.
10. Discuss the challenges and considerations in the manufacturing of OTC tablets, including formulation strategies, equipment selection, and quality control measures.

Answer Key for MCQ Questions

1. b) To bind powders or granules together to form a solid mass
2. c) Dry Granulation
3. b) Rotary Press
4. b) To improve the flowability and compressibility of powders
5. b) Plastic Deformation
6. b) To improve powder flow and reduce friction
7. b) Rotary Tablet Press Compaction
8. a) Density vs. Pressure
9. b) Die Fill
10. b) It increases the surface area of the particles

11.d) Isostatic Compaction"

12.b) It improves flowability

13.c) Inhibiting cyclooxygenase enzymes

14.b) Microcrystalline Cellulose

15.b) To bind powders together

16.b) Consolidation

17.b) It causes sticking or binding of the tablet to the die

18.b) Elastic Deformation

19.a) Roller Compactor

20.a) By decreasing the surface tension between particles and solvent

CHAPTER – 8

STUDY OF CONSOLIDATION PARAMETERS

INTRODUCTION:

In the study of local anesthetics, consolidation parameters refer to the key factors that contribute to the efficacy, safety, and overall effectiveness of these drugs. These parameters are essential for understanding how local anesthetics work and how to optimize their use in clinical settings. Here's an overview of the consolidation parameters for local anesthetics:

1. Chemical Structure

a. **Esters vs. Amides:** Local anesthetics are generally classified into two groups based on their chemical structure. Esters (e.g., Procaine) and amides (e.g., Lidocaine) differ in their metabolism and potential for allergic reactions.

b. **Structure-Activity Relationship (SAR):** The chemical structure of local anesthetics affects their potency, duration of action, and metabolic pathways.

2. Mechanism of Action

a. **Blockade of Nerve Conduction:** Local anesthetics work by blocking sodium channels in the neuronal cell membrane. This prevents the propagation of nerve impulses, resulting in a loss of sensation in the targeted area.

b. **Receptor Binding:** Understanding how these drugs interact with sodium channels and other receptors can help optimize their use.

3. Onset and Duration of Action

a. **Onset Time:** This refers to how quickly the anesthetic starts to take effect after administration. Factors influencing onset include pH of the solution, pKa of the anesthetic, and tissue pH.

b. **Duration of Action:** This depends on the drug's affinity for the sodium channel, its metabolism, and its ability to bind to plasma proteins. For example, Bupivacaine has a longer duration of action compared to Lidocaine.

4. Pharmacokinetics

a. **Absorption:** The rate at which the anesthetic is absorbed into the bloodstream can affect its effectiveness and potential for systemic toxicity.

b. **Distribution:** The extent to which the drug spreads through the body, including its ability to cross the blood-brain barrier.

c. **Metabolism:** Esters are typically hydrolyzed by plasma cholinesterase, while amides are metabolized in the liver. This affects their duration of action and potential for systemic side effects.

d. **Excretion:** The route and rate of excretion can influence the drug's duration and potential accumulation in the body.

5. Toxicity and Side Effects

a. **Systemic Toxicity:** Overdose or excessive absorption can lead to CNS and cardiovascular toxicity. Monitoring and understanding dose limits are crucial.

b. **Allergic Reactions:** Esters are more likely to cause allergic reactions compared to amides due to their metabolic byproducts.

6. Clinical Applications

a. **Types of Anesthesia:** Different local anesthetics are used for various types of procedures, including topical anesthesia, infiltration anesthesia, nerve blocks, and epidural anesthesia.

b. **Choice of Anesthetic:** Selection depends on factors such as the required duration of action, the procedure being performed, and patient-specific considerations.

7. Concentration and Dosage

a. **Concentration:** Higher concentrations can increase the potency but may also increase the risk of toxicity.
b. **Dosage:** Correct dosing is critical to ensure effectiveness while minimizing adverse effects.

8. Interactions with Other Drugs

a. **Drug Interactions:** Local anesthetics can interact with other medications, which can affect their efficacy and safety profile. For instance, interactions with vasoconstrictors like epinephrine can influence the drug's action and side effects.

DIFFUSION PARAMETERS

In the study of local anesthetics, diffusion parameters are critical for understanding how these drugs spread through tissues and achieve effective anesthesia. Here's a detailed overview of diffusion parameters in this context:

1. Rate of Diffusion

a. **Initial Rate:** The speed at which the anesthetic spreads from the site of administration to the target nerve fibers. This can be influenced by factors such as the concentration of the anesthetic, the volume injected, and the tissue characteristics.
b. **Tissue Penetration:** The ability of the anesthetic to penetrate various tissues, including skin, subcutaneous fat, and muscle, which affects how quickly and effectively it reaches the nerve fibers.

2. Volume of Distribution

a. **Spread in the Tissue:** The volume of distribution refers to the extent to which the anesthetic spreads through the local tissue. A larger volume of distribution can lead to broader anesthesia but may also increase the risk of systemic absorption and toxicity.
b. **Injection Site:** The location of the injection affects the volume of distribution. For instance, an injection into a highly vascular area may lead to faster systemic absorption.

3. Rate of Absorption

a. **Systemic Absorption:** After diffusion through the tissues, the anesthetic may be absorbed into the bloodstream. The rate of absorption can affect both the efficacy of the anesthesia and the risk of systemic toxicity.

b. **Vasoconstriction:** Adding vasoconstrictors (like epinephrine) to the anesthetic solution can reduce blood flow in the area, slowing absorption and prolonging the duration of action.

4. Local Tissue Factors

a. **pH of the Tissue:** The pH of the tissue affects the ionization of the anesthetic. A lower pH (more acidic) can decrease the amount of anesthetic in its active form, potentially slowing the onset of action.

b. **Blood Flow:** Areas with higher blood flow can lead to more rapid absorption of the anesthetic, reducing its duration of action. Conversely, areas with lower blood flow may retain the anesthetic longer.

5. Drug Properties

a. **Lipophilicity:** The ability of the anesthetic to dissolve in lipids affects its diffusion through nerve membranes. More lipophilic drugs tend to penetrate nerves more effectively.

b. **Molecular Size:** Smaller molecules can diffuse more easily through tissues, potentially improving the speed of onset and depth of anesthesia.

6. Impact of Local Anesthesia Techniques

a. **Infiltration Anesthesia:** Diffusion parameters are critical as the anesthetic spreads through the tissue surrounding the injection site.

b. **Nerve Block:** Effective diffusion is essential for achieving complete nerve blockade, as the anesthetic must diffuse to the nerve trunk or branches.

c. **Epidural and Spinal Anesthesia:** Diffusion through the cerebrospinal fluid and spinal tissues is key for effective anesthesia.

7. Influence of Adjuvants

a. **Vasoconstrictors:** Agents like epinephrine can modify diffusion parameters by reducing blood flow, which prolongs the duration of action and decreases systemic absorption.
b. **Additives:** Other additives, such as steroids or opioids, can influence the effectiveness and duration of local anesthesia by affecting the diffusion and binding of the anesthetic.

8. Clinical Implications

a. **Effectiveness of Anesthesia:** Proper understanding of diffusion parameters helps in achieving adequate anesthesia for various procedures.
b. **Prevention of Complications:** Awareness of how diffusion affects drug distribution can help in avoiding complications such as inadequate anesthesia or systemic toxicity.

DISSOLUTION PARAMETERS

In the study of local anesthetics, dissolution parameters are crucial for understanding how these drugs dissolve and disperse once they are administered. These parameters influence the onset, efficacy, and safety of local anesthesia. Here's a detailed overview of dissolution parameters:

1. Solubility

a. **In Water:** The solubility of a local anesthetic in water determines how well it can be prepared for injection. Highly soluble anesthetics are easier to dissolve and prepare in solution form.
b. **In Lipids:** Since local anesthetics need to cross nerve membranes, their lipid solubility impacts their ability to diffuse through lipid-rich nerve membranes and achieve effective blockade.

2. pH of the Solution

a. **Impact on Solubility:** The pH of the anesthetic solution affects its solubility and ionization. Local anesthetics are weak bases, and their solubility is influenced by the pH of the solution and the surrounding tissues.

b. **pKa and Ionization:** The pKa of the anesthetic determines the ratio of ionized to non-ionized forms. The non-ionized (free base) form is more lipid-soluble and can cross nerve membranes more effectively. The pH of the solution helps in determining this ratio.

3. Rate of Dissolution

a. **Immediate vs. Slow Dissolution:** The rate at which the anesthetic dissolves in the tissue fluid can impact the speed of onset of anesthesia. Fast dissolution leads to quicker onset, while slow dissolution can delay the onset but may provide a more prolonged effect.

b. **Formulation Factors:** The rate of dissolution can be influenced by factors such as the concentration of the anesthetic, the presence of additives (e.g., buffers), and the viscosity of the solution.

4. Concentration of the Anesthetic

a. **Higher Concentrations:** Higher concentrations generally increase the potency of the anesthetic but may also lead to higher systemic absorption and risk of toxicity.

b. **Dilution Effects:** Dilution of the anesthetic can affect its efficacy and the duration of action. Understanding the optimal concentration helps in achieving effective anesthesia while minimizing risks.

5. Formulation Factors

a. **Additives and Stabilizers:** Additives such as preservatives, buffering agents, and vasoconstrictors can influence the dissolution rate and stability of the anesthetic solution. For example, buffering agents can adjust the pH to improve the solubility and onset time.

b. **Type of Solution:** Solutions can vary in terms of their formulation, such as isotonic or hypertonic solutions, which affect how the anesthetic dissolves and disperses.

6. Viscosity of the Solution

a. **Impact on Injection:** The viscosity of the solution affects how easily it can be injected and how it disperses in the tissue. High viscosity solutions may require more force for injection and can impact the spread of the anesthetic.
b. **Modification of Viscosity:** Adding certain agents to the anesthetic solution can alter its viscosity to achieve a desired flow rate and distribution pattern.

7. Temperature

a. **Effect on Dissolution:** Temperature can impact the solubility and dissolution rate of the anesthetic. Warmer solutions generally dissolve more readily, which can influence the onset of anesthesia.

8. Clinical Implications

a. **Efficacy and Onset:** Understanding dissolution parameters helps in predicting and controlling the onset and efficacy of local anesthesia.
b. **Safety and Side Effects:** Proper dissolution and concentration control help in minimizing potential side effects and toxicity.

PHARMACOKINETIC PARAMETERS

In the study of local anesthetics, pharmacokinetic parameters are crucial for understanding how these drugs are absorbed, distributed, metabolized, and excreted by the body. These parameters help in optimizing the use of local anesthetics to achieve effective and safe anesthesia. Here's a detailed overview of pharmacokinetic parameters for local anesthetics:

1. Absorption

a. **Rate of Absorption:** The rate at which the anesthetic is absorbed from the site of injection into the bloodstream. This can be influenced by factors such as the site of injection, blood flow, and the presence of vasoconstrictors.
b. **Systemic Absorption:** Local anesthetics can be absorbed systemically if they leak into the bloodstream, potentially leading to systemic effects or

toxicity. Understanding systemic absorption helps in managing and mitigating risks.

2. **Distribution**
   a. **Volume of Distribution (Vd):** The extent to which the drug spreads throughout the body's tissues. A higher volume of distribution indicates that the drug is widely distributed beyond the bloodstream and into various tissues.
   b. **Tissue Binding:** Local anesthetics may bind to various tissues, including fat and muscle, affecting their distribution and duration of action. Lipid-soluble anesthetics tend to have a higher volume of distribution in fatty tissues.
3. **Protein Binding**
   a. **Plasma Protein Binding:** Local anesthetics often bind to plasma proteins like albumin. The degree of binding affects the free (active) concentration of the drug. High protein binding can reduce the amount of free drug available for action but may also impact the duration of action and the potential for toxicity.
4. **Metabolism**
   a. **Biotransformation:** Local anesthetics are metabolized in the body to inactive forms.
      i. **Esters:** Metabolized primarily by plasma cholinesterase. Rapid hydrolysis in the blood means shorter duration of action and lower risk of systemic toxicity.
      ii. **Amides:** Metabolized in the liver by cytochrome P450 enzymes. This usually results in a longer duration of action and requires careful monitoring in patients with liver dysfunction.
   b. **Rate of Metabolism:** The rate at which the anesthetic is broken down can impact its duration of action and potential for toxicity.
5. **Excretion**

a. **Route of Excretion:** The primary route of excretion for local anesthetics is through the kidneys. Metabolites and some unchanged drug are eliminated in the urine.

b. **Rate of Excretion:** The rate at which the drug is eliminated from the body influences its overall duration of action and potential for accumulation, especially in patients with impaired renal function.

6. Half-Life

a. **Elimination Half-Life:** The time it takes for the concentration of the anesthetic in the bloodstream to reduce by half. This parameter is crucial for understanding how long the drug will remain effective and helps in planning repeated dosing if necessary.

7. Clearance

a. **Total Clearance (Cl):** The volume of plasma from which the drug is completely removed per unit time. It reflects the efficiency of both metabolic and excretory processes in eliminating the drug from the body.

8. Effect of Adjuvants

a. **Vasoconstrictors:** Agents like epinephrine can affect the pharmacokinetics by reducing local blood flow, which slows systemic absorption and prolongs the duration of action.

b. **Buffering Agents:** Adjusting the pH of the solution can affect the drug's ionization and absorption, impacting its onset and duration of action.

9. Clinical Implications

a. **Dosing and Administration:** Understanding pharmacokinetic parameters helps in determining the appropriate dosing regimen and administration route for effective anesthesia.

b. **Safety and Efficacy:** Monitoring these parameters helps in minimizing adverse effects and optimizing therapeutic outcomes.

HECKEL PLOTS

Heckel plots are used primarily in the field of powder compaction and tablet formulation, but their principles can be applied to the study of local anesthetics and other pharmacological agents in terms of their solid-state properties and how they impact drug formulation and delivery. Here's a detailed look at how Heckel plots can be relevant:

What is a Heckel Plot?

A Heckel plot is a graphical representation used to analyze the relationship between the applied pressure during compaction and the resulting reduction in tablet volume. It is primarily used to understand the compaction behavior of powders and materials, which can be critical in drug formulation.

Components of a Heckel Plot

1. **Pressure (P):** The applied compaction pressure during the tablet formation process. It is plotted on the x-axis of the Heckel plot.
2. **Relative Density or Compressibility (1/V):** The relative change in volume or density of the powder due to compaction. It is plotted on the y-axis of the Heckel plot.

Interpreting Heckel Plots

1. **Compression Behavior:**
    a. **Initial Linear Region:** The initial part of the plot where the relationship between applied pressure and volume reduction is linear. This region reflects the elastic deformation of the powder particles.
    b. **Deformation Region:** As pressure increases, the plot often shows a region where volume reduction occurs at a slower rate. This reflects the plastic deformation and rearrangement of particles.
2. **Heckel Equation:**
    a. The Heckel equation relates the density of the powder during compression to the applied pressure. It is often expressed as:

$$\ln\left(\frac{1}{1-\frac{V}{V_0}}\right) = kP + C$$

3. **Parameters Derived from Heckel Plots:**
    a. **Heckel Constant (k):** Indicates the material's plasticity. A higher value suggests greater plastic deformation.
    b. **Yield Pressure (P_y):** The pressure at which the material begins to undergo significant plastic deformation.

Application to Local Anesthetics

1. **Formulation of Solid Dosage Forms:**
    a. **Powder Compaction:** Understanding the compaction behavior of local anesthetics in powder form is crucial for designing tablets or other solid dosage forms.
    b. **Optimization of Formulations:** Heckel plots help in optimizing the formulation by providing insights into how different excipients and drug properties affect the compaction process.
2. **Impact on Drug Delivery:**
    a. **Controlled Release:** The compaction behavior affects how the drug is released from tablets. Understanding these properties helps in designing formulations with desired release profiles.
    b. **Stability:** Proper compaction and formulation ensure that the drug maintains its stability and efficacy throughout its shelf life.

Practical Considerations

1. **Material Properties:** The properties of the local anesthetic powder, such as particle size, shape, and cohesiveness, can significantly affect the Heckel plot results.
2. **Processing Conditions:** Factors like compaction speed, temperature, and equipment settings influence the compaction behavior and should be controlled to achieve consistent results.

Clinical Implications

1. **Effective Dosage Forms:** Proper understanding of compaction and dissolution characteristics ensures that local anesthetic tablets or powders perform effectively in clinical settings.
2. **Patient Safety:** Optimizing the formulation based on Heckel plot analysis helps in minimizing issues such as inconsistent dosing or poor drug release.

SIMILARITY FACTORS – F2 AND F1

Similarity factors, such as f2 and f1, are important metrics used in pharmaceutical sciences to evaluate the similarity between two drug formulations, particularly in terms of their dissolution profiles. These factors help in comparing the release characteristics of different formulations or between a test formulation and a reference formulation. Here's a detailed explanation of f2 and f1:

Similarity Factor (f2)

1. Definition:

a. **Similarity Factor (f2f_2f2)** is a measure used to assess the similarity between the dissolution profiles of two formulations. It provides a quantitative assessment of how closely the release profiles of the test and reference formulations match.

3. **Formula:**

$$f_2 = 50 \cdot \log \left[\frac{1+\frac{1}{n}\sum_{t=1}^{n}(R_t-T_t)^2}{1+\frac{1}{n}\sum_{t=1}^{n}(R_t-T_t)^2} \right]$$

where:

a. Rt = Cumulative percentage of drug released from the reference formulation at time t
b. Tt = Cumulative percentage of drug released from the test formulation at time t
c. n = Number of time points

3. Interpretation:

a. **f2Value Range:** An f2 value between 50 and 100 indicates that the dissolution profiles of the test and reference formulations are similar. Values less than 50 suggest differences between the profiles.

b. **Higher f2Values:** Indicate greater similarity between the dissolution profiles of the test and reference formulations.

Difference Factor (f1)

1. Definition:

a. **Difference Factor (f1)** measures the absolute difference between the dissolution profiles of the test and reference formulations. It helps to quantify the extent of deviation between the two profiles.

3. **Formula:**

$$f_1 = \frac{1}{n}\sum_{t=1}^{n}|R_t - T_t|$$

where:

a. Rt = Cumulative percentage of drug released from the reference formulation at time t

b. Tt = Cumulative percentage of drug released from the test formulation at time ttt

c. n = Number of time points

3. Interpretation:

a. **f1 Value Range:** An f1 value of 0 indicates perfect similarity, while higher values suggest greater differences between the dissolution profiles.

b. **Lower f1 Values:** Indicate that the profiles are more similar.

Application in Drug Formulation

1. **Evaluating Bioequivalence:**

a. **Regulatory Requirement:** In the development of generic drugs, similarity factors are used to demonstrate that the generic formulation has a dissolution profile similar to the reference (brand-name) drug, which is a requirement for regulatory approval.

2. **Optimizing Formulations:**
   a. **Formulation Development:** During formulation development, f2 and f1 help in assessing how changes in the formulation or manufacturing process affect the drug release characteristics.
3. **Comparing Different Dosage Forms:**
   a. **Dissolution Profile Comparison:** When comparing different dosage forms (e.g., tablets vs. capsules), similarity factors provide insight into how formulation changes impact drug release.

Practical Considerations

1. **Time Points:**
   a. **Selection of Time Points:** The number and timing of the sampling points in the dissolution study can affect the calculation of f2 and f1. Adequate time points should be chosen to accurately capture the dissolution profile.
2. **Methodology:**
   a. **Standardization:** Ensuring standardized dissolution testing conditions is crucial for obtaining reliable f2 and f1 values.
3. **Data Interpretation:**
   a. **Statistical Analysis:** In addition to similarity factors, statistical analyses may be used to support conclusions about the similarity or differences between dissolution profiles.

HIGUCHI AND PEPPAS PLOT

Higuchi and Peppas plots are used to analyze and understand drug release mechanisms from various dosage forms, particularly those with controlled-release or extended-release properties. These plots help in determining how drugs are released from matrices or devices over time. Here's a detailed explanation of Higuchi and Peppas plots:

Higuchi Plot

1. **Purpose:**
   a. **Drug Release Kinetics:** Higuchi plots are used to describe the drug release from a matrix system where the release is governed by diffusion. This is commonly applied to matrix tablets or films where the drug is dispersed within a polymer matrix.
2. **Higuchi Equation:**
   a. **Equation:** The Higuchi equation describes drug release from a planar matrix based on Fickian diffusion:

$$Q = \frac{A \cdot D \cdot t^{1/2}}{H}$$

where:

i. Q = Amount of drug released at time ttt
ii. A = Surface area of the matrix
iii. D = Diffusion coefficient of the drug in the matrix
iv. H = Thickness of the matrix
v. t = Time

3. **Plotting:**
   a. **Higuchi Plot:** The plot typically involves plotting Q (the cumulative amount of drug released) versus t1/2. A linear relationship indicates that the release follows Higuchi's model.
4. **Interpretation:**
   a. **Linear Relationship:** If the plot of Q versus t1/2 is linear, it suggests that the drug release follows diffusion-controlled kinetics.
   b. **Non-linear Relationship:** Deviations from linearity may indicate that other mechanisms are influencing the release, such as swelling or erosion.

Peppas Plot

1. **Purpose:**

a. **Release Mechanism:** Peppas plots are used to analyze drug release from matrices where both diffusion and erosion might play a role. It helps in understanding the mechanism of drug release more comprehensively.

2. **Peppas Equation:**

a. **Equation:** The Peppas equation generalizes the drug release rate to account for various release mechanisms:

$$M(t) = M_\infty \cdot (k \cdot t^n)$$

where:

i. M(t) = Cumulative amount of drug released at time t

ii. $M\infty$ = Total amount of drug in the system

iii. k = Release rate constant

iv. n = Release exponent (indicative of the release mechanism)

v. t = Time

3. **Plotting:**

a. **Peppas Plot:** Plot $M(t)/M\infty$ versus t on a log-log scale. The slope of the plot helps determine the value of nnn, which is used to identify the release mechanism.

4. **Interpretation:**

a. **Release Exponent n:** The value of nnn can indicate different release mechanisms:

i. **n<0.5:** Fickian diffusion (purely diffusion-controlled release).

ii. **0.5<n<1.0:** Anomalous diffusion (both diffusion and erosion).

iii. **n=1.0:** Case II transport (zero-order release, primarily due to erosion).

iv. **n>1.0:** Super Case II transport (release rate accelerates with time, often due to swelling).

Application in Drug Formulation

1. **Controlled-Release Formulations:**

a. **Matrix Tablets and Films:** Higuchi and Peppas plots are crucial for evaluating the release kinetics from matrix systems, helping to design formulations with desired release profiles.

2. **Optimization of Formulations:**

   a. **Formulation Development:** These plots help in optimizing the formulation by providing insights into how different excipients and drug loading levels affect the release mechanism.

3. **Predicting Drug Release:**

   a. **Long-Term Release:** Understanding the release mechanism is essential for predicting how a drug will behave over time, which is crucial for ensuring consistent therapeutic effects.

Practical Considerations

1. **Sampling and Data Collection:**

   a. **Time Points:** Accurate and regular sampling is needed to construct meaningful Higuchi and Peppas plots. Ensure that sampling times are appropriate to capture the entire release profile.

2. **Mathematical Modeling:**

   a. **Model Validation:** It's important to validate the fit of the Higuchi and Peppas models to experimental data. If the models do not fit well, consider additional mechanisms or modifications in the formulation.

3. **Release Mechanism:**

   a. **Complex Systems:** In cases where multiple mechanisms are at play, both models might need to be used together with other analytical techniques to fully understand the release dynamics.

LINEARITY CONCEPT OF SIGNIFICANCE

In the study of consolidation parameters, the concept of linearity plays a crucial role in various aspects, including the analysis of drug release profiles, the validation of analytical methods, and the interpretation of pharmacokinetic data. Here's a detailed exploration of the significance of linearity in the context of consolidation parameters:

1. Linearity in Drug Release Profiles

a. **Definition:**

i. **Linearity** refers to a direct proportional relationship between two variables. In drug release studies, it often pertains to the relationship between the cumulative amount of drug released and time, or between drug concentration and other parameters.

b. **Significance:**

i. **Release Kinetics:** A linear relationship in a plot of cumulative drug release versus time (or t1/2 for Higuchi plots) suggests that the release follows a predictable pattern, such as diffusion-controlled release. Deviations from linearity may indicate that other mechanisms, such as swelling or erosion, are affecting the release profile.

c. **Interpretation:**

i. **Consistency:** Linear release profiles are desirable in controlled-release formulations as they indicate consistent drug release rates over time.

ii. **Predictability:** Linear relationships help in predicting the drug release over extended periods and in scaling up the formulation for commercial production.

2. Linearity in Analytical Methods

a. **Definition:**

i. **Linearity** in analytical methods refers to the ability of a method to provide results that are directly proportional to the concentration of the analyte within a given range. This is crucial for accurate and reliable quantification of drug concentrations in various samples.

b. **Significance:**

i. **Calibration Curves:** Establishing a linear calibration curve is essential for quantifying drug concentrations accurately. The linearity of the curve ensures that the method can reliably measure drug levels across a range of concentrations.

ii. **Method Validation:** Linearity is a key criterion in method validation, ensuring that the analytical method performs consistently and accurately within the specified concentration range.

c. **Interpretation:**

i. **Accuracy and Precision:** Linear calibration curves indicate that the method is accurate and precise for the concentrations tested, which is vital for ensuring the reliability of analytical results.

ii. **Dynamic Range:** The linear range of the method determines the concentration range over which the method can be used effectively. Extrapolating beyond this range may lead to inaccuracies.

3. Linearity in Pharmacokinetic Data

a. **Definition:**

i. **Linearity** in pharmacokinetic studies refers to the proportional relationship between dose and drug concentration or between drug concentration and time. It is crucial for understanding how drug levels in the body change over time.

b. **Significance:**

i. **Dose-Response Relationship:** Linear dose-response relationships indicate predictable changes in drug concentration with changes in dose, which is important for dose optimization.

ii. **Drug Clearance and Volume of Distribution:** Linearity in concentration-time profiles helps in accurately determining pharmacokinetic parameters such as clearance and volume of distribution.

c. **Interpretation:**

i. **Predictive Modeling:** Linear pharmacokinetic data facilitate predictive modeling of drug behavior, aiding in dose adjustments and predicting drug interactions.

ii. **Drug Development:** Understanding linearity helps in designing dosing regimens and in evaluating the potential for non-linear pharmacokinetics, which can affect drug efficacy and safety.

4. Practical Considerations

a. **Data Quality:**

i. **Accurate Measurements:** Ensure accurate and precise measurements to maintain linearity in both release profiles and analytical methods.

ii. **Sampling Frequency:** Regular and appropriate sampling is crucial to accurately capture and interpret linearity in drug release profiles and pharmacokinetic data.

b. **Method Optimization:**

i. **Calibration and Validation:** Regular calibration and validation of analytical methods ensure that linearity is maintained over time and across different conditions.

ii. **Formulation Adjustments:** If non-linearity is observed, consider adjustments in formulation or experimental conditions to achieve desired release characteristics.

c. **Regulatory Compliance:**

i. **Standards and Guidelines:** Adherence to regulatory standards for linearity in analytical methods and pharmacokinetic studies ensures compliance and supports the credibility of the results.

STANDARD DEVIATION

Standard deviation (SD) is a key statistical measure used to quantify the amount of variation or dispersion in a set of data points. In the context of the study of consolidation parameters, standard deviation provides insights into the consistency and reliability of data related to drug release, formulation, and other pharmaceutical processes. Here's a detailed exploration of the significance and application of standard deviation in this context:

1. Standard Deviation in Drug Release Studies

a. **Definition:**

i. **Standard Deviation (SD):** A measure that indicates how much individual data points deviate from the mean (average) value of the dataset. It is calculated as:

$$SD = \sqrt{\frac{\sum_{i=1}^{n}(x_i - \bar{x})^2}{n-1}}$$

where:

i. xi = Each individual data point

ii. x¯ = Mean of the data points

iii. n = Number of data points

b. **Significance:**

i. **Consistency of Release:** A low standard deviation in drug release data indicates consistent release profiles across different samples or batches, while a high standard deviation suggests variability.

ii. **Formulation Quality:** Monitoring the standard deviation helps in ensuring the quality and uniformity of drug formulations.

c. **Application:**

i. **Comparing Formulations:** Standard deviation is used to compare the consistency of drug release profiles between different formulations or manufacturing processes.

ii. **Quality Control:** It is used in quality control to ensure that the drug release falls within the acceptable range of variability.

2. Standard Deviation in Analytical Method Validation

a. **Definition:**

i. **Analytical Precision:** Standard deviation measures the precision of an analytical method, reflecting how consistently the method produces similar results when repeated measurements are taken.

b. **Significance:**

i. **Accuracy and Reliability:** A low standard deviation indicates that the analytical method provides reliable and reproducible results, which is essential for accurate quantification of drug concentrations.

ii. **Validation Criteria:** Standard deviation is a critical component of method validation and is used to assess the precision and reproducibility of the analytical method.

c. **Application:**

i. **Calibration Curves:** In calibration curve analysis, standard deviation helps in determining the reliability of the calibration points and the method's overall performance.

ii. **Repeatability and Reproducibility:** Standard deviation is used to evaluate the repeatability (same operator, same equipment) and reproducibility (different operators, different equipment) of the method.

3. Standard Deviation in Pharmacokinetic Data

a. **Definition:**

i. **Pharmacokinetic Variability:** Standard deviation helps in understanding the variability in pharmacokinetic parameters such as drug concentration over time, volume of distribution, and clearance rates.

b. **Significance:**

i. **Dose Adjustment:** A high standard deviation in pharmacokinetic data may indicate variability in drug absorption, distribution, metabolism, or excretion, which can affect dosing regimens and therapeutic efficacy.

ii. **Patient Safety:** Understanding variability helps in predicting and managing potential side effects and optimizing drug therapy for individual patients.

c. **Application:**

i. **Data Interpretation:** Standard deviation is used to interpret pharmacokinetic data and assess the consistency of drug behavior across different subjects or conditions.

ii. **Clinical Trials:** In clinical trials, standard deviation helps in evaluating the variability of drug responses among participants and in designing studies with appropriate sample sizes.

4. Practical Considerations

a. **Data Quality:**

i. **Accurate Measurement:** Ensure accurate and consistent measurement techniques to obtain reliable standard deviation values.

ii. **Sample Size:** Larger sample sizes provide more reliable estimates of standard deviation and reduce the impact of outliers.

b. **Statistical Analysis:**

i. **Normal Distribution:** Standard deviation assumes that the data follows a normal distribution. If the data is not normally distributed, other statistical methods may be needed.

ii. **Interpreting Results:** Consider the context of the standard deviation and the specific requirements of the study or application to interpret the results appropriately.

c. **Regulatory Compliance:**

i. **Standards and Guidelines:** Adherence to regulatory standards for statistical analysis and reporting ensures that the data is presented accurately and complies with industry requirements.

CHI SQUARE TEST

The chi-square test is a statistical method used to determine if there is a significant association between categorical variables or to assess the goodness-of-fit of observed data to a theoretical distribution. In the study of consolidation parameters, the chi-square test can be particularly useful in various contexts, including analyzing categorical data related to drug release, formulation quality, and other pharmaceutical processes. Here's a detailed explanation of how the chi-square test is applied in this context:

1. Chi-Square Test for Goodness-of-Fit

a. **Definition:**

i. **Goodness-of-Fit Test:** The chi-square test for goodness-of-fit assesses whether the observed distribution of data matches an expected distribution. This is useful for testing if experimental data follows a theoretical distribution, such as a normal distribution or a predefined pattern.

b. **Application in Drug Release Studies:**

i. **Release Profiles:** To determine if the observed release profile of a drug matches the expected release profile based on a theoretical model or formulation specification.

ii. **Statistical Analysis:** For instance, if you expect a drug to release in a certain pattern (e.g., linear or exponential) and have observed data, the chi-square test can help determine if deviations are statistically significant.

b. **Formula:**

$$\chi^2 = \sum \frac{(O_i - E_i)^2}{E_i}$$

where:

a. Oi = Observed frequency in category i
b. Ei = Expected frequency in category i
c. The sum is taken over all categories.

d. **Interpretation:**

i. **Significance:** A high chi-square value indicates a significant difference between observed and expected values, suggesting that the data does not fit the expected distribution well.

ii. **P-Value:** Compare the chi-square statistic to the chi-square distribution with the appropriate degrees of freedom to obtain a p-value. A low p-value (typically <0.05) indicates a significant difference.

2. Chi-Square Test for Independence

a. **Definition:**

i. **Independence Test:** The chi-square test for independence examines if two categorical variables are independent or if there is a significant association between them.

b. **Application in Drug Formulation and Quality Control:**

i. **Categorical Data Analysis:** For instance, assessing whether different formulation batches produce significantly different release profiles or whether the presence of certain excipients is associated with specific drug release characteristics.

ii. **Quality Control:** Evaluating if the observed proportions of different quality categories (e.g., pass/fail, high/low release rates) are independent of batch or formulation variables.

d. **Formula:**

$$\chi^2 = \sum \frac{(O_{ij} - E_{ij})^2}{E_{ij}}$$

where:

a. Oij = Observed frequency in cell (i,j)

b. Eij = Expected frequency in cell (i,j)

c. The sum is taken over all cells in the contingency table.

d. **Interpretation:**

i. **Significance:** A high chi-square value indicates that the variables are not independent, suggesting a significant association between them.

ii. **P-Value:** The p-value is used to determine the significance level. A p-value less than the chosen alpha level (e.g., 0.05) suggests that the variables are significantly associated.

3. Practical Considerations

a. **Data Requirements:**

i. **Categorical Data:** The chi-square test requires categorical data. For continuous data, it may need to be categorized or transformed into frequency counts.

ii. **Sample Size:** Adequate sample size is necessary to ensure the reliability of the chi-square test. Small sample sizes can lead to inaccurate results.

b. **Assumptions:**

i. **Expected Frequencies:** For the goodness-of-fit test, expected frequencies should generally be greater than 5 to ensure the validity of the test. If this condition is not met, consider using Fisher's exact test or combining categories.

ii. **Independence:** For the test of independence, each observation should be independent of others. This means each data point should not influence or be influenced by other data points.

c. **Limitations:**

i. **Non-Normal Data:** The chi-square test may not be suitable for non-normal or skewed data without proper categorization.

ii. **Small Frequencies:** If expected frequencies are very low, the chi-square test may not be accurate, and alternative tests should be considered.

4. Application Examples

a. **Drug Release Analysis:**

i. **Comparing Release Profiles:** Comparing the observed release profile of different drug formulations to expected profiles to assess if differences are statistically significant.

b. **Formulation Studies:**

i. **Quality Control:** Analyzing whether the proportions of different quality outcomes (e.g., stable vs. unstable formulations) are independent of factors such as production conditions or ingredient variations.

STUDENTS T-TEST

The Student's t-test is a statistical test used to determine whether there is a significant difference between the means of two groups. It is particularly useful when dealing with small sample sizes and is commonly applied in various fields, including pharmaceutical studies. Here's a detailed exploration of how the Student's t-test is applied in the study of consolidation parameters:

1. Purpose of the Student's t-Test

a. **Definition:**

i. **Student's t-Test:** A parametric test used to compare the means of two groups to determine if they are significantly different from each other. The test is named after William Sealy Gosset, who published under the pseudonym "Student."

b. **Types of t-Tests:**

i. **Independent Samples t-Test:** Compares the means of two independent groups (e.g., different formulations or different batches).

ii. **Paired Samples t-Test:** Compares the means of two related groups (e.g., measurements taken before and after a treatment on the same subjects).

2. Application in Drug Release Studies

a. **Independent Samples t-Test:**

i. **Purpose:** To determine if there is a significant difference in drug release profiles between two different formulations or batches.

ii. **Example:** Comparing the average release rates of two different drug formulations to assess if the formulations release the drug at significantly different rates.

b. **Paired Samples t-Test:**

i. **Purpose:** To assess changes in drug release profiles within the same sample group under different conditions or over time.

ii. **Example:** Comparing the drug release rate from a formulation before and after a stability study to determine if there are significant changes due to storage conditions.

3. Conducting the Student's t-Test

a. **Independent Samples t-Test:**

i. **Hypotheses:**

1. **Null Hypothesis (H0):** There is no significant difference between the means of the two groups.
2. **Alternative Hypothesis (H1):** There is a significant difference between the means of the two groups.

ii. **Formula:**

$$t = \frac{\bar{x}_1 - \bar{x}_2}{\sqrt{\frac{s_1^2}{n_1} + \frac{s_2^2}{n_2}}}$$

where:

1. x¯1 and x¯2 = Means of the two groups
2. s12 and s22 = Variances of the two groups
3. n1 and n2 = Sample sizes of the two groups

iii. **Degrees of Freedom:** Calculated using:

$$\mathrm{df} = \frac{\left(\frac{s_1^2}{n_1} + \frac{s_2^2}{n_2}\right)^2}{\frac{\left(\frac{s_1^2}{n_1}\right)^2}{n_1 \; 1} + \frac{\left(\frac{s_2^2}{n_2}\right)^2}{n_2 \; 1}}$$

b. **Paired Samples t-Test:**

i. **Hypotheses:**

1. **Null Hypothesis (H0):** The mean difference between paired observations is zero.
2. **Alternative Hypothesis (H1):** The mean difference between paired observations is not zero.

ii. **Formula:**

$$t = \frac{\bar{d}}{s_d / \sqrt{n}}$$

where:

1. $\bar{d}$ = Mean of the differences between paired observations
2. sd = Standard deviation of the differences
3. n = Number of pairs

iii. **Degrees of Freedom:** n−1n - 1n−1, where nnn is the number of pairs.

4. Interpreting the Results

a. **P-Value:**

i. **Significance Level:** Compare the calculated t-value to the critical t-value from the t-distribution table with the appropriate degrees of freedom. Alternatively, use the p-value associated with the t-value to determine significance.

ii. **Threshold:** A p-value less than the chosen alpha level (e.g., 0.05) indicates a significant difference between the groups.

b. **Effect Size:**

i. **Cohen's d:** Measure of the effect size which quantifies the magnitude of the difference between the means. It helps in understanding the practical significance of the results.

ii. **Calculation:** For independent samples t-test:

$$d = \frac{\bar{x}_1 - \bar{x}_2}{\sqrt{\frac{s_1^2 + s_2^2}{2}}}$$

5. Practical Considerations

a. **Assumptions:**

i. **Normality:** The t-test assumes that the data in each group is approximately normally distributed. For small sample sizes, normality is particularly important.

ii. **Equality of Variances:** The independent samples t-test assumes equal variances between the two groups. If this assumption is violated, consider using the Welch's t-test, which does not assume equal variances.

b. **Sample Size:**

i. **Adequate Sample Size:** Ensure that the sample sizes are adequate to achieve reliable results. Small sample sizes may lead to less reliable conclusions.

c. **Data Preparation:**

i. **Data Cleaning:** Ensure that the data is clean and properly prepared before conducting the t-test. Outliers and data errors can impact the results.

6. Application Examples

a. **Comparing Drug Release Rates:**

i. **Formulation Comparison:** Use the independent samples t-test to compare the release rates of two different drug formulations to determine if they produce significantly different release profiles.

b. **Assessing Stability:**

i. **Formulation Stability:** Apply the paired samples t-test to compare drug release rates before and after stability testing to evaluate the impact of storage conditions on drug release.

ANOVA TEST

The Analysis of Variance (ANOVA) test is a statistical method used to determine if there are significant differences among the means of three or more groups. It helps in assessing whether any of the group means are different from each other and is widely used in various fields, including pharmaceutical studies. Here's a detailed look at how ANOVA is applied in the study of consolidation parameters:

1. Purpose of ANOVA

a. **Definition:**

i. **ANOVA:** A statistical technique used to compare the means of three or more groups to determine if at least one group mean is significantly different from the others.

b. **Types of ANOVA:**

i. **One-Way ANOVA:** Used when comparing means across one categorical independent variable with three or more levels (e.g., different drug formulations).

ii. **Two-Way ANOVA:** Used when comparing means across two categorical independent variables (e.g., different formulations and different storage conditions) and their interaction effects.

2. Application in Drug Release Studies

a. **One-Way ANOVA:**

i. **Purpose:** To evaluate if there are significant differences in drug release profiles among three or more different formulations or batches.

ii. **Example:** Comparing the average release rates of drugs from three different formulations to determine if they produce significantly different release profiles.

b. **Two-Way ANOVA:**

i. **Purpose:** To assess the impact of two factors on drug release and their interaction effects.

ii. **Example:** Examining the effect of both formulation type and storage conditions on drug release rates to understand how these factors interact and influence the release profile.

3. Conducting ANOVA

a. **One-Way ANOVA:**

i. **Hypotheses:**

1. **Null Hypothesis (H0):** All group means are equal.
2. **Alternative Hypothesis (H1):** At least one group mean is different.

ii. **Formula:**

$$F = \frac{\text{Between-Group Variance}}{\text{Within-Group Variance}}$$

where:

1. **Between-Group Variance:** Variability due to differences between group means.
2. **Within-Group Variance:** Variability within each group.

iii. **Steps:**

1. **Calculate Group Means:** Determine the mean of each group.
2. **Calculate Overall Mean:** Compute the mean of all data points combined.
3. **Compute Between-Group Variance:** Measure variability between group means and the overall mean.
4. **Compute Within-Group Variance:** Measure variability within each group.
5. **Calculate F-Statistic:** Use the variances to compute the F-statistic.

b. **Two-Way ANOVA:**

i. **Hypotheses:**

1. **Main Effects:**
   a. **Null Hypothesis (H0):** No significant effect of each factor on the dependent variable.
   b. **Alternative Hypothesis (H1):** Significant effect of each factor on the dependent variable.
2. **Interaction Effect:**
   a. **Null Hypothesis (H0):** No interaction effect between the factors.
   b. **Alternative Hypothesis (H1):** Significant interaction effect between the factors.

ii. **Steps:**

1. **Calculate Main Effects:** Evaluate the effect of each independent variable separately.
2. **Calculate Interaction Effects:** Assess how the combination of factors influences the dependent variable.

3. **Compute F-Statistics:** For each effect (main and interaction), calculate the F-statistic using the respective variances.

4. Interpreting the Results

a. **F-Statistic:**

i. **Calculation:** The F-statistic is calculated as the ratio of between-group variance to within-group variance.

ii. **Significance:** A high F-statistic indicates significant differences between group means.

b. **P-Value:**

i. **Threshold:** Compare the F-statistic to the critical value from the F-distribution table to obtain the p-value.

ii. **Significance Level:** A p-value less than the chosen alpha level (e.g., 0.05) indicates that there are significant differences among the group means.

c. **Post-Hoc Tests:**

i. **Purpose:** If ANOVA indicates significant differences, post-hoc tests (e.g., Tukey's HSD, Bonferroni) are used to identify which specific groups differ from each other.

ii. **Application:** Use post-hoc tests to perform pairwise comparisons between groups to pinpoint significant differences.

5. Practical Considerations

a. **Assumptions:**

i. **Normality:** Data should be approximately normally distributed within each group.

ii. **Homogeneity of Variances:** Variances should be approximately equal across groups. Levene's test can be used to assess this assumption.

b. **Sample Size:**

i. **Adequate Sample Size:** Ensure that the sample sizes are sufficient to achieve reliable and valid results. Small sample sizes may affect the accuracy of the ANOVA results.

c. **Data Preparation:**

i. **Data Cleaning:** Ensure that the data is properly cleaned and prepared before conducting ANOVA. Outliers and errors can impact the results.

6. Application Examples

a. **Comparing Drug Formulations:**

i. **Release Rates:** Use one-way ANOVA to compare the average drug release rates from three or more different formulations to assess if there are significant differences.

b. **Assessing Factors Affecting Drug Release:**

i. **Formulation and Storage Conditions:** Apply two-way ANOVA to evaluate how different formulations and storage conditions impact drug release rates and if there are interactions between these factors.

Multiple-Choice Questions (Objective)

1. Which of the following classifications is based on the chemical structure of local anesthetics?
   a) Sodium channels
   b) Esters and Amides
   c) Bioavailability
   d) Receptor Binding
2. What is the primary mechanism of action of local anesthetics?
   a) Blockade of potassium channels
   b) Inhibition of protein synthesis
   c) Blockade of sodium channels
   d) Activation of calcium channels
3. Which factor influences the onset time of a local anesthetic?

a) Tissue pH
b) Duration of action
c) Metabolism rate
d) Excretion rate

4. How are esters typically metabolized in the body?
   a) By the liver
   b) By plasma cholinesterase
   c) By the kidneys
   d) By the pancreas
5. What is the primary risk associated with systemic absorption of local anesthetics?
   a) Increased potency
   b) Allergic reactions
   c) Systemic toxicity
   d) Reduced efficacy
6. Which local anesthetic has a longer duration of action compared to Lidocaine?
   a) Procaine
   b) Bupivacaine
   c) Benzocaine
   d) Mepivacaine
7. What is the significance of the pKa of a local anesthetic?
   a) It determines the lipid solubility
   b) It determines the protein binding
   c) It affects the onset of action
   d) It influences the duration of action
8. Which factor can reduce the rate of absorption of a local anesthetic into the bloodstream?
   a) Increased tissue pH

b) Addition of a vasoconstrictor
c) Increased drug concentration
d) Increased tissue perfusion

9. What does the volume of distribution (Vd) indicate in pharmacokinetics?
a) The rate of drug absorption
b) The extent of drug distribution in the body
c) The rate of drug metabolism
d) The rate of drug excretion

10. Which parameter is primarily responsible for the lipophilicity of a local anesthetic?
a) Molecular weight
b) Chemical structure
c) Ionization state
d) Protein binding

11. What type of plot is used to analyze the compaction behavior of powders?
a) Higuchi plot
b) Peppas plot
c) Heckel plot
d) ANOVA plot

12. Which similarity factor is used to compare the dissolution profiles of two formulations?
a) f1
b) f2
c) f3
d) f4

13. Which equation is used in Higuchi plots to describe drug release from a matrix?
a) Q = k * t^n
b) Q = A * D * t^1/2 / H

c) Q = K * t^1/2

d) Q = D * t / H

14. What does a linear relationship in a Higuchi plot suggest?

a) Zero-order release

b) First-order release

c) Diffusion-controlled release

d) Erosion-controlled release

15. In the Peppas equation, what does a release exponent (n) value of 0.5 indicate?

a) Case II transport

b) Super Case II transport

c) Fickian diffusion

d) Anomalous diffusion

16. What is the purpose of a chi-square test for goodness-of-fit?

a) To compare means between two groups

b) To determine the independence of variables

c) To assess if observed data matches an expected distribution

d) To evaluate correlation between variables

17. When is an independent samples t-test used?

a) To compare means within the same group

b) To compare means between two unrelated groups

c) To analyze categorical data

d) To evaluate the fit of a theoretical distribution

18. What does a high F-statistic in ANOVA indicate?

a) Significant differences between group means

b) No significant differences between group means

c) A high degree of correlation

d) A low degree of correlation

19. What is the primary use of post-hoc tests following ANOVA?

a) To confirm normality of data

b) To validate the assumptions of ANOVA

c) To identify which specific groups differ

d) To compute the F-statistic

20. What is the significance of standard deviation in drug release studies?

a) It indicates the average drug release rate

b) It measures the consistency of release profiles

c) It calculates the mean drug release

d) It determines the total drug released

Short Answer Type Questions (Subjective)

1. Define the mechanism of action of local anesthetics.
2. Explain the difference between esters and amides in local anesthetics.
3. What factors influence the onset time of local anesthetics?
4. Describe the process of metabolism for ester-based local anesthetics.
5. What is systemic toxicity in the context of local anesthetics?
6. How does the addition of vasoconstrictors affect the pharmacokinetics of local anesthetics?
7. What role does pKa play in the efficacy of local anesthetics?
8. Explain the significance of the volume of distribution (Vd) in pharmacokinetics.
9. Describe the importance of lipophilicity in the diffusion of local anesthetics.
10. What are Heckel plots used for in pharmaceutical studies?
11. Explain the purpose of similarity factors f1 and f2.
12. How is the Higuchi equation used in drug release studies?
13. What does a linear relationship in a Peppas plot indicate about the release mechanism?
14. Define the chi-square test for independence.
15. When is a paired samples t-test used in drug studies?

16. What does the F-statistic represent in ANOVA?
17. Why are post-hoc tests necessary after conducting ANOVA?
18. Describe the significance of standard deviation in quality control of drug formulations.
19. Explain the practical considerations when conducting an ANOVA test.
20. How can the Student's t-test be applied to compare drug release rates?

Long Answer Type Questions (Subjective)

1. Discuss the factors that influence the onset and duration of action of local anesthetics, providing examples of different anesthetics.
2. Explain the pharmacokinetic parameters of absorption, distribution, metabolism, and excretion for local anesthetics.
3. Describe the application of Heckel plots in analyzing the compaction behavior of pharmaceutical powders.
4. Discuss the significance of similarity factors f1 and f2 in evaluating the dissolution profiles of drug formulations.
5. Explain the role of Higuchi and Peppas plots in understanding drug release mechanisms from matrix systems.
6. Describe the purpose and interpretation of the chi-square test for goodness-of-fit in pharmaceutical studies.
7. Discuss the application of the Student's t-test in comparing means between two groups in drug release studies.
8. Explain the process and significance of conducting ANOVA to compare multiple groups in pharmaceutical research.
9. Discuss the role of standard deviation in ensuring the quality and consistency of drug formulations.
10. Explain the practical considerations and challenges in applying statistical tests such as ANOVA and t-tests in pharmaceutical studies.

Answer Key for MCQ Questions

1. b) Esters and Amides
2. c) Blockade of sodium channels
3. a) Tissue pH
4. b) By plasma cholinesterase
5. c) Systemic toxicity
6. b) Bupivacaine
7. c) It affects the onset of action
8. b) Addition of a vasoconstrictor
9. b) The extent of drug distribution in the body
10. b) Chemical structure
11. c) Heckel plot
12. b) f2
13. b) Q = A * D * t^1/2 / H
14. c) Diffusion-controlled release
15. c) Fickian diffusion
16. c) To assess if observed data matches an expected distribution
17. b) To compare means between two unrelated groups
18. a) Significant differences between group means
19. c) To identify which specific groups differ
20. b) It measures the consistency of release profiles

www.ingramcontent.com/pod-product-compliance
Lightning Source LLC
LaVergne TN
LVHW021135160826
845679LV00023B/1920
* 9 7 9 8 8 9 5 8 8 4 2 9 4 *